FIAT - PININFARINA 124 & 2000 SPIDER 1968 - 1985

Compiled by
R.M. Clarke

ISBN 1 870642 244

Distributed by
Brooklands Book Distribution Ltd.
'Holmerise', Seven Hills Road,
Cobham, Surrey, England

BROOKLANDS BOOKS

BROOKLANDS BOOKS SERIES

AC Ace & Aceca 1953-1983
AC Cobra 1962-1969
Alfa Romeo Alfasud 1972-1984
Alfa Romeo Alfetta Coupes GT.GTV.GTV6 1974-1987
Alfa Romeo Giulia Berlinas 1962-1976
Alfa Romeo Giulia Coupés 1963-1976
Alfa Romeo Spider 1966-1987
Aston Martin Gold Portfolio 1972-1985
Austin Seven 1922-1982
Austin A30 & A35 1951-1962
Austin Healey 100 1952-1959
Austin Healey 3000 1959-1967
Austin Healey 100 & 3000 Collection No. 1
Austin Healey 'Frogeye' Sprite Collection No. 1
Austin Healey Sprite 1958-1971
Avanti 1962-1983
BMW Six Cylinder Coupés 1969-1975
BMW 1600 Collection No. 1
BMW 2002 1968-1976
Bristol Cars Gold Portfolio 1946-1985
Buick Riviera 1963-1978
Cadillac Automobiles 1949-1959
Cadillac Automobiles 1960-1969
Cadillac Eldorado 1967-1978
Cadillac in the Sixties No. 1
Camaro 1966-1970
High Performance Camaros 1982-1988
Chevrolet 1955-1957
Chevrolet Camaro Collection No. 1
Chevelle & SS 1964-1972
Chevy II Nova & SS 1962-1973
Chrysler 300 1955-1970
Citroen Traction Avant 1934-1957
Citroen DS & ID 1955-1875
Citroen 2CV 1949-1982
Cobras & Replicas 1962-1983
Cortina 1600E & GT 1967-1970
Corvair 1959-1968
Daimler Dart & V-8 250 1959-1969
Datsun 240z 1970-1973
Datsun 280Z & ZX 1975-1983
De Tomaso Collection No. 1
Dodge Charger 1966-1974
Excalibur Collection No. 1
Ferrari Cars 1946-1956
Ferrari Cars 1962-1966
Ferrari Cars 1969-1973
Ferrari Dino 1965-1974
Ferrari Dino 308 1974-1979
Ferrari 308 & Mondial 1980-1984
Ferrari Collection No. 1
Fiat-Bertone X1/9 1973-1988
Ford Falcon 1960-1970
Ford Mustang 1964-1967
Ford Mustang 1967-1973
High Performance Mustangs 1982-1988
Ford RS Escort 1968-1980
Honda CRX 1983-1987
High Performance Escorts MkI 1968-1974
High Performance Escorts MkII 1975-1980
Hudson & Railton Cars 1936-1940
Jaguar Cars 1957-1961
Jaguar Cars 1961-1964
Jaguar Cars 1964-1968
Jaguar MK2 1959-1969
Jaguar E-Type 1961-1966
Jaguar E-Type 1966-1971
Jaguar E-Type V12 1971-1975
Jaguar XKE Collection No. 1
Jaguar XJ6 1968-1972
Jaguar XJ6 Series II 1973-1979
Jaguar XJ6 & XJ12 Series III 1979-1985
Jaguar XJ12 1972-1980
Jaguar XJS 1975-1980
Jensen Cars 1946-1967
Jensen Cars 1967-1979
Jensen Interceptor Gold Portfolio 1966-1986
Lamborghini Cars 1964-1970
Lamborghini Cars 1970-1975
Lamborghini Countach Collection No. 1
Lamborghini Countach & Urraco 1974-1980
Lamborghini Countach & Jalpa 1980-1985
Lancia Stratos 1972-1985
Land Rover 1948-1973
Land Rover Series II & IIa 1958-1971
Land Rover Series III 1971-1985
Lotus Cortina 1963-1970
Lotus Elan 1962-1973
Lotus Elan Collection No. 1
Lotus Elan Collection No. 2
Lotus Elite 1957-1964
Lotus Elite & Eclat 1974-1981
Lotus Turbo Esprit 1980-1986
Lotus Europa 1966-1975
Lotus Europa Collection No. 1
Lotus Seven 1957-1980
Lotus Seven Collection No. 1
Maserati 1965-1970
Maserati 1970-1975
Mazda RX-7 Collection No. 1
Mercedes 190 & 300SL 1954-1963
Mercedes 230/250/280SL 1963-1971
Mercedes 350/450SL & SLC 1971-1980
Mercedes Benz Cars 1949-1954
Mercedes Benz Cars 1954-1957
Mercedes Benz Cars 1957-1961
Mercedes Benz Competition Cars 1950-1957
Metropolitan 1954-1962
MG Cars 1929-1934

MG TC 1945-1949
MG TD 1949-1953
MG TF 1953-1955
MG Cars 1957-1959
MG Cars 1959-1962
MG Midget 1961-1980
MG MGA 1955-1962
MGA Collection No. 1
MGB Roadsters 1962-1980
MGB GT 1965-1980
Mini Cooper 1961-1971
Morgan Cars 1960-1970
Morgan Cars 1969-1979
Morris Minor Collection No. 1
Old's Cutlass & 4-4-2 1964-1972
Oldsmobile Toronado 1966-1978
Opel GT 1968-1973
Packard Gold Portfolio 1946-1958
Pantera 1970-1973
Pantera & Mangusta 1969-1974
Plymouth Barracuda 1964-1974
Pontiac Fiero 1984-1988
Pontiac GTO 1964-1970
Pontiac Firebird 1967-1973
High Performance Firebirds 1982-1988
Pontiac Tempest & GTO 1961-1965
Porsche Cars 1960-1964
Porsche Cars 1964-1968
Porsche Cars 1968-1972
Porsche Cars in the Sixties
Porsche Cars 1972-1975
Porsche 356 1952-1965
Porsche 911 Collection No. 1
Porsche 911 Collection No. 2
Porsche 911 1965-1969
Porsche 911 1970-1972
Porsche 911 1973-1977
Porsche 911 Carrera 1973-1977
Porsche 911 SC 1978-1983
Porsche 911 Turbo 1975-1984
Porsche 914 1969-1975
Porsche 914 Collection No. 1
Porsche 924 1975-1981
Porsche 928 Collection No. 1
Porsche 944 1981-1985
Porsche Turbo Collection No. 1
Reliant Scimitar 1964-1986
Rolls Royce Silver Cloud 1955-1965
Rolls Royce Silver Shadow 1965-1980
Range Rover 1970-1981
Rover P4 1949-1959
Rover P4 1955-1964
Rover 2000 + 2200 1963-1977
Rover 3 & 3.5 Litre 1958-1973
Rover 3500 1968-1977
Rover 3500 & Vitesse 1976-1986
Saab Sonett Collection No. 1
Saab Turbo 1976-1983
Singer Sports Cars 1933-1934
Studebaker Hawks & Larks 1956-1963
Sunbeam Alpine & Tiger 1959-1967
Thunderbird 1955-1957
Thunderbird 1958-1963
Thunderbird 1964-1976
Toyota MR2 1984-1988
Triumph 2000-2.5-2500 1963-1977
Triumph Spitfire 1962-1980
Triumph Spitfire Collection No. 1
Triumph Stag 1970-1980
Triumph Stag Collection No. 1
Triumph TR2 & TR3 1952-1960
Triumph TR4.TR5.TR250 1961-1968
Triumph TR6 1969-1976
Triumph TR6 Collection No. 1
Triumph TR7 & TR8 1975-1982
Triumph GT6 1966-1974
Triumph Vitesse & Herald 1959-1971
TVR Gold Portfolio 1959-1988
Volkswagen Cars 1936-1956
VW Beetle 1956-1977
VW Beetle Collection No. 1
VW Golf GTi 1976-1986
VW Karmann Ghia 1955-1982
VW Scirocco 1974-1981
VW Bus-Camper-Van 1954-1967
VW Bus-Camper-Van 1968-1979
Volvo 1800 1960-1973
Volvo 120 Series 1956-1970

BROOKLANDS MUSCLE CARS SERIES

American Motors Muscle Cars 1966-1970
Buick Muscle Cars 1965-1970
Camaro Muscle Cars 1966-1972
Capri Muscle Cars 1969-1983
Chevrolet Muscle Cars 1966-1972
Dodge Muscle Cars 1967-1970
Mercury Muscle Cars 1966-1971
Mini Muscle Cars 1961-1979
Mopar Muscle Cars 1964-1967
Mopar Muscle Cars 1968-1971
Mustang Muscle Cars 1967-1971
Shelby Mustang Muscle Cars 1965-1970
Oldsmobile Muscle Cars 1964-1970
Plymouth Muscle Cars 1966-1971
Pontiac Muscle Cars 1966-1972
Muscle Cars Compared 1966-1971
Muscle Cars Compared Book 2 1965-1971

BROOKLANDS ROAD & TRACK SERIES

Road & Track on Alfa Romeo 1949-1963
Road & Track on Alfa Romeo 1964-1970

Road & Track on Alfa Romeo 1971-1976
Road & Track on Alfa Romeo 1977-1984
Road & Track on Aston Martin 1962-1984
Road & Track on Auburn Cord & Duesenberg 1952-1984
Road & Track on Audi 1952-1980
Road & Track on Audi 1980-1986
Road & Track on Austin Healey 1953-1970
Road & Track on BMW Cars 1966-1974
Road & Track on BMW Cars 1975-1978
Road & Track on BMW Cars 1979-1983
Road & Track on Cobra, Shelby &
   Ford GT40 1962-1983
Road & Track on Corvette 1953-1967
Road & Track on Corvette 1968-1982
Road & Track on Corvette 1982-1986
Road & Track on Datsun Z 1970-1983
Road & Track on Ferrari 1950-1968
Road & Track on Ferrari 1968-1974
Road & Track on Ferrari 1975-1981
Road & Track on Ferrari 1981-1984
Road & Track on Fiat Sports Cars 1968-1987
Road & Track on Jaguar 1950-1960
Road & Track on Jaguar 1961-1968
Road & Track on Jaguar 1968-1974
Road & Track on Jaguar 1974-1982
Road & Track on Lamborghini 1964-1985
Road & Track on Lotus 1972-1981
Road & Track on Maserati 1952-1974
Road & Track on Maserati 1975-1983
Road & Track on Mazda RX7 1978-1986
Road & Track on Mercedes 1952-1962
Road & Track on Mercedes 1963-1970
Road & Track on Mercedes 1971-1979
Road & Track on Mercedes 1980-1987
Road & Track on MG Sports Cars 1949-1961
Road & Track on MG Sports Cars 1962-1980
Road & Track on Mustang 1964-1977
Road & Track on Peugeot 1955-1986
Road & Track on Pontiac 1960-1983
Road & Track on Porsche 1951-1967
Road & Track on Porsche 1968-1971
Road & Track on Porsche 1972-1975
Road & Track on Porsche 1975-1978
Road & Track on Porsche 1979-1982
Road & Track on Porsche 1982-1985
Road & Track on Rolls Royce & Bentley 1950-1965
Road & Track on Rolls Royce & Bentley 1966-1984
Road & Track on Saab 1955-1985
Road & Track on Toyota Sports & G T Cars 1966-1986
Road & Track on Triumph Sports Cars 1953-1967
Road & Track on Triumph Sports Cars 1967-1974
Road & Track on Triumph Sports Cars 1974-1982
Road & Track on Volkswagen 1951-1968
Road & Track on Volkswagen 1968-1978
Road & Track on Volkswagen 1978-1985
Road & Track on Volvo 1957-1974
Road & Track on Volvo 1975-1985

BROOKLANDS CAR AND DRIVER SERIES

Car and Driver on BMW 1955-1977
Car and Driver on BMW 1977-1985
Car and Driver on Cobra, Shelby & Ford GT40
   1963-1984
Car and Driver on Datsun Z 1600 & 2000
   1966-1984
Car and Driver on Corvette 1956-1967
Car and Driver on Corvette 1968-1977
Car and Driver on Corvette 1978-1982
Car and Driver on Ferrari 1955-1962
Car and Driver on Ferrari 1963-1975
Car and Driver on Ferrari 1976-1983
Car and Driver on Mopar 1956-1967
Car and Driver on Mopar 1968-1975
Car and Driver on Pontiac 1961-1975
Car and Driver on Porsche 1955-1962
Car and Driver on Porsche 1963-1970
Car and Driver on Porsche 1970-1976
Car and Driver on Porsche 1977-1981
Car and Driver on Porsche 1982-1986
Car and Driver on Saab 1956-1985
Car and Driver on Volvo 1955-1986

BROOKLANDS MOTOR & THOROUGHBRED & CLASSIC CAR SERIES

Motor & T & CC on Ferrari 1966-1976
Motor & T & CC on Ferrari 1976-1984
Motor & T & CC on Lotus 1979-1983
Motor & T & CC on Morris Minor 1948-1983

BROOKLANDS PRACTICAL CLASSICS SERIES

Practical Classics on Austin A 40 Restoration
Practical Classics on Land Rover Restoration
Practical Classics on Metalworking in Restoration
Practical Classics on Midget/Sprite Restoration
Practical Classics on Mini Cooper Restoration
Practical Classics on MGB Restoration
Practical Classics on Morris Minor Restoration
Practical Classics on Triumph Herald/Vitesse
Practical Classics on Triumph Spitfire Restoration
Practical Classics on VW Beetle Restoration
Practical Classics on 1930S Car Restoration

BROOKLANDS MILITARY VEHICLES SERIES

Allied Military Vehicles Collection No. 1
Allied Military Vehicles Collection No. 2
Dodge Military Vehicles Collection No. 1
Military Jeeps 1941-1945
Off Road Jeeps 1944-1971
V W Kubelwagen 1940-1975

CONTENTS

BROOKLANDS
BOOKS

ACKNOWLEDGEMENTS

It has been a pleasurable and revealing task compiling this book. I had no idea when I started that the Fiat Spider was so universally liked and attracted such praise when it made its debut in the sixties. I suppose this is naive of me as any car that can remain in production for over two decades must be special.

For readers who enjoy a formal introduction I would suggest that you turn to page 96 and read Richard Sutton's excellent historical piece 'Forgotten Flair' which first appeared in Classic and Sportscar in 1986.

The Brooklands series of books, which now exceed 300 titles, are intended to fulfill the needs of owners of interesting cars by making available, road tests and other articles that were written about their automobiles. We are fortunate that authors, photographers and publishers understand our motives and generously allow us to include their copyright photographs and stories.

We are sure that Fiat enthusiasts will wish to join with us in thanking, amongst others, the management of Autocar, Car and Driver, Classic and Sportscar, Foreign Car Guide, Modern Motor, Motor, Motor Trend, Popular Imported Cars, Road & Track, Road & Track Specials, Road Test, Sports Car Graphic and Sports Car World for their continued support.

R.M. Clarke

Fiat 124 Spider

Be now informed that the delightful Italian automotive personality exists in a modestly priced Fiat 124.

A lady. A lovely, sensual, responsive Italian lady. There is no other way of thinking about the Fiat 124 Spider, it's time you knew it.

Like women to dream about, the really good Italian cars have always had a mysterious irresistibility and an eagerness to please. Somehow, they seem to exist solely for the pleasure of their drivers. There are moments of passing poignancy, a gentle, soft scent of perfume in the lush evening air of summer and those moments *are* the Ferraris and the Maseratis and the Lamborghinis. Be now informed that the de-

lightful Italian automotive personality exists in a modestly priced Fiat.

For $3230.50 there is an exclusive mistress waiting named Fiat 124. Fierce enough, subject to a flashing kaleidoscope of moods, submissive, even occasionally demanding; a more-or-less permanent dalliance with the 124 is in vivid contrast to assignations with the bluff, obvious, straightforward life to be led with the likes of the Datsun 2000, or Triumph TR-250. Where there are moments of tight-jawed hardship with the British cars, all is sweet willingness with Italy's 124.

The substantial advances in automotive technology in the last 15 years have almost completely passed by the medium-priced sports cars. "Refinement" has meant putting frosting on a two-by-four and calling it cake. It tastes a little better but it's still a board.

The 124 Spider is not a warmed over traditional sports car. Although it does share some mechanical parts with the 124 sedan, the car itself is entirely new and totally different than anything currently available in its price class. In fact, it just seems like too good a car for its price. In these days, when you can't even touch an Alfa Duetto for less than four grand and a naked Porsche 912 goes for over five, the 124 Spider is a bargain.

Why bother with a sports car at all if it's not an exciting, performance-oriented machine? Where is the love affair, the endless poring over mechanical intricacies, the quiet bragging about your car's delectable —almost unique—virtues? Stand tall in the saloon, even the office, puffed with pride and the envy of lesser folk who somehow don't understand. *That* is where owning a sports car counts as much as on the road. Because today you seldom have the opportunity to drive a sports car in the true let-it-all-hang-out tradition. And a major portion of the owner's satisfaction comes from appreciating the mechanical sophistication of the love-object. Delights like 4-wheel disc brakes and 5-speed transmissions and double overhead cams are all part of the sports car thing and the Fiat 124 Spider has them all.

Fiat has firmly resisted the current trend of stuffing a big 6-cylinder engine into its sports machine and, instead, has made extensive modifications to the smallish 124 sedan engine. The bore has been increased from 2.87 to 3.15 inches, with no change in the stroke, to enlarge the displacement to 1438cc. The compression ratio remains a mild 8.9 to one. Instead of using the sedan's pushrod cylinder head however, the Spider gets a new aluminum, double overhead cam head with pent-roof combustion chambers. It does wonders for the output of the small displacement engine. The cams are driven by a fiberglass-reinforced rubber

. . . a more-or-less permanent dalliance with the Fiat 124 is in vivid contrast to assignations with the bluff, obvious, straightforward life to be led with the likes of the Datsun 2000 or Triumph TR-250.

timing belt under an elaborate cast aluminum shield at the front of the engine. A 2-bbl. Weber carburetor with a progressive secondary and a cast iron four-into-two exhaust header complete the engine picture. According to Fiat, 96 horsepower is available at the flywheel, 31 more than the sedan—which is no small improvement.

We know what you're thinking. With only a 1.5-liter engine the Spider is another one of those pretty, but slow, Fiats. Little Fiats have always substituted charm for performance until Abarth gets a hold of them and rips things out and stuffs things in until the softness is all gone and they're blatant snorting devices, wailing up a mountainside in a European mountain-climbing championship.

The 124 Spider shouldn't have been any different. At least, that's what *we* thought and we turned out to be all wrong. Our test Spider would do a standing quarter mile in 17.5 seconds at 77.0 mph with 0-60 times of 10.1 seconds. We're not saying this is earthshaking performance, but the Fiat can show its tailpipe to its six-cylinder competition in a side-by-side, wheel-to-wheel discussion and that's no small surprise. Top speed is of little importance in this world of 70 mph speed limits, but, just for the record, we did see an honest 104 mph in fifth gear. Fifth is really a bit too long for top speed runs since the engine never quite reaches its peak power point. Fiat claims the Spider will actually go 2 mph faster in fourth and, judging from the ratios, we believe it.

By this time you've gotten a hint that the 124 has a 5-speed gearbox, but we can't resist talking about it anyway. Five speeds are great devices; great to dream about and great to slice through on that curvy country road. But even more important, with a relatively small displacement engine like the Fiat's, all those ratios allow you to more effectively stay in the engine's prime operating range. Shift effort is exceptionally light and, since the lever must be lifted for reverse, there is no danger of a 5-R shift—a *distinct* possibility with some other 5-speeds. Most 5-speed gearboxes have centering springs which push the lever into the 3-4 slot so the driver can easily tell which gear he is about to select by feel alone. The Fiat's spring is a bit weak, however, so more attention must be paid to the position of the lever. Care is required on 2-3 upshifts and 5-4 downshifts to make sure the lever goes into the right slot. With a stronger spring it would be perfect—except for the ratios, that is. The test car had a fairly short first gear and a noticeable hole between second and third. In fact, it felt very much like the ratios in the 4-speed

box on the 124 Coupe. Here's where the intrigue starts.

According to the owner's manual the Spider ratios are completely different than the Coupe ratios, the Spider having an even lower first gear. When we questioned the Fiat factory representative he assured us that neither of the gear sets we spoke of were correct and that all Spiders coming into the U.S. had yet another set. Italians are, by constitution, diplomats—even conspirators—so we never reached any sort of agreement. But while we're convinced the test Spider had the Coupe gears we hope the new gear set-up is genuine, because it supposedly has closer ratios with a longer first.

The Spider has 4-wheel disc brakes with vacuum assist. They perform flawlessly, making perfect straight line stops from 80 mph at a rate of 0.88G with only light pedal pressure. Unfortunately, they tended to be noisy, particularly after the brake test. Three of them were content with a faint squeak but the right front liked to moan a lot (the mistress image again) whenever we tried to stop, which is a fault probably peculiar to this one car.

The Spider's rigid axle rear suspension, using trailing arms and a Panhard rod to locate the axle, is so effective that we see no need for improvement for street driving. The ride is soft by traditional sports car standards and yet firm enough for precise control in any situation we encountered. Although supremely predictable, the Spider has a very strong understeering nature which definitely reduces its cornering speed. The scrubbing of the front tires in tight corners absorbs more power than the engine can produce, so the car is fated to slow all the way through. This characteristic is much less noticeable in high speed corners, say 70-80 mph, but those aren't the ones you normally pick to have fun with either. Ideally, for really quick cornering, power available and understeer should be in proportion to each other. Low powered cars should be very nearly neutral so you can get the tail out with power when required. This is virtually impossible with the Fiat. A rear anti-sway bar is part of the standard suspension but we definitely feel a stiffer one is required for *optimum* handling.

Radial ply tires are also standard equipment on the Spider. The test car had 165 SR 13 Pirelli Cinturatos but Michelins are also available. Fiat recommends 23 psi all around but we suspect 5 psi more in the front would go a long way toward curing the understeer ailment.

The real beauty of the Fiat can only be realized in driving. The car is low, just a

bit over 49 inches, but entry is no problem because of the long doors. The instant you touch down on the driver's seat you feel that Italian personality. The seat is beautifully comfortable, covered with a soft leather-like material, and supports your anatomy in just the way God intended. The back rests adjust through a wide angle simply by turning a knob.

The roominess of the Spider's interior comes as a surprise. Elbow and shoulder room is plentiful and you can even see your feet—as opposed to just sticking them down into long dark tunnels—a feature of traditional sports cars. The reason for all of this unexpected interior space is that while the Spider has approximately the same wheelbase and overall length as its competitors, it's nearly five inches wider. Don't get the idea that it's too wide for your garage, though, because it's still nine inches narrower than a Camaro.

As you look around the interior it seems that everything is padded, but most noticeable is the soft roll on the door window sills at shoulder level. Each door has a large arm rest, the front of which turns up at a 45-degree angle to form a grab handle.

The unpadded portion of the instrument panel is made of real wood, and real wood is nice to see. It seems exactly in keeping with the superb quality of the interior. The instruments are grouped directly in front of the driver, easily readable and labeled in both English and Italian. (How's your *benzina* supply?) The oil pressure and fuel gauges even have warning lights to indicate a dangerously low condition. Most remarkable is that the steering wheel doesn't obscure the driver's view of a single gauge, a rarity that doesn't occur even in a Porsche.

When speaking of the Spider's driving position, the old road tester's cliche of "everything falls readily to hand" would have to be modified slightly to read "with possible exception of the steering wheel which is slightly out of reach to anyone with less than 35-inch arms." You don't know the meaning of straight arm driving until you try the 124 Spider. That wheel is so far away you can hardly see it, much less touch it—ah, the Farina-Fangio tradition. The staff was divided as to whether or not they liked it, but all agreed it was part of the Italian personality.

Out on the road the Fiat hums quietly along; none of the precise mechanical whir of a BMW; none of the belligerent roar of the traditional sports cars but a nice, refined hum. In fact, engine noise at less than full throttle is almost indiscernible. It's

CONTINUED ON PAGE **64**

ACCELERATION standing ¼ mile, seconds

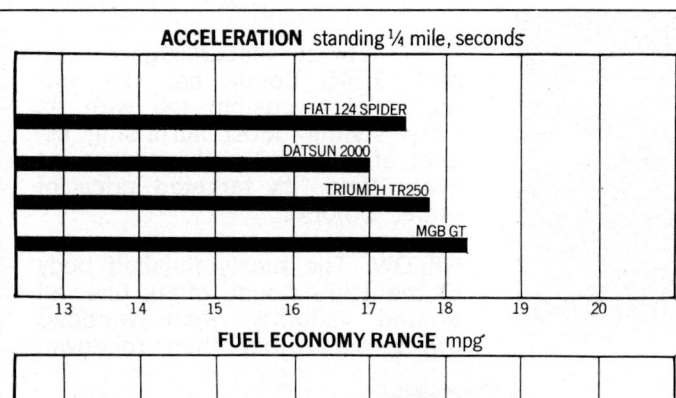

FIAT 124 SPIDER
DATSUN 2000
TRIUMPH TR250
MGB GT

13 14 15 16 17 18 19 20

BRAKING 80-0 mph panic stop, feet

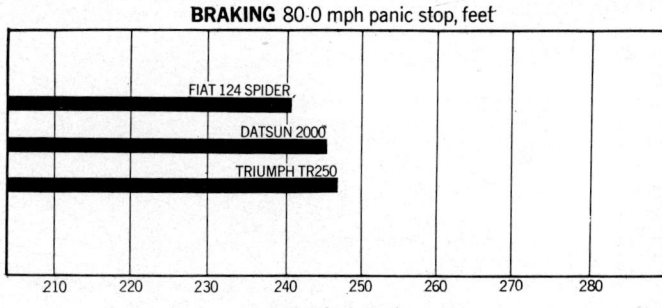

FIAT 124 SPIDER
DATSUN 2000
TRIUMPH TR250

210 220 230 240 250 260 270 280

FUEL ECONOMY RANGE mpg

FIAT 124 SPIDER
DATSUN 2000
TRIUMPH TR250

6 10 14 18 22 26 30 34

PRICE AS TESTED dollars x 1000

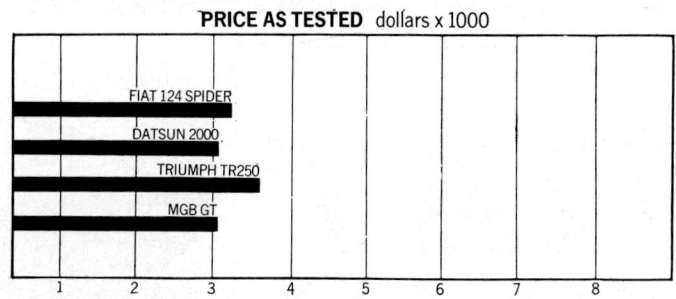

FIAT 124 SPIDER
DATSUN 2000
TRIUMPH TR250
MGB GT

1 2 3 4 5 6 7 8

FIAT 124 SPIDER

Importer: Fiat Roosevelt
532 Sylvan Avenue
Englewood Cliffs, N.J.

Vehicle type: Front-engine, rear-wheel-drive, 2-passenger convertible

Price as tested: $3265.50
(Manufacturer's suggested retail price, including all options listed below, Federal excise tax, dealer preparation and delivery charges; does not include state and local taxes, license or freight charges)

Options on test car: Radio $35.00

ENGINE

Type: 4-in-line, water-cooled cast iron block, aluminum head, 5 main bearings
Bore x stroke...3.15 x 2.81 in, 80.0 x 71.5 mm
Displacement..............87.8 cu in, 1438 cc
Compression ratio.....................8.9 to one
Carburetion.....1 x 2 bbl Weber 26/34 DHS A
Valve gear.................Timing belt driven double overhead cam
Power (SAE)..............96 bhp @ 6500 rpm
Torque (SAE)........82.5 lbs/ft @ 4000 rpm
Specific power output.........1.09 bhp/cu in, 66.8 bhp/liter
Max. recommended engine speed...6800 rpm

DRIVE TRAIN

Transmission............5-speed, all-synchro
Final drive ratio....................4.10 to one

Gear	Ratio	Mph/1000 rpm	Max. test speed
I	3.75	4.4	30 mph (6800 rpm)
II	2.30	7.1	48 mph (6800 rpm)
III	1.49	11.0	74 mph (6800 rpm)
IV	1.00	16.4	101 mph (6150 rpm)
V/OD	0.91	18.0	104 mph (5800 rpm)

DIMENSIONS AND CAPACITIES

Wheelbase...........................89.8 in
Track....................F: 53.2 in, R: 51.9 in
Length.................................156.3 in
Width...................................63.5 in
Height..................................49.2 in
Ground clearance.......................N.A.
Curb weight.........................2093 lbs
Weight distribution, F/R.........56.4/43.6%
Battery capacity.........12 volts, 60 amp/hr
Generator capacity.................527 watts
Fuel capacity........................11.5 gal
Oil capacity...........................4.0 qts
Water capacity........................8.0 qts

SUSPENSION

F: Ind., unequal length wishbones, coil springs, anti-sway bar.
R: Rigid axle, trailing arms, panhard rod, coil springs, anti-sway bar.

STEERING

Type........................ Worm and roller
Turns lock-to-lock.......................2.7
Turning circle curb to curb.............34.1 ft

BRAKES

F:............8.93 Solid disc, vacuum assist
R:............8.93 Solid disc, vacuum assist

WHEELS AND TIRES

Wheel size.........................13 x 5.0-in
Wheel type...........Stamped steel, 4-bolt
Tire make and size.Pirelli Cinturatos, 165 x 13
Tire type ....Tube type
Test inflation pressures...F: 23 psi, R: 23 psi
Tire load rating......710 lbs per tire @ 24 psi

PERFORMANCE

Zero to	Seconds
30 mph	2.9
40 mph	4.8
50 mph	7.3
60 mph	10.1
70 mph	13.8
80 mph	19.0
90 mph	25.0

Standing ¼-mile.......17.5 sec @ 77.0 mph
Top speed........................104 mph
80-0 mph....................241 ft (.88 G)
Fuel mileage.....22-26 mpg on premium fuel
Cruising range..................253–299 mi

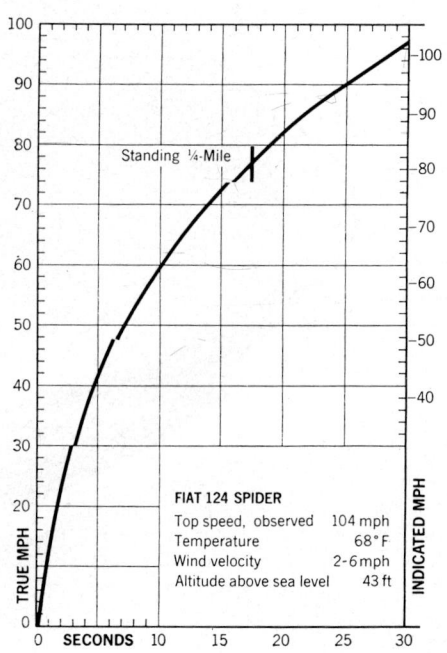

Standing ¼-Mile

FIAT 124 SPIDER
Top speed, observed   104 mph
Temperature   68°F
Wind velocity   2-6 mph
Altitude above sea level   43 ft

TRUE MPH   INDICATED MPH

SECONDS

NEW 1968 MODELS

LEFT: Latest Fiat designed and built 124S Coupe has the earmarks of a custom job with its crisp styling. Most surprising aspect of this 100 mph car was, at press time, its targeted price of under $3,000.

BELOW: The nicely finished body of the 124S Coupe offers fine, all around visibility. Rear windows swing out rather than rolldown.

FIAT 124S

By EMMET GREENE

Styled by Pinin Farina, the Sports Spider shares the 96 hp double overhead camshaft, four-cylinder engine with the pretty Coupe above. Its 95.3 inch wheelbase is 4.5 inches less than the Coupe, and it is 5.5 inches shorter overall, and some 84 lbs. lighter, yet the Coupe has higher top speed. Spider has 5-speed gearbox with overdrive 5th and Coupe has 4 gears.

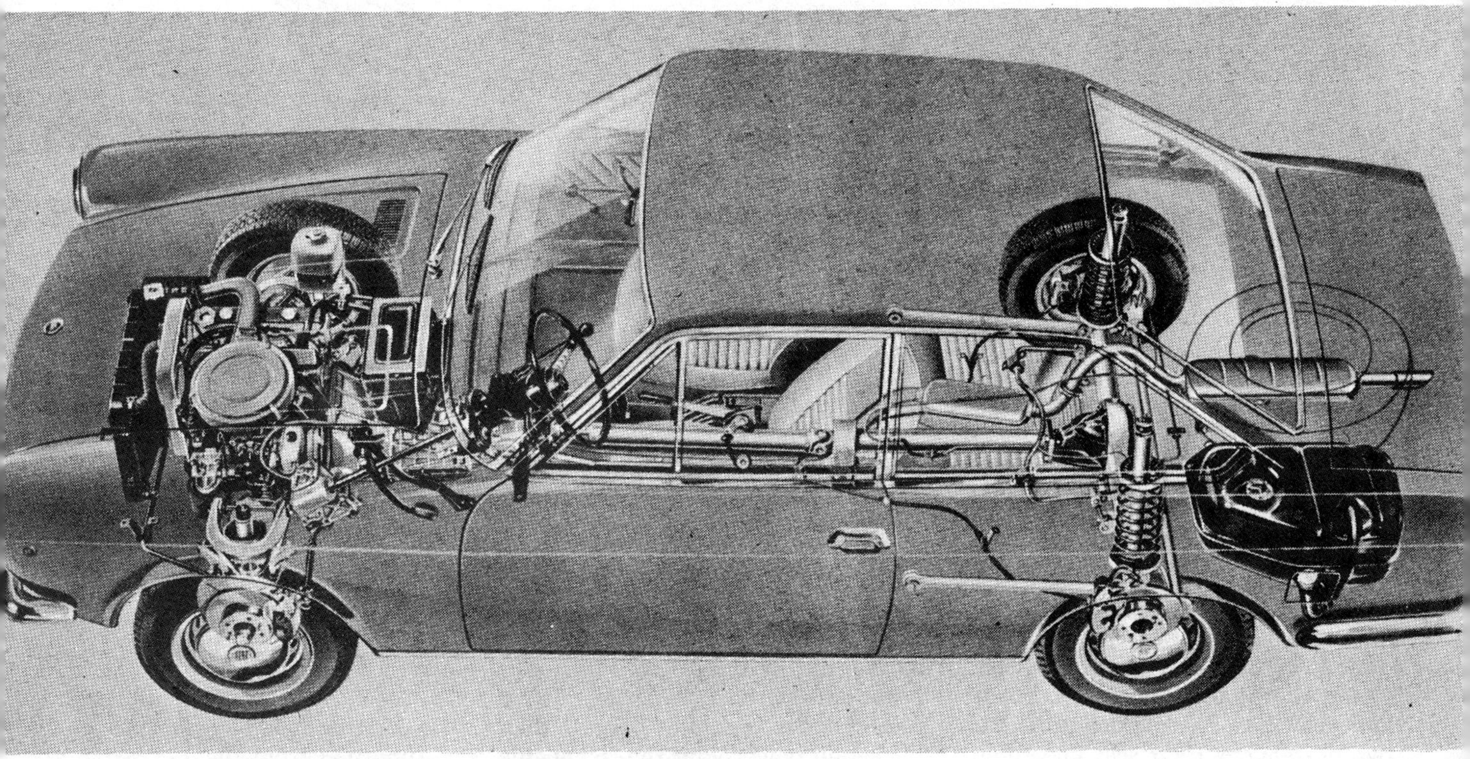

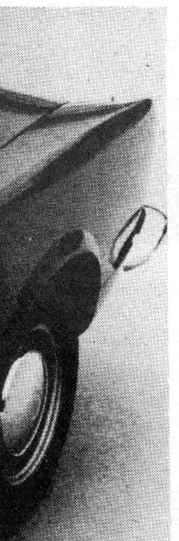

ABOVE: Phantom view of pretty Coupe. Disc brakes and coil springs on all fours. Fine handling attributable to front and rear sway bars, and at rear dual torque arms and transverse panhard rod at back of axle. Braking effort distribution valve controlled by riding height or loading helps reduce rear wheel lockup or skids.

LEFT: Rear seat of Coupe offers more knee room than many close coupled or 2 plus 2 coupes. However, Spider convertible has less knee room in back.

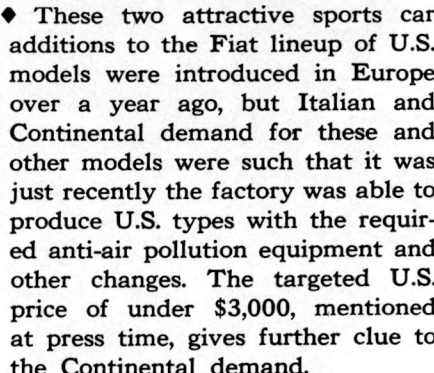

♦ These two attractive sports car additions to the Fiat lineup of U.S. models were introduced in Europe over a year ago, but Italian and Continental demand for these and other models were such that it was just recently the factory was able to produce U.S. types with the required anti-air pollution equipment and other changes. The targeted U.S. price of under $3,000, mentioned at press time, gives further clue to the Continental demand.

Besides the appealing styling they are well equipped and finished, have nice interiors and comfortable seating. The Coupe with its elegant but simple lines was designed by the factory's styling studio, and the Spider is the work of Pinin Farina.

Both 124S types are based on Fiat's most successful international sedan, the 124, that went on sale here about two years ago. Unlike most sedan-based sports versions, the 124S models offer an entirely different engine and an appealing character that belies their sedan lineage.

The coupe shares the sedan's 95.27 inch wheelbase, but the stance of the Spider is foreshortened nearly 5½ inches to 89.7 inches. The graceful design goal of the coupe resulted in its being slightly more than 3 inches longer (162 inches)

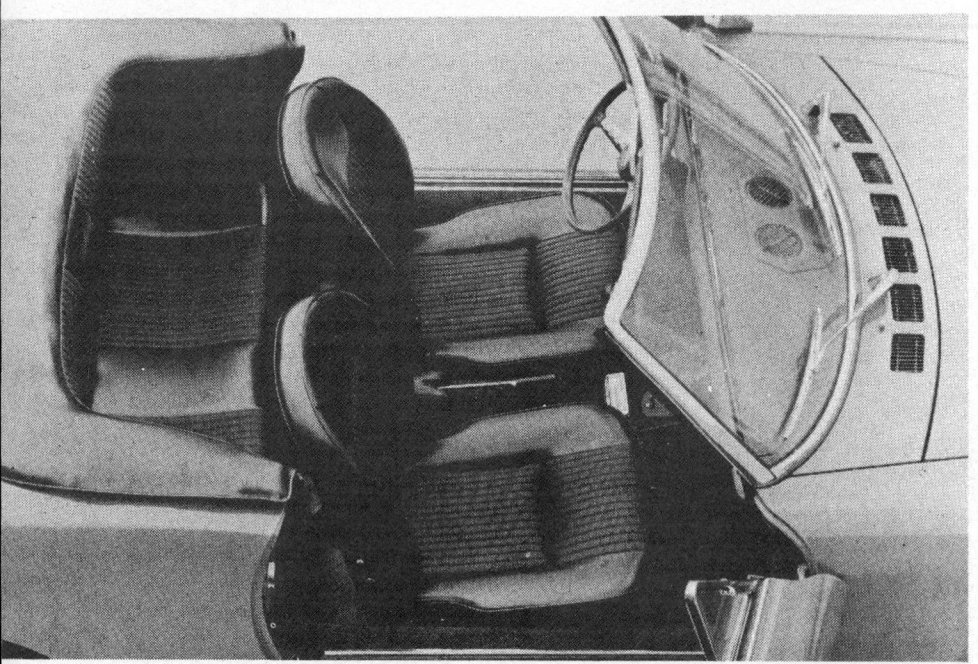

LEFT: The bucket seats of the Spider convertible offer good side support in keeping with the car's cornering abilities. Shorter wheelbase of Spider reduces rear seat knee room. Rotatable vents on top of dash have directional vanes and serve as fresh air vents or defrosters.

than the somewhat boxy 124 sedan. The 124S coupe is about the size of the Karmann Ghia Coupe, but it has rear seat accommodation for two passengers. Rear seat kneeroom ranges from about 5 to 11 inches dependent on the adjustment position of the front seats. The shorter wheelbase convertible is cramped for rear kneeroom.

Most notable difference is, of course, the advance design high output, dual overhead camshaft, 96 hp four-cylinder engine. Larger than the sedan powerplant the "S" engine has a 1438cc (87.8 cu. in.) versus the 65 hp 1197cc (73 cu. in.) unit used in the sedan. The added power boosts the top speed of both sports models to the 105 mph area, and

zero to 60 mph acceleration of continental models of the coupe is under 13 seconds—a very creditable figure for this type of chariot.

Inherited from the 124 sedan are such features as four wheel disc brakes and a two piece driveshaft with a center steady bearing. The brakes have a load sensitive brake pressure regulating valve to mini-

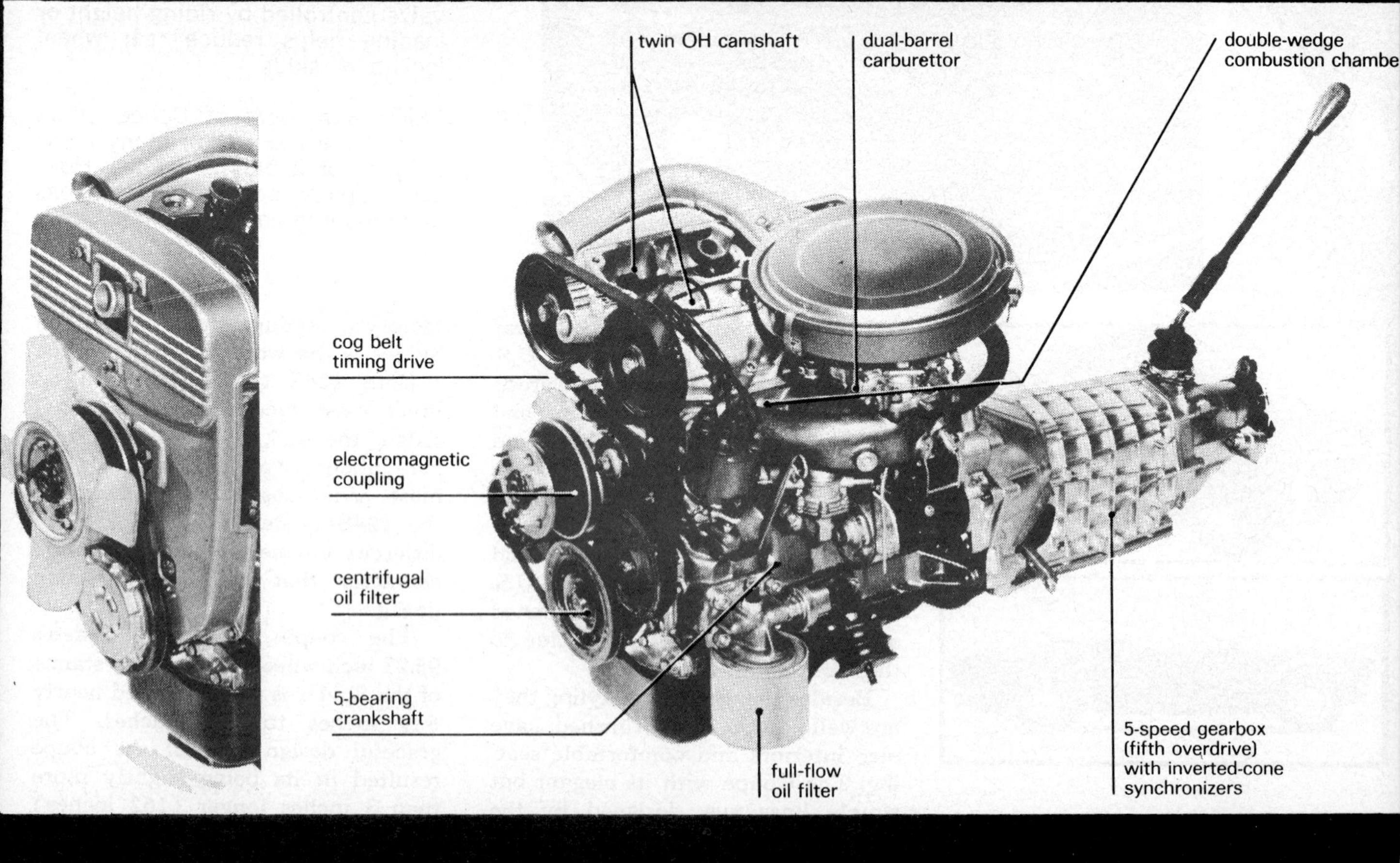

twin OH camshaft

dual-barrel carburettor

double-wedge combustion chamber

cog belt timing drive

electromagnetic coupling

centrifugal oil filter

5-bearing crankshaft

full-flow oil filter

5-speed gearbox (fifth overdrive) with inverted-cone synchronizers

 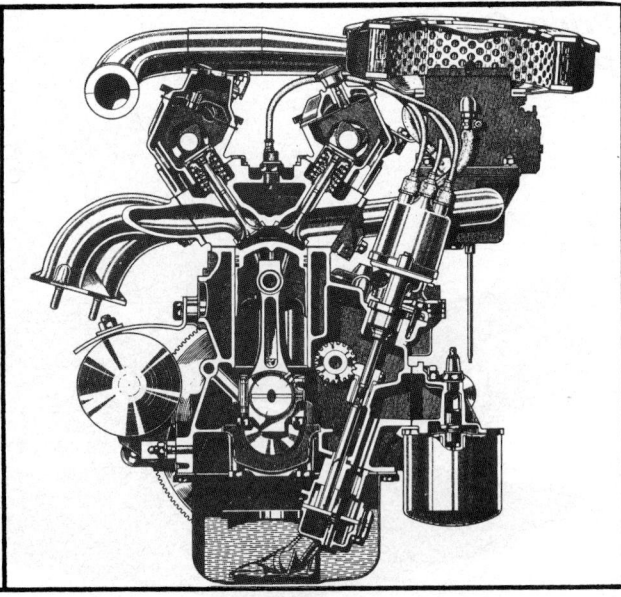

mize wheel lock-up or skidding and contribute to straight line stopping. The discs have power assistance through a vacuum servo.

Interior trim and finish is very attractive and is not in any way related to the more spartan sedan. Upholstery is in leatherette vinyl, and the comfortable, deeply contoured front bucket seats are of the

ABOVE LEFT: Front suspension and steering assembly of Spider shows front sway bar, disc brakes and angled coil springs surrounding shock absorbers. Safety steering has a universal jointed column.

ABOVE RIGHT: Double overhead camshaft, seen at top of overhead valves, very efficient crossflow cylinder head, dual wedge combustion chambers allow this 87.7 cu. in. (1438 cc) engine to produce 96 hp @ 6500 rpm with only 8.9 to 1 compression ratio.

LEFT: Very efficient five main bearing engine. Fiat is the first to use cog belt to drive dual overhead cams. Far left shows timing or belt cover in place and centrifugal oil filter below fan.

reclining type. Their side bolster construction offers fine side support when cornering rapidly, and seats also have a bolster type construction for support of the thighs.

Instrumentation is complete in that it provides a trip recorder speedometer, an 8000 rpm electronic tachometer, and gauges for oil pressure, water temperature and fuel along with the usual indicator lights. The dashboard, padded at upper and lower edges, has a simulated wood finish to complement the competition type steering wheel.

An attractive floor console carries the stout, positive acting shift lever to operate the four-speed floor shift on the coupe or the five-speed unit that is standard on the convertible. To the rear of the console, between the seats, is a pull-up handbrake and a group of heater control levers. The interior is fully carpeted, and this helps enhance the rich looking sporty or GT interior.

Seated at the wheel of the coupe one becomes aware of the excellent all-around vision and the large glass area. The interesting thin rear quarter pillar and large rear window just about eliminate any blindspots. The window is of the swing-out type that is hinged in front.

Other interesting aspects of the car are the fresh-air vents on the dashboard. On the coupe they are mounted on the dash panel, on the convertible they're on top of the dash. As our short trial and photographic run was during sub-zero temperature we did not sample the effectiveness of vents. However, the

heater on the coupe proved to be very effective.

The high point of mechanical interest is the dual overhead camshaft engine. Fiat is the world's first manufacturer to adopt a cogged belt to drive two camshafts. Pioneer, perhaps, was Glas in Germany and the Pontiac 6 in the U.S., but they, of course, are single cams. Unlike the wire reinforced belt of the Glas, Fiat uses a neoprene belt with a fiberglas reinforced center section that is not subject to corrosion.

Moving the valve operating camshaft from its usual position inside the engine onto the cylinder head contributes to the engine's mechanical efficiency and is a method of gaining horsepower. In current U.S. engines the sole application of overhead cams, other than racing powerplants, is the Pontiac Six.

It is a more costly design but it eliminates the array of push rods and rocker arms needed for the remote control of the engine's valves. The overhead cams operate virtually directly on the valve stems and eliminate the reciprocating weight and the wear and expansion factors of the conventional rocker arm set-up.

One of the drawbacks of some overhead camshaft designs has been the difficulty or expense of valve clearance adjustment and the high labor cost of replacing or servicing the former chain drive.

Fiat neatly solves these potential drawbacks by providing shim adjustment of valve clearances and a

CONTINUED ON PAGE 64

PHOTOS BY BOB MC KAY

FIAT 124 SPORT COUPE AND SPIDER

The phrase quoted above, "... an amazing price /quality/performance ratio," appears in a multi-lingual full line brochure prepared by the prolific Fiat *Stampa e Propaganda* department. The same paragraph also describes the 124 Coupe as having, "... an appealingly new sporty line and lively spirit" so it is highly doubtful that Madison Avenue's Ivory hunters are scouting the twisted streets of Turin to find this new copy writing genius. I mean, his work is a little uneven.

Nonetheless, and despite the fact that it swings a little less than "Somewhere West Of Laramie ..." this phrase pretty well pigeonholes the pair of cars referred to hereinafter.

We'll even buy "amazing" ... a word seldom employed in this magazine except to express horror or indignation ... because the kicker here is definitely *price*. Fiat has come up with something which looks, feels, smells and drives like something which costs a bundle more. You can't call the 124s "poor man's Ferraris" because that handle really belongs to the Dinos. But, we'll guarantee that your less sensitive neighbors will at least ask you if this car is related to a Ferrari should you bring one home.

FUNCTIONAL DESIGN WITH GRACE

After throwing out the snob appeal, and getting down to the factual aspects, it is apparent that the styling of the Coupe, in particular, must be given some high marks because it is functional without being ungraceful. The greenhouse is about as open as is possible. The pillars are extremely

12

Panic stop with locked wheels produces only slight deviation. Braking capabilities of both Coupe and Spider are rated very high at 27 to 28 fps deceleration rate.

Even with live rear axle, both Fiats stick like glue on most surfaces. Fuel consumption averages 25.5 mpg.

into the driver's position with no problems. Artist Dave Deal, a bit shorter but weighing 240 pounds, felt that the seats are a little skimpy for the very big man. However the average sized members of the staff were well satisfied both with the seats and knee stretch out and floorboard room. Rear seat headroom is also adequate except for the outsize person.

The Spider has the same front seating as the Coupe, but rear seat legroom and luggage space are diminished. Rear seats are for small kids or casual jaunts.

A TOUCH OF CLASS

Interior appointments and details also set the Fiats apart from other entries in this price bracket. There is a true touch of class, both in the coupe which is a factory design and the spider, a Pininfarina design. For example: the real-wood dash panel in the spider is removable (via four knurled screws) for access to instruments; an under-hood light is provided; fresh air is delivered at floorboard level for cooling where it is needed; there are generous map (or junk) bins; the convertible top is a

narrow and visibility is unmatched in a closed car. The backlight is not so slanted as to create great heat or frost problems, but it opens up the roofline tremendously.

Whether the styling appeals to you or not is a matter of preference, but, from a practical standpoint, the space between the wheel centers has been quite well used. There is decent legroom in the rear seats and a couple of youngsters can ride all day without the paralysis which would afflict them in the average "plus two" of

this type. Adults can be comfortable for reasonable distances and the deck will accommodate a couple of suitcases.

The front seats are sensibly shaped and well constructed. Although not as big and padded as the Porsche for instance, these buckets offer much more comfort than most of those found in comparably priced machines. The backs are adjustable for rake and there is 7" of travel. Our tallest consultant fit his leggy six foot four inch frame carrying 205 pounds

Cockpit layout combines the functional with the aesthetic. Instruments and controls are sensibly located. Seating is very comfortable.

No contortions required, instrument panel is removable for easy access.

Optional Mag wheels are popular extra. Disc brakes are 9 inch diameter and power assisted.

one-man, one-hand type operation; the optional radio has a disappearing antenna, with key and the windshield wiper has provision for intermittent operation. Carpeting is another in a long list of no-cost "extras" included in the base prices.

These items are set forth because they upgrade the cars quite a bit over the normal concept of a sports car in this range — which tends to be on the Spartan side. Even leaving styling out of it, the sensible instrument panel and controls layout, cannot help being attractive and reminiscent of much more expensive Italian cars.

The twin overhead cam engine, displacing 1438 cc (88 cubic inches), might also qualify as a "class" item. Double knockers aren't all that common and this little instrument wails a pretty tune . . . right up to 7,000 rpm.

NOT MICKEY MOUSE

Although one review of the 124 ascribed a "certain mousy character" to the engine, we cannot agree. True, it requires some activity with

the gearchange lever to extract best performance, but certainly not to an excessive degree. And, we found that it will lug around 2,000 rpm nicely. In fact, the ROAD TEST group was unanimous in its praise of the car's performance on the highway and none of them considered its dragstrip acceleration times the least bit inferior.

The figures quoted incidentally are for the Coupe. We did not run acceleration tests on the Spider, but reports from Paul Frere and other European writers whose opinions we respect, indicate that there is very little to choose between the two.

With our test cars having around 5,000 miles on the odometer, the best e.t. recorded was 17.76 seconds for the standing start quarter. The highest top speed through the traps was 74.40 mph. This is MGB, Triumph GT-6, Sunbeam Alpine type performance.

The Coupe has a four speed gearbox as standard equipment with a five speed as an option. The Spider utili-

zes the five speed as a stock item and its contribution is welcome but we couldn't call it mandatory. Fifth gear is not just an overdrive tacked onto the four speed. The gearsets are entirely different in the two boxes. Closer-spaced and with a "higher" first, the five speed's final ratio is .912 to 1. Both cars use a 4.1 to 1 ring and pinion. The use of 5th causes about a 400 rpm drop in engine speed at 70 mph, which may make you feel a little better at cruising but which doesn't seem too important to either the engine's comfort or that of the driver. Actually, the Spider's flat-out top speed is higher in 4th than it is in 5th.

The engine is not identical to that in the Fiat 125 sedan (available in Europe only) although both employ

Underhood space is snug with twin cam engine and accessories. Dipstick and plugs are easy to reach, however. Fan is electric, thermostatically controlled.

Coupe trunk is 14 inches deep and measures 35 inches from front to back. With 60 inch width, two suitcases and miscellaneous items can be carried.

the notched "Gilmer" belt cam drive. The 124 Sport models have a shorter stroke and different carburetion.

THOROUGHLY MODERN MILLIEU

Clearly the reason that such a luxurious package can be delivered for this price is the fact that so many sedan components can be used. This also accounts for much of the price differential between coupe and Spider. The latter is five inches shorter in wheelbase and is not built on the stock sedan platform which serves the Coupe. Otherwise, drive, suspension, and accessories are taken right off the fast-moving Fiat sedan pro-

duction lines.

As any faithful reader of ROAD TEST knows, the Fiat 124 sedan has been well thought of in these quarters. It is a thoroughly modern version of a standard design with emphasis on good braking and handling.

Four-wheel discs, and rear-front proportioning valve, combined with radial tires (stock) add up to quick, controllable stops. We were able to maintain 27 to 28 fps deceleration rates without rear wheel lockup. Panic stop skids resulted in straight-line halting. This puts the 124s in a top bracket for brake effectiveness.

The brakes are power-assisted but steering is not. This makes for a little wheel heaviness at low speeds, such as in parking. However steering from 10 or 15 mph on up is light, positive and quite responsive.

Naturally, the true appraisal of a car lies not in its technical achievements but in how well it satisfies the requirements.

A small displacement sports car, (*Small Turismo*, perhaps?) is obviously for fun and inexpensive but distinguished transportation. Whereas the "fun" plainly comes from an ability to maneuver in a much nimbler fashion than something larger and more powerful.

The Coupe and Spider fulfill the requirements in excellent style. Outside of the Lancia Fulvia, the staff of the magazine couldn't come up with a recently-tested sports car which had provoked such an uninhibited reaction in the person behind the wheel. These little cars handle beautifully under all conditions and there just isn't any fault to be found in their road behavior.

Give the Michelin 'X' and Pirelli Cinturato tires full credit, but both

ROAD PERFORMANCE GOOD

the Coupe and Spider stick like glue in steady state turns and in transition. They have enough power to go exhilaratingly fast, except on the steepest uphill stretches, and don't worry, you can get from here to there at the speed limit.

With the announcement that integrated air conditioning will be available for the Coupe, Fiat has just about rubbed out the last of our notes on the squawk sheet.

In truth, there were fewer negative comments on these cars than anything recent. This stemmed from two reasons. One: The price, for a car of this concept, particularly the Coupe, is more than right.

Two: The quality in all appointments is so high that there was never any need to excuse anything on the basis of price. We have always maintained the idea that for a car to be outstanding the *value* has to be there. Thus, there are occasions when it is necessary to balance something which may not be perfection against the overall benefit and decide whether the annoyance or shortcoming is not consistent with the price.

But, in the case of the Fiat 124 Coupe and Spider, no apologies are needed. Unless high mileage produces some problems (and this would be unusual considering the sedan's record) we will have to rate them as outstanding. ♠

FIAT 124 Sport Coupe
$2,923.90   West Coast P.O.E.

DIMENSIONS

Overall length (in.)	162
Width (in.)	65.8
Height (in.)	52.2
Wheelbase (in.)	95.3
Tread, front (in.)	53
Tread, rear (in.)	51.8
Turning diameter (ft.)	35
Fuel tank capacity (gal.)	14.2
Trunk capacity (cu. ft.)	17.1

WEIGHT, TIRES, BRAKES

Weight, curb (lb.)	2 030
Weight distribution front	53 %
Weight distribution rear	47 %
Tires, Pirelli radial	165 x 13
Brakes, front	disc
Brakes, rear	disc

ENGINE

Type	dohc in-line 4
Displacement (cu. in.)	87
Displacement (cc)	1438
Horsepower (at 6500 rpm)	96
Torque (at 4000 rpm)	82.42 lb/ft

SUSPENSION

Front . . . . independent: wishbones, coil springs, anti-roll bar

Rear . . . . . live, longitudinal radius arms, torque tube, Panhard rod, anti-roll bar

PERFORMANCE & ACCELERATION

0-30 mph (sec.)	3.4
0-40 mph (sec.)	5.9
0-50 mph (sec.)	7.4
0-60 mph (sec.)	11.6
0-70 mph (sec.)	17.8
0-80 mph (sec.)	24.8

PASSING

30-50 mph (sec.)	4.0
40-60 mph (sec.)	5.7
50-70 mph (sec.)	10.4
60-80 mph (sec.)	13.2
Standing ¼ mile (sec.)	17.76
Speed at end of ¼ mile (mph)	74.40
Top speed (est. mph)	103

BRAKING

From 60 mph (ft.)	138.2

Fiat 124 Spider
$3,225.50   West Coast P.O.E.

DIMENSIONS

Overall length (in.)	156
Width (in.)	63
Height (in.)	49
Wheelbase (in.)	89
Tread, front (in.)	53
Tread, rear (in.)	51
Turning diameter (ft.)	34.2
Fuel Tank capacity (gal.)	14.4
Trunk capacity (cu. ft.)	14.0

WEIGHT, TIRES, BRAKES

Weight, curb (lb.)	2080
Weight distribution front	53 %
Weight distribution rear	47 %
Tires, Pirelli radial	165 x 13
Brakes, front	disc
Brakes, rear	disc

ENGINE

Type	dohc in-line 4
Displacement (cu. in.)	87
Displacement (cc)	1438
Horsepower (at 6500 rpm)	96
Torque (at 4000 rpm)	82.42 lb/ft

SUSPENSION

Front . . . . independent: wishbones, coil springs, anti-roll bar

Rear . . . . . live, trailing arms, transverse Panhard rod coil springs, anti-roll bar

PERFORMANCE & ACCELERATION (times estimated)

0-30 mph (sec.)	3.4
0-40 mph (sec.)	6.2
0-50 mph (sec.)	8.1
0-60 mph (sec.)	11.8
0-70 mph (sec.)	19.6
0-80 mph (sec.)	25.0

PASSING

30-50 mph (sec.)	4.7
40-60 mph (sec.)	5.6
50-70 mph (sec.)	11.5
60-80 mph (sec.)	13.2
Standing ¼ mile (sec.)	n.a.
Speed at end of ¼ mile (mph)	n.a.
Top speed (est. mph)	106

BRAKING

From 60 mph (ft.)	142.3

FIAT 124 SPORT COUPE & SPIDER

A pair that sets new standards of refinement for medium-price sports/GT cars

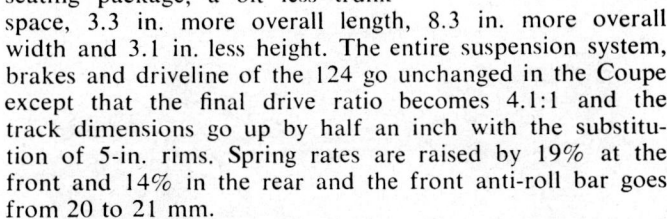

Sometime in 1966 Fiat became the 4th largest producer of automobiles in the world, surpassing Volkswagen. The company has progressively introduced new models until nearly its entire line is composed of up-to-date, attractive cars; only the largest models plus the revised 1100 and the tiny 500-600s are old designs and the large ones (2300, 1800 and 1500L) are due to be replaced this year by the 130.

The 124, introduced in 1964, is the mainstay of the line. A conventional front-engine, rear-drive car, it is nevertheless one of the best and most modern sedans in the 1.0/1.5-liter range, and it was only natural that Fiat should use it as a basis for a new sports model to replace the aging 1500 Spider. The 124 Sport, available as a 4-seater Coupe and a Spider, has been out for a year but is just now arriving on the American scene because of the work involved in conforming it to the legal standards. With the introduction of these two highly attractive models, Fiat this year is seriously setting out to market large quantities of cars in the U.S. for the first time. And, no question about it, with cars like the already popular 850 Spider, the 850 Coupe, the 124 Sedan and station wagon and the 124 Sport, Fiat is going to sell a lot of cars in the U.S.

Engineering

As with many small and middle-sized European sedans, the basic sedan chassis handles so well that little change is needed to make it suitable for a sports car. Therefore the basic points of departure from the 124 sedan are (1) the completely different bodies; (2) a highly modified engine, still based on 124 reciprocating parts but with its own light alloy double-overhead-cam head and Weber carburetor; and for the Spider, a 5-speed gearbox and a shortened wheelbase.

To relate the 124 Sport models to the 124 sedan, however, is not to denigrate their position among contemporary sports and GT cars. Quite the contrary, they amount to the most modern and attractive designs in the field anywhere near the $3000 mark. To review the mass-production basis, consider the 124 sedan; a boxy, 4-door sedan on a 95.3-in. wheelbase with front and rear track dimensions of 52.4/51.2 in., overall length of 158.7 in., curb weight of 1930 lb. The 124's body is of unit steel construction and the body structure was designed with no strength margin for cutting off its top (a platform strong enough to allow cutting off the top and still retain adequate rigidity would have meant extra weight). The 124 has conventional unequal-arm-and-coil-spring independent front suspension, a live rear axle on trailing arms with coil springs and a Panhard rod, and disc brakes at all four wheels with pressure to the rear brakes modified by a linkage that senses the car's rear loading.

The 124 powerplant is a modern, only slightly oversquare inline pushrod four of 1197 cc and 65 bhp and drives through a 4-speed gearbox and a 4.3:1 final drive ratio (for gearing of 15.1 mph/1000 rpm). When we tested it we found the 124 sedan to have exceptionally good handling and braking and very lively performance for an $1800 sedan at the expense of high revs and a lot of "buzz."

For the 124 Sport Coupe, Fiat uses the same platform as the sedan, sticking to the 95.3-in. wheelbase. In the name of style and sport, an entirely new body (styled by Fiat) is laid over the platform with a slightly tighter seating package, a bit less trunk space, 3.3 in. more overall length, 8.3 in. more overall width and 3.1 in. less height. The entire suspension system, brakes and driveline of the 124 go unchanged in the Coupe except that the final drive ratio becomes 4.1:1 and the track dimensions go up by half an inch with the substitution of 5-in. rims. Spring rates are raised by 19% at the front and 14% in the rear and the front anti-roll bar goes from 20 to 21 mm.

Ahead of the clutch are the big mechanical changes in the 124 Sport. The bore is increased from 73 mm to 80, giving 1438 cc and doing away with the 124's water space between the bores. The 124's timing chain, however, is replaced by a toothed belt drive for the distributor and a totally different twin-cam head. This makes the 124 Sport the first production car to use a toothed belt for twin overhead camshafts; only one belt is used too, so the engine must surely set a new record for low production cost for a dohc. However, the belt must be replaced every 36,000 miles, according to Fiat.

The cylinder head is of light alloy, with pentroof combustion chambers. The intake valves are inclined at 31.8 degrees to the vertical and are on the left side; the exhausts are at 33.5 degrees for an included angle of 65.3 degrees and a slightly asymetrical layout. The usual bucket tappets go between cam lobe and valve, with discs atop the buckets for clearance adjustment. The intake and exhaust systems are arranged for "cross flow."

Transverse section of twin-cam engine shows exhaust valves at greater angle to vertical than intakes, cross-flow ports.

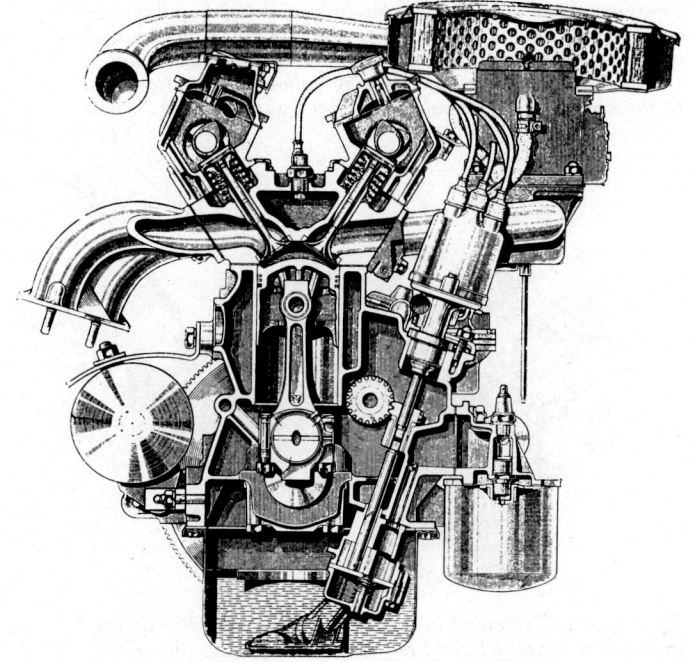

Carburetion is by a single 2-V Weber 34 DFH 1 with a vacuum-operated secondary butterfly and manual choke and throttle controls, and on the exhaust side a smooth cast-iron header feeds all four ports into a single pipe. It's significant that this engine meets the U.S. emission regulations with practically no modifications at all—no air pump, no dual-diaphragm distributor, no retarded spark at idle—in spite of the fact that it's a high-output engine developing 67 bhp/liter or almost 1.1 bhp/cu in. Surely low emissions were taken into account in the basic design of the engine, and many manufacturers who have had such trouble meeting the standards might not suffer so much if their engines had been designed in the last five years! A dry-element air cleaner filters the air to the carburetor and is held in place

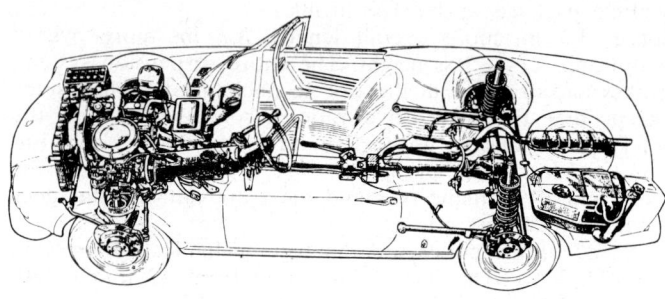

FIAT 124 SPORT COUPE & SPIDER

Live rear axle, left, is exceedingly well located and sprung, handles 124 Sports' power admirably. Linkage on top works brake proportioning valve at right end. Front suspension, steering and pedals, right; steering column terminates well to the rear of front wheel centerline, a safety factor.

Timing belt is shielded only at front by cover; idler drives distributor shaft. Electric fan clutch lets plastic fan coast.

by an incredible number of nuts and bolts; Italian engineers just don't seem to trust simple over-center clamps or wing nuts. The air cleaner has a large bent intake horn that must be swivelled down to proximity with the exhaust header for winter operation.

Output of the engine, then, is drastically increased by the fancy cylinder head and displacement increase: from 65 at 5600 to 96 at 6500. Torque goes up from 70 lb-ft at 3800 to 82.5 at 4000, and the useful rev range to 6600 rpm.

Behind the twin-cam engine are the 124's normal 7.9-in. diaphragm-spring clutch and 4-speed all-synchro gearbox. Though both Coupe and Spider use the same engine version, the Spider gets a gearbox extension containing an overdrive 5th gear, whereas the Coupe uses the sedan's ratios. This means gearbox ratios of 3.750, 2.300, 1.490 and 1.000:1 for the Coupe; the Spider gets taller ratios all the way with 3.422, 2.100, 1.361 and 1.000 for the first four, plus a much-needed 0.912:1 5th for highway cruising. We understand that later the Coupe will be available with the 5-speed box as an option.

Interior arrangement of both Coupe and Spider is not particularly efficient in the use of body width; both cars have flat side windows and rather bulbous sides, unusual for such recent designs. They're both good in the utilization of lengthwise space, however. Both have driver layouts that are ergonomically among the best today, with carefully thought-out placement of instruments, controls and seats. I would say that the Coupe seating package is slightly superior to that of a Mustang coupe, and for a car 21.5-in. shorter and 5 in. narrower that's not bad at all. The Spider interior benefits from the fact that Fiat (and Pininfarina) haven't tried to perpetuate the long-hood sports car motif of bygone days; thus the dash can be well forward for extra cockpit space.

The Spider is on a shortened platform, having a wheelbase 5.5 in. shorter than the sedan or Coupe, and this fact is primarily responsible for its $300 price premium over the Coupe—the lack of interchangeability makes it more costly to produce. Certainly the 5-speed box contributes no more than about $75 to the price difference, and the trimmings and fittings are pretty much equal for the two. It comes as a mild surprise that both the Coupe and Spider are heavier than the sedan: the sedan weighs in at 1930 lb curb, the Spider 2090 and the Coupe 2110 lb. Strange, you say, that the sporting models should weigh more and be larger than the basic sedan, but it must be remembered that these cars are much more luxurious and sound-deadened than the sedan, and that their larger size couldn't in any way be considered a liability in maneuvering. Incidentally, both Sports are more rigid than the sedan.

Weight distribution, which is 53/47% front/rear on the sedan is 54/46 on the Coupe and 55/45 on the Spider. Therefore these cars follow the long-standing practice followed by Fiat and Alfa, with relatively front-heavy distribution, a well located live axle and small radial tires (165-13 in this case)—all adding up to very precise control and a lot of understeer.

Fuel capacity is greater in the sports models than for the sedan, at 11.9 gal (sedan carries 10.3), and the tank is located in the left rear body quarter on both. Both cars also use the 8.9-in. single-piston swinging-caliper disc brakes of the 124, with 297 sq in. area and a vacuum booster.

Parking brake is by cable actuation of the rear calipers, not as satisfactory as those arrangements using auxiliary drums for the purpose, but this works better with a swinging caliper than with the older opposed-piston designs.

The best summary of the 124 Sport Coupe would be that it appears to a really advanced sporting 4-seater for a reasonable price; as for the Spider, it is the *only* car of its type being built today that is mechanically modern—and by "car of its type" we simply mean a popular-priced open sports car in the 1.5-liter class.

NEW MODEL ANALYSIS AND ROAD & TRACK ROAD TEST

FIAT 124 SPORT COUPE & SPIDER

W E'VE WAITED a long time to test the two Fiat 124 Sports. The Spider appeared first in late 1966 and the Coupe in the spring of 1967, but it has taken all this time for Fiat to conform them to the U.S. safety and smog regulations. But they were worth the wait: our 2000-odd-miles' experience with both of them was a thoroughly enjoyable experience.

The first impression upon driving either Coupe or Spider is that these cars are *refined,* especially in the chassis but also in the engine and powertrain department. Unfortunately along with the refinement comes a certain mousy character too, for the twincam 1438-cc engine produces rather meager torque at any speed. The engine is smooth for a four, and it's mechanically quiet as long as it's not pressed. But one winds up pressing it much of the time; free use of the gearbox and the engine's willingness to rev (to 6600, its redline) are assumed, and if so used not only does the engine emit a purposeful buzz up through the gears but its through-the-gears acceleration is actually a bit quicker than the more "torquey" MGB. There is no camdrive noise, thanks to the belt drive, and only a light tappet click. The engine warms up very quickly and needs little manipulating of the manual choke and throttle, but its idle quality is never any better than lumpy. When getting on the throttle hard, the Weber carburetor's vacuum-operated secondary butterfly comes in with a slight bump.

The Coupe comes with the standard Fiat 124 sedan's 4-speed gearbox, and though we found this smooth and quiet (with the exception of 3rd gear) we think the Coupe needs an overdrive 5th gear just as much as the Spider does, but only the Spider offers it currently. The Coupe's 1st, 2nd and 3rd gears are also steeper than the open car's, making it buzzier but quicker off the mark—as shown on the acceleration curves. The real deficiency of the 4-speed, however, is its 3970 rev/mi in the coupe; at 4450 rpm (in-

dicated 4600) an exhaust boom sets in, effectively limiting cruising speed to 4400 rpm or 68 mph, not to mention the generally noisy cruising. The Spider's 0.912:1 5th gear allows it to cruise at just over 4000 rpm at 70 mph—not exactly long-legged but much better. The Spider's taller first three ratios, practical because it will not be loaded as heavily as the Coupe, are also more useful on winding roads. As an aside, the Spider also benefits from the 5-speed box in that its shift lever sprouts from a point farther back on the unit; the 5-speed is made by substituting a tail housing containing the extra ratio for the normal rear section of the gearbox.

As for the rest of the drive train, the 7.9-in. clutch is smooth and positive with no slip encountered any time during the brutal acceleration runs; there is some final-drive noise in both cars but this is worse in the Spider, heard as a grinding at low speeds and a mild whine at high.

Regardless of whether or not the engine and transmission make for sparkling performance, they are both pleasant to the senses. What is even more pleasant to the senses is the modern, refined chassis. Both cars ride extremely well for sports cars—the springing is relatively soft, the damping firm on the rebound rather than on bounce, the spring travel generous. They are particularly good on bad roads, riding only fairly well over such minor disturbances as tar strips on smooth pavement. Whatever good ride qualities the two cars have is very much enhanced by their rigid and absolutely rattle-free bodies—even the Spider has no tendency to squeaks and rattles. None of this should be construed as saying the 124s ride like large sedans; rather, they just show how well a small sports car can ride in these modern times.

The handling of the two Fiats is as outstanding as their ride. They handle in a typical Italian fashion, with moderate body roll, a lot of understeer, an intimate relationship of feel between tires and steering wheel, and ultra-light steer-

SCALE: 10" DIVISIONS

Spider top is a model of good design. Procedure is to release two latches over windshield, fold back; side windows go along.

Spider, left, and Coupe have identical instruments and . . .   *. . . controls in their totally different facia arrangements.*

ing. The tires are small (165-13) radials and thus the absolute cornering bite isn't great, but these cars are tremendously stable and predictable through any corner and we'll guarantee they will make a better driver out of any novice. Our Spider had Michelin X tires (not the asymetrical kind), the Coupe Pirelli Cinturatos—accounting for the discrepancy in mph/1000 figures if you happened to notice it—the Michelins offering slightly greater cornering power at a slight cost in ride quality.

Over really bad surfaces the rear live axle, located by trailing arms and a Panhard rod and sprung by coils, shows itself to be very much the equal of its job. Even its tendency to make the car hop when cornering hard on a rough road is minimal, thanks to the soft spring rates. We'd venture the conclusion that the 124 Sports have as fine a suspension system as anyone could expect at their prices.

Like the 124 sedan, the sports models are unusual in their category in having disc brakes at all four wheels. On early 124 sedans the swinging-caliper brakes suffered from a spongy pedal feel, presumably because of some deflection in the system; this fault has been eliminated now and the

vacuum-assisted brakes in these cars give light, well modulated braking in all normal driving. The unusual (and beautifully simple) linkage between the rear axle and a pressure-modulating valve in the rear hydraulic lines apparently does its job too, as we never experienced rear-wheel lockup in either car regardless of load; perhaps a little too well in the Spider, as its front wheels locked on emergency braking at a mere 20 ft/sec/sec (62%-g) resulting in a straight-line skid. Carefully controlling the pedal effort would raise the deceleration rate to 23 fps^2, still mediocre. The Coupe, on the other hand, turned in a respectable 26 fps^2 (81%-g) with no conscious control and 27 with; as the measured weight distribution isn't that much different between the two perhaps the different tires that should get the credit. Both cars have considerable front-end dive on braking. The parking brake, operated by a slightly awkward lever (too far back) between the seats, works on the rear calipers and is not strong enough to hold on a 30% grade.

Both 124 Sports back up their excellent chassis with really good driver and passenger accommodation. The driving position is one of the best we've encountered (and is

SCALE: 10" DIVISIONS

PRICE

	Coupe	Spider
Basic list	$2924	$3226
As tested	$2994	$3296

ENGINE

Type	4 cyl inline, dohc
Bore x stroke, mm	80.0 x 71.5
Equivalent in	3.15 x 2.81
Displacement, cc/cu in	1438/87.8
Compression ratio	8.9:1
Bhp @ rpm	96 @ 6500
Equivalent mph	105 113
Torque @ rpm, lb-ft	82.5 @ 4000
Equivalent mph	62 69
Carburetion	one Weber 34 DCF 2V
Type fuel required	premium

DRIVE TRAIN

Clutch diameter, in	7.9
Gear ratios: 5th (n.a., 0.912)	3.73:1
4th (1.00, 1.00)	4.10:1 ..... 4.10:1
3rd (1.49, 1.36)	6.11:1 ..... 5.58:1
2nd (2.30, 2.10)	9.42:1 ..... 8.60:1
1st (3.75, 3.42)	15.35:1 ..... 14.02:1
Synchromesh	on all 4 ..... on all 5
Final drive ratio	4.10:1

INSTRUMENTATION

Instruments: 120-mph speedo, 999.0 trip odo, 99,999 odo, 8000-rpm tach, fuel level, oil pressure, water temperature

Warning lights: fuel level, directional signals, headlights on, high beam, alternator, parking brake, oil pressure, emergency flasher

ACCOMMODATION

	Coupe	Spider
Seating capacity, persons	4	2+1
Seat width	2x19.0/54.5	2x19.0/47.0
Head room	40.0/37.0	39.0/29.0
Seat back adjustment, deg	25	
Driver comfort rating (scale of 100):		
Driver 69 in. tall	85	
Driver 72 in. tall	80	
Driver 75 in. tall	75	

CHASSIS & BODY

Body/frame: unit steel construction

Brake type: 8.9-in. disc at all wheels, single piston swinging calipers

Swept area, sq in	297
Wheels	13 x 5K
Tires	Cinturato 165-13 .. Michelin 165-13
Steering type	worm & roller
Overall ratio	16.4:1
Turns, lock-to-lock	2.75
Turning circle, ft	36.1 ..... 34.1

Front suspension: unequal-length A-arms, coil springs, tube shocks, anti-roll bar

Rear suspension: live axle on trailing arms, Panhard rod, coil springs

MAINTENANCE

Engine oil capacity, qt	4.0
Change interval, mi	6000
Filter change interval, mi	6000
Chassis lube interval, mi	12,000
Tire pressures, psi	23/26 ..... 23/23

GENERAL

	Coupe	Spider
Curb weight, lb	2110	2090
Test weight	2435	2420
Weight distribution		
front/rear, %	54/46	55/45
Wheelbase, in	95.3	89.8
Track, front/rear	53.0/51.8	
Overall length	162.0	156.3
Width	65.8	63.5
Height	52.8	49.2
Frontal area, sq ft	19.3	17.4
Ground clearance, in	4.7	4.7
Overhang, front/rear	28.5/38.2	29.8/36.7
Trunk space, cu ft	9.6	6.2
Fuel tank capacity, gal	11.8	

CALCULATED DATA

	Coupe	Spider
Lb/hp (test wt)	25.3	25.2
Mph/1000 rpm	15.1	17.5
Engine revs/mi	3970	3430
Piston travel, ft/mi	1860	1610
Rpm @ 2500 ft/min	5330	
Equivalent mph	83	92
Cu ft/ton mi	82.8	71.8
R&T wear index	74	55
Brake area, sq in/ton	245	

MISCELLANEOUS

Body styles available: coupe and roadster as tested

Warranty period, mo/mi 12/12000

ROAD TEST RESULTS

ACCELERATION

	Coupe	Spider
Time to distance, sec:		
0-100 ft	3.9	3.9
0-250 ft	6.5	6.5
0-500 ft	10.0	10.0
0-750 ft	13.1	12.9
0-1000 ft	10.7	10.4
0-1320 ft (¼ mi)	18.6	18.3
Speed at ¼ mi	74	76
Time to speed, sec:		
0-30 mph	3.7	4.1
0-40 mph	5.5	5.9
0-50 mph	8.3	8.3
0-60 mph	11.3	11.9
0-70 mph	15.6	15.5
0-80 mph	23.0	21.1
0-90 mph	35.9	31.0
Passing exposure time, sec:		
To pass car going 50 mph	7.7	7.2

FUEL CONSUMPTION

	Coupe	Spider
Normal driving, mpg	22-26	23-27
Cruising range, mi	260-305	270-320

SPEEDS IN GEARS

	Coupe	Spider
4th gear, (6550, 6700 rpm), mph	104	106
5th (6000)	n.a.	104
3rd (6600)	68	77
2nd (6600)	43	50
1st (6600)	27	30
Panic stop from 80 mph:		
Deceleration, % g	81	62
Control	good	fair

BRAKES

Fade test: percent of increase in pedal effort required to maintain 50%-g deceleration rate in six stops from 60 mph .. 54 ... 54

Parking: hold 30% grade .. no ..... no

Overall braking performance .. very good ... good

SPEEDOMETER ERROR

	indicated	actual
30 mph	28.3	30.0
40 mph	38.2	40.2
60 mph	57.2	59.4
80 mph	75.6	77.9
90 mph	84.2	86.9
Odometer, 10.0 mi	9.59	actual 9.82

ACCELERATION & COASTING

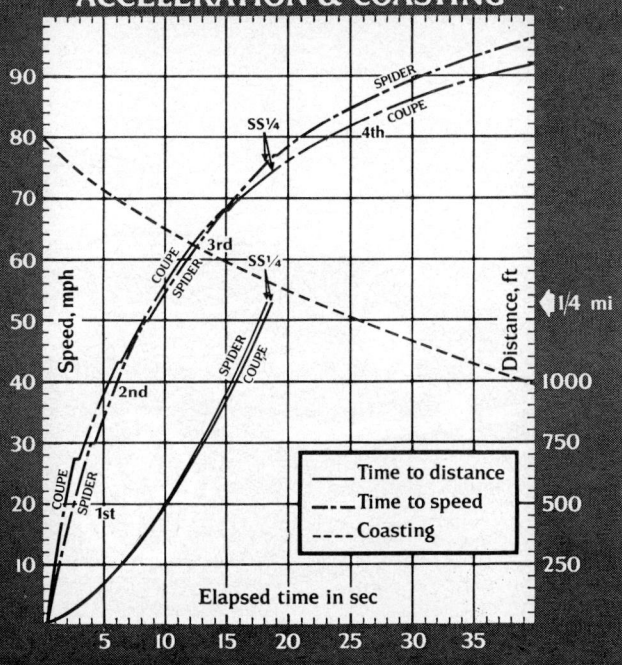

Time to distance
Time to speed
Coasting

Elapsed time in sec

FIAT 124 SPORT COUPE & SPIDER

almost exactly the same for the two dissimilar bodies): steering wheel well forward and slightly horizontal for arms-out driving with good support for the weight of hands and arms; seats with excellent contouring, plenty of side location and 25 degrees of seatback adjustment; and pedals that are, if a bit too close together, not too close to the driver as they are on many Italian cars. The only thing more we could ask here would be a telescoping steering column, but that would be gilding the chrysanthemum, as most people can drive for an hour without needing to change position as it is.

Though the layout and styling of the dash is different for the two cars, both have the same instrumentation and switches, with the Spider placing all instruments directly in front of the driver and the Coupe getting them so close as not to matter. Instruments are traditional, readable, circular white-on-black, set into simulated wood on the Coupe and real wood on the Spider. The minor instruments (fuel level, oil pressure, water temp) are bilingual with metric and Centigrade markings as well as English and Fahrenheit; Fiat and others steadfastly refuse to fit an ammeter, which we still feel too valuable to be without. All the switches and knobs are easy to reach in both cars though the shoulder-belted driver will have to loosen up to reach such things as the fresh-air vent on the opposite side.

Both cars have moderate-sized, locking gloveboxes plus large map trays on the underdash quarter panels; the Coupe offers a rear seating package that if not generous is certainly more satisfactory than an American ponycar 20 in. longer on the outside. Trunks are well shaped and finished on both cars, the Coupe offering a generous 9.6 cu ft of capacity.

Weather protection is a give-and-take proposition with the two 124s. Raw-air ventilation is mediocre in the Coupe (which really needs it because of its huge glass area), quite good in the Spider. The main heating-ventilation controls are between the seats, perhaps hazardous in a crash but convenient to work by touch without looking; a 2-speed blower is provided but it's noisy on both speeds, and temperature control is by a water valve rather than by the more satisfactory air-mixing system. An especially nice touch on both cars is the intermittent wiper operation for drizzly weather: one position of the wiper switch cycles the wipers only once every few seconds, the frequency of cycling regulated by a rheostat on the dash.

Vision outward from both Spider and Coupe deserves special mention. The Coupe comes about as close to 360-degree vision as is possible today, and the Spider is the only 2-seater roadster we know of with glass quarter windows built into its top. These fold down with the top which, as the photo shows, is a model for any and all who would design a roadster top. It is also worth mentioning that the Spider is relatively free of wind noise and buffeting with its top down, making that sort of motoring extremely pleasant.

On the minus side, our Coupe had a set of 3-point belts that were impossible to adjust correctly—either they're incredibly dumb or we are, for we could never figure them out. In both cars the belt buckles rattle fiercely when not in use—the only rattles to be found.

Another benefit of a car with a newly designed chassis and powertrain is low maintenance requirements. The 124s require only an oil and filter change every 6000 mi (though the maker suggests checking oil, gearbox, rear axle and steering box fluid levels every 3000).

There's no denying that the Fiat 124 Sports are extremely attractive cars, enjoyable to drive, easy to maintain and highly practical. Both are pleasant to look at too, even if the Spider is rather old-fashioned looking. Our only major criticism is that their on-the-road performance is not quite up to their looks, and we would respectfully suggest that Fiat consider making the 125 (1608-cc) version of the dohc engine, which develops 100 lb-ft torque, standard equipment for the American market.

The 124 Coupe styling is excellent, combining practicality and an appealing GT look. The roof, nearly symmetrical in side aspect, gives excellent rear headroom. Frontal appearance suffers a bit from the low grille but forward vision benefits.

FIAT 124 SPIDER

TWIN CAMS, 5-SPEED GEAR BOX, FINE HANDLING PLUS DISC BRAKES AND YET IT'S PRICED RIGHT!

By THE EDITOR ■ Everytime we've decided we've driven just about the ultimate in automobiles in a particular price category along comes still another new car which rates all kinds of rave notices. The Fiat 124 Spider is just such a car. Of course, you could make any sports car buff's mouth water by saying, "Twin Cams—5-speed box" but his throat might go dry immediately when you quote him a driveaway price. This is not the case with the Spider. It has all kinds of exotic engineering and

styling appointment that you normally don't come by for less than four thousand dollars.

First of all, a convertible is not a convertible unless you can run it any time you want to with the top down. The only thing we've found that beats this Fiat's top is a sunroof! We actually sat in the driver's seat, pulled the two clamps at the top of the windshield, pushed up and the whole top went back and settled down right where it ought to be. We had to get out and stand up to get enough lever-

age to raise it but even this was easier than in any other soft top we've handled recently. Flip the top back like that, feel the sun all around you and you just know you're in for a good day out there on the turnpike. The Fiat 124 Spider didn't let us down here either.

Pull away from the curb. Ho, Ho! The steering's kind of light yet positive as you dash around the corner. A beach ball in the street? Tap the brake and feel the Fiat come to a halt. Sure

Fiat's done it again! The Spider's a tight little rig with excellent performance.

FIAT 124 SPIDER

enough, here comes the kid who belongs to the ball. You can smile at his startled face in front of you. You've got everything under control—he and the beach ball are safe. Back in first now and off about your business with him looking at the wild Positrano yellow paint job on this rig. In the Holland Tunnel between New York and New Jersey shortly thereafter someone uplls up alongside and yells across the lanes about what they call this color. We can't tell him then because we had to check with the company to find out that this particular yellow is named after a little town in Italy in which most of the buildings are painted this shade of yellow. We came upon an Alfa painted with the identical yellow which is somewhat unusual.

Anyway, by now we're convinced this is going to be a good day. We've got a fine set of wheels under us and, surprisingly, this little Fiat grooves along quietly— that's what we said—quietly. The gear box functions effortlessly although you have to be cruising out there on the highway to get into that fifth gear. The fifth's an overdrive anyway anf it'll drop 500 rpms without moving the needle on the speedometer.

The steering wheel is far enough away from the driver that you can do your straight-arm bit "a la Sterling Moss" and the pedals are placed well enough, too, so that you can depress the clutch right down to ghe floorboard yet drive without having your knees tucked up under your ears. Both thighs rest on the seat, your back is fitted into the squab and you're ready for the twistiest road once you've buckled your seat belt. The 124 Spider's a true two-seater, of course, but we squeezed another person into the back when we did the cover shots with model

The engine has four cylinders, in line, a water-cooled cast iron block with an aluminum head. It has five main bearings and twin overhead cams. It develops 96 horsepower at 6500 rpm with a 87.8 cu. in. displacement. The transmission is 5-speed with all gears synchronized. Carburetion is a 2 barrel Weber. The suspension is independent in front with rigid axle in the rear with coil springs all around and anti-sway bars front and back. The gas tank holds 11½ gals. and oil sump takes 4 qts.

Ann Pettibone. This would have been at least difficult if not impossible with the top up even for a quick junket around the block. The 124 is 63½ inches wide which adds up to making the seats eminently comfortable in all directions.

Visibility all around was quite good for a soft top of this type. The top fitted quite well over the windshield and with the windows rolled up. The side vents open to pump air into the interior which gladens the eye. The dash is polished wood with the instruments on the left visible through the steering wheel. The radio is housed in a console in front of the short shift lever, between the seats. If the girls didn't notice our Fiat by the wild yellow paint job, incidentally, we could get their attention with the horn. The car is fitted with the Fiamm elector-compressor horns which may be illegal in some states but which we hope to get for personally owned vehicle after the baby gets the shoes she needs. These horns are the greatest.

We could not find any fault with

CONTINUED ON PAGE 85

FIAT SPYDER — A SEXY SOFT TOP

It's as true a sports car as you'll find anywhere today.

The rear of the Fiat is very well-balanced although conglomeration of overseas stickers and plates make it a little cluttered. Michelins are the original equipment.

Left hand drive is a little tricky at first. The car will eventually have to be converted from left to right. Vision with hood up is very good. Seats adjust to any position fore and aft.

Kevan Wolfe talks about the Fiat 124 convertible with owner, Pixie Curry, a Sydney Fashion designer. The car has excellent lines and is really longer than it appears, owing to use of telephoto lens.

WHILE other consumer magazines were striving to obtain the Fiat 124S Coupe, we were carrying out a rather sneaky operation — although it did take more time to put into effect than we had first anticipated.

It happened that a young, very-with-it fashion designer, Pixie Curry, was lumbering around Sydney town in a Fiat 124S convertible. Lovely, it was. All in that modern mustard paint with black interior which it seems everyone is going for these days. And, we might add, Miss Curry certainly didn't detract from the image either, thank you.

Finally we did get to grips (?) with Pixie and this beautifully-proportioned Fiat drophead after months of researching the whereabouts of the car, and had some pleasant hours galloping all over the eastern headlands of Sydney. If the Fiat 124S Coupe is a poor man's love (WHEELS November, 1968), the convertible has got to go one better.

It looks more like the Fiat Dino than the 124 Coupe, but without the accentuated bulge of the fenders. The grille is slightly different to the 124S with triangulated ends while the parking lights are elongated and set into the body panel beneath the headlights — whereas the 124 Coupe has circular, small lights at each end of the grille.

One slight difficulty we ran into was that of left hand drive. It's quite easy to get used to apart from trying not to snick the gears through the unfamiliar right hand change. The dashboard is quite different with the gauges being grouped directly in front of the driver while the tumbler switches of the coupe are replaced with push/pull knobs, also located differently. The overall pattern of the dash extends right across the cockpit in a complete oval using padding along the top, whereas the coupe has everything in a separate section occupying slightly more than half the dash. While the coupe has air flow through the face of the dash, the convertible has rotational discs mounted in the top centre of the vertical plane. Ineffective with the hood down, they do work well with it up.

Before moving into the mechanicals of the car, we should point out that this particular convertible was first bought in Germany. Pixie was, at that time, having a semi-world jaunt, and she took the car to Britain, then back through Europe, down through Arabia to Bombay where it was shipped to Australia. After traversing such countryside, the Fiat was little the worse for wear. A couple of minor dings here, a dent there and you wouldn't know it from any other slightly used car.

The mechanicals are identical with the Fiat 124S coupe, but somehow the convertible doesn't have the same pulling power. With three aboard the difference was very marked and we needed to make more use of the gearbox than is usual with the 124 range. The tyre pressures were set according to the book but the car was a definite and positive understeerer. This trait was accompanied by tyre squeal which is quite unusual for Michelin tyres when motoring rather sedately around suburban streets. Obviously the tyres require some overpressure than what the makers indicate in the little book.

Mustard in color, the little Fiat 124 convertible was a pretty thing. The black hood and black upholstery really did things for it. The hood folds down quickly and without fuss, held by a small, tailored cover which clips in place and drops behind the front seats to form a backing for the (very) occasional rear seat.

Although the car isn't generally available in Australia — except possibly on special order — we found it to be quite ideally suited to Australian conditions. We won't tell you what Pixie paid for her little Fiat cutie, but even at retail prices here in Australia, you've got a swingin' little convertible indeed! #

FIAT 124 VERSUS FIAT 124

CAN A TOPLESS SPIDER FIND HAPPINESS AMID A
WORLD OF HARD-CLAD COUPES?

MAYBE WE GET TO A POINT where just plain good isn't enough. Trying to figure out how to write a story we've repeated many times in the past few years is sometimes almost more than our cluttered minds can cope with.

Well, let's see . . . . We could begin in the wearily straight *R&T* style: "The Fiat 124 Sport Spider and 124 Coupe are really darn swell cars . . ." But then, there is always the possibility you'd fall asleep. The other approach, a la *C&D,* would be: "The political, social and sexual implications of selling two Fiat body styles, both designated 124 . . ." And that would fail because we lack a staff psychologist.

Now, here's the problem as we see it: How do you say that Fiat 124s are nice, but relatively unexciting? And further, how do you keep those dyed-in-the-wool, imported-car cuckoos you work with on the magazine from tearing at your throat if you say the car is mild as mother's milk? No matter how you look at it, though, we're still looking at a pair of slight upstages of the traditionally bland British propensity for plain vanilla transportation. Yet,

maybe that's the problem — there isn't enough *nice* vanilla transportation around.

Let's face it, these Fiats are *good* cars, and if you are a *nice* fellow or a *personable* girl, you would be very happy with one. But . . . you guys in the office next door . . . they don't happen to be particularly exciting or innovative in technology, performance or appearance in this age of screaming psychedelia.

We found Fiat's 850 Racer (July, SCG) to be a real kicky car — it was different, miniscule, economical, stylish, but it could have used the bigger ohc engine out of the 124. Oh yes, the 124s have dual overhead camshafts; very impressive. That, along with the five-speed gearboxes, is probably what caught our attention most. And there aren't a lot of cars in this price range ($3200-$3600) that have both those talking-points. Not that they do much for you that a little more displacement wouldn't, but they do show that you're getting something for your dollars. However, with the increasing interest in small cars with small engines, increased displacement might not be a valid selling point in today's value market. The ohc drive is fairly modern too, with rubber toothed-belts similar to General Motors', instead of the standard noisy European

chains (as Oldsmobile and Cadillac also use) or gear trains. The result is an engine so smooth and quiet that there's a terrible tendency to over-rev in city traffic.

The five-speed is a definite contributor with the 1438-cc engine. It shifts slick, except that we occasionally went from first to second-and-a-half (figure that one out!), but with five available gears you devote more consciousness to which one you're using. The shift lever is mounted so far back that it falls readily to hand. Fifth gear is, for all plausible purposes, no more than a fuel-saving overdrive for flat-out freeways.

The styling of both cars can best be called "traditional." However, for being Italian, you'd expect a little more. Our first impression was that the two were cleverly disguised orange crates, but after spending some days with them, the cars don't look half bad. As they say, "Beauty is in the eye of the beholder." Fiat is doing its utmost to produce an Alfa at less cost . . . and less flair.

The interiors are good. Staid maybe, but pleasant and comfortable. In the Spider, the bucket seats are well padded and spongy, and upholstered in standard

FIAT 124 SPIDER

PRICE
Base $3427
As tested $3527
With options .... AM-FM radio

ENGINE
Type ...... 4-cylinder, in-line, water-cooled, cast-iron block, aluminum head
Displacement .... 87.8 cu. in. (1438 cc)
Horsepower .... 96 hp @ 6500 rpm
Torque .... 82.4 lbs.-ft. @ 4000 rpm
Bore & stroke .... 3.16 in. x 2.81 in. (80.3 mm x 71.5 mm)
Compression ratio .... 8.9 to 1
Valve actuation .... Dual overhead cam
Induction system .... One 2V Weber
Exhaust system ... Cast-iron headers, 4 into 1
Electrical system ...... 12-volt alternator, point distributor
Fuel .... Premium
Recommended redline 6800

DRIVE TRAIN
Clutch .... Single dry plate

Transmission	Gear Ratio	Overall Ratio
1st Synchro	3.42	14.02
2nd Synchro	2.10	8.61
3rd Synchro	1.36	5.57
4th Synchro	1.00	4.10
5th Synchro	0.91	3.73

Differential .... Hypoid, 4.10 ratio

CHASSIS
Frame .... Unitized, front engine, rear drive
Front suspension .... Wishbone control arms, coil springs, hydraulic shocks, anti roll bar
Rear suspension .... Rigid axle, trailing arms, transverse Panhard rod, stabilizer bar
Steering .... Worm and roller, 3.0 turns, overall ratio 16.4 to 1, turning circle 34 feet
Brakes ..... Four wheel disc, power assisted. dual independent systems, 8.9-in. dia. front, 8.9-in. dia. rear
Wheels .... 13-in. dia.; 5.0-in. wide
Tires .... Pirelli 165 SR 13, pressures F/R: 23/23 (rec.), 27/27 (test)

BODY
Type .... Unitized, 2-door, 2-passenger
Seats .... Front bucket, rear boot
Windows .... 2 manual, 2 vents
Luggage space ...... Rear trunk, 6.0 cu. ft.
Instruments .... 140 mph speedo, 8000 rpm tach
Gauges ..... fuel, oil pressure, temp
Lights ...... oil pressure, ignition, emergency brake

WEIGHTS AND MEASURES
Weight .... 2085 lbs. (curb), 2310 lbs. (test)
Weight distribution F/R 56%/44%
Wheelbase .... 89.5 in.
Track F/R .... 53.0 in./51.8 in.
Height .... 49.0 in.
Width .... 63.5 in.
Length .... 156 in.
Ground clearance .... 6.0 in.
Oil capacity .... 5 qt.
Fuel capacity .... 12 gal.
Coolant capacity .... 8 qt.

MISCELLANEOUS
Weight/power ratio (curb/advertised) .... 21.8 lbs. per hp
Advertised hp/cu. in. 1.09
Speed per 1000 rpm (top gear) ..... 18.3 mph
Warranty .... 12 months/12,000 miles

AERODYNAMIC FORCES AT 100 MPH

CORNERING CONDITIONS

PERFORMANCE

Acceleration .... 0-30 (3.6 sec.), 0-60 (10.6 sec.), 0-quarter mile (17.6 sec., 77.2 mph)

Top speed .... 110 mph (est.) at 6500 rpm (hp limited)

Braking .... Distance from 60 mph: 137 ft. (0.87 g av.)
Number of stops to fade: Not attainable
Stability: Excellent
Maximum pitch angle: 0.6°

Handling .... Maximum lateral: 0.71 g right, 0.73 g left
Skidpad understeer: 6.9° right, 9.7° left
Maximum roll angle: 5.4°
Reaction to throttle, full: More understeer; off: Less understeer

Speedometer	30.0	40.0	50.0	60.0	70.0	80.0	90.0
Actual mph	33.0	42.0	51.0	60.0	69.0	78.5	87.5

Aerodynamic forces at 100 mph:
Drag .... 275 lbs. (includes tire drag)
Lift F/R .... 215 lbs./0 lbs.

TEST EXPLANATIONS

Fade test is successive maximum g stops from 60 mph each minute until wheels cannot be locked. Understeer is front minus rear tire slip angle at maximum lateral on 200-ft. dia. Digitek skidpad. Autoscan chassis dynamometer supplied by Humble Oil.

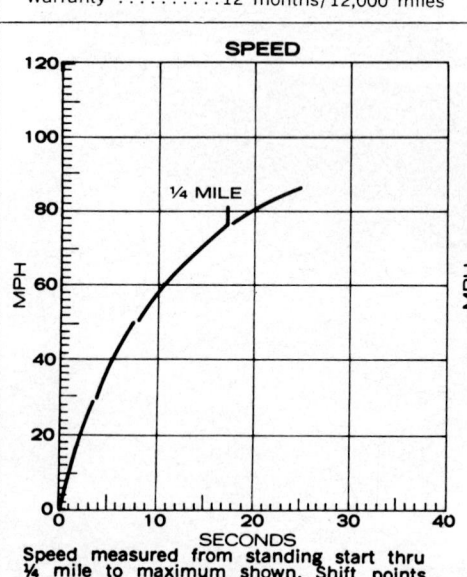

SPEED

Speed measured from standing start thru ¼ mile to maximum shown. Shift points indicated by line breaks.

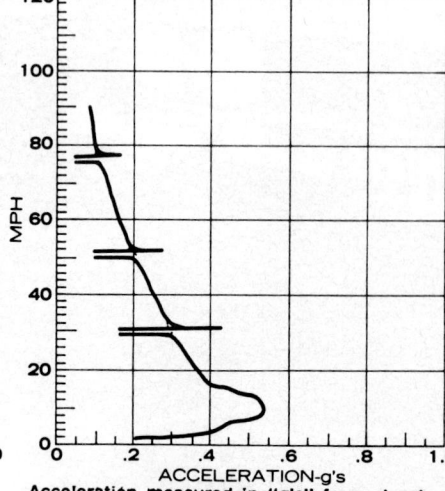

ACCELERATION

Acceleration measured in "g's" from standing start to speed shown. Shift points indicated by "spikes" on graph.

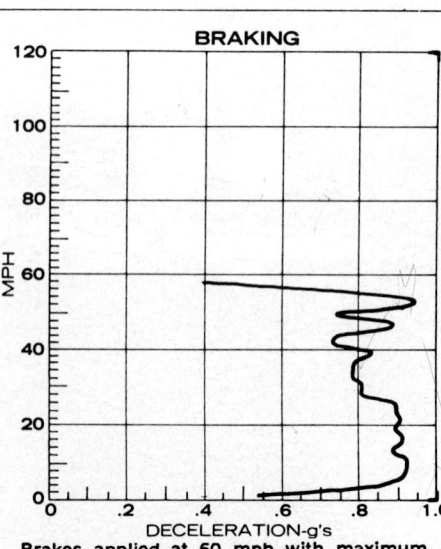

BRAKING

Brakes applied at 60 mph with maximum force, but using pedal "feathering" technique to prevent wheel lockup.

FIAT 124 COUPE

PRICE
Base $3133
As tested $3133
With options ....None

ENGINE
Type ......4-cylinder, in-line, water-cooled, cast-iron block, aluminum head
Displacement ....87.8 cu. in. (1438 cc)
Horsepower ....96 hp @ 6500 rpm
Torque ....82.4 lbs.-ft. @ 4000 rpm
Bore & stroke ....3.16 in. x 2.81 in. (80.3 mm x 71.5 mm)
Compression ratio ....8.9 to 1
Valve actuation ....Dual overhead cam
Induction system ....One 2V Weber
Exhaust system ..Cast-iron headers, 4 into 1
Electrical system ....12-volt alternator, point distributor
Fuel ....Premium
Recommended redline 6800

DRIVE TRAIN
Clutch ....Single dry plate

Transmission	Gear Ratio	Overall Ratio
1st Synchro	3.80	15.59
2nd Synchro	2.18	8.94
3rd Synchro	1.41	5.78
4th Synchro	1.00	4.10
5th Synchro	0.91	3.73

Differential ....Hypoid, 4.10 ratio

CHASSIS
Frame ....Unitized, front engine, rear drive
Front suspension ....Wishbone control arms, coil springs, hydraulic shocks, anti-roll bar
Rear suspension ... Rigid axle, trailing arms transverse Panhard rod, stabilizer bar
Steering ....Worm and roller, 3.0 turns, overall ratio 16.4 to 1, turning circle 36 feet
Brakes .....Four wheel disc, power assisted, dual independent systems, 8.9-in. dia. front, 8.9-in. dia. rear
Wheels ....13-in. dia.; 5-in. wide
Tires ....Pirelli 165 SR 13 pressures F/R: 26/29 (rec.), 29/32 (test)

BODY
Type ....Unitized, 2-door, 4-passenger
Seats ....Front bucket, rear bench
Windows ....2 manual, 4 vents
Luggage space ....Rear trunk, 11 cu. ft.
Instruments .140 mph speedo, 8000 rpm tach
Gauges: ....fuel, oil pressure, temp
Lights: ....oil pressure, ignition, emergency brake

WEIGHTS AND MEASURES
Weight .....2185 lbs. (curb), 2410 lbs. (test)
Weight distribution F/R 56%/44%
Wheelbase ....95.3 in.
Track F/R ....53.0 in./51.8 in.
Height ....52.7 in.
Width ....65.7 in.
Length ....161.8 in.
Ground clearance ....6.0 in.
Oil capacity ....5 qt.
Fuel capacity ....12 gal.
Coolant capacity ....8 qt.

MISCELLANEOUS
Weight/power ratio (curb/advertised) ....22.8 lbs. per hp
Advertised hp/cu. in. 1.09
Speed per 1000 rpm (top gear) ....18.3 mph
Warranty ....12 months/12,000 miles

AERODYNAMIC FORCES AT 100 MPH

CORNERING CONDITIONS

PERFORMANCE

Acceleration ....0-30 (4.2 sec.), 0-60 (11.7 sec.), 0-quarter mile (18.2 sec., 76.3 mph)

Top speed ....110 mph (est.) at 6500 rpm (hp limited)

Braking ....Distance from 60 mph: 154 ft. (0.78 g av.)
Number of stops to fade: Not attainable
Stability: Very good
Maximum pitch angle: 2.0°

Handling ....Maximum lateral: 0.68 g right, 0.70 g left
Skidpad understeer: 8.7° right, 12.5° left
Maximum roll angle: 6.8°
Reaction to throttle, full: More understeer; off: Less understeer

Speedometer	30.0	40.0	50.0	60.0	70.0	80.0	90.0
Actual mph	31.5	42.0	51.5	61.5	71.5	81.0	91.5

Aerodynamic forces at 100 mph:

Drag ....290 lbs. (includes tire drag)
Lift F/R ....250 lbs./125 lbs.

TEST EXPLANATIONS

Fade test is successive maximum g stops from 60 mph each minute until wheels cannot be locked. Understeer is front minus rear tire slip angle at maximum lateral on 200-ft. dia. skidpad. Autoscan chassis dynamometer supplied by Humble Oil.

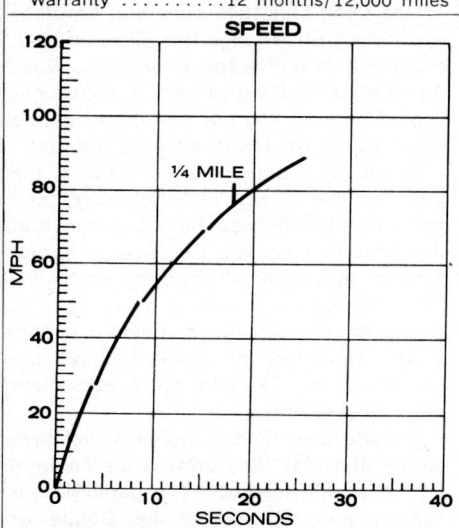

SPEED

Speed measured from standing start thru ¼ mile to maximum shown. Shift points indicated by line breaks.

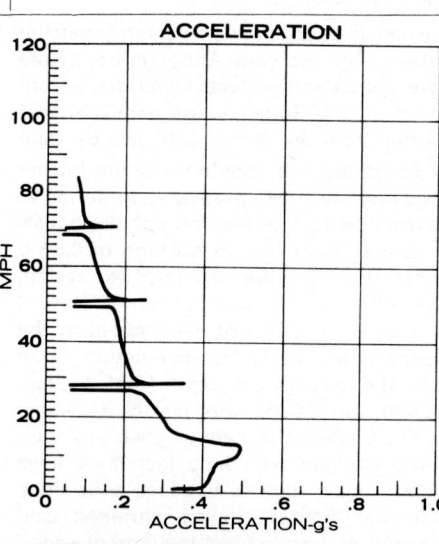

ACCELERATION

Acceleration measured in "g's" from standing start to speed shown. Shift points indicated by "spikes" on graph.

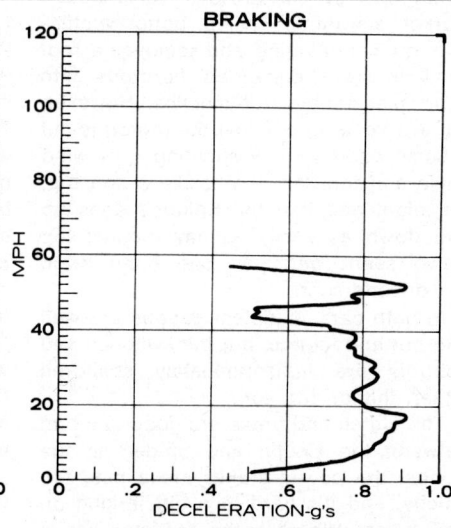

BRAKING

Brakes applied at 60 mph with maximum force, but using pedal "feathering" technique to prevent wheel lockup.

Instrumentation on Spider (left) and Coupe is legible and easy to see, although the layouts are different. The Spider uses sporty wood tone throughout the dash assembly, while the Coupe's is matte black.

roadster blister-your-butt, black leatherette. There's plenty of travel and reclinability within the limits of the plus-two back seat, but we've run out of anecdotes about +2 seating, so we'll just say that rear legroom is limited by the front seatbacks, which rest against the rear cushion at full travel. It makes for lots of space up front, however, to the extent that the top of the steering wheel can't be reached. The roadster also has the same "comfortable" seatbelts we panned in the 850. So comfortable you can't even feel them — only the obese can tighten them to within 6 inches of their laps.

For being some $300 cheaper, the Coupe is far more pleasant to drive. The seats, with genuine cloth inserts, breathe easier and fit better, and there's *real* rear seating. The well-contoured semi-buckets in back provide plenty of room for the un-leggy, but the rear head restraint is a very rigid piece of trim above the backlite. Actually, one of the nicest points about the Coupe is the seats, and their luxury is almost out of proportion with the overall concept and price of the car.

Ventilation and wind noise are more than acceptable in the Coupe — at least compared with the roadster. This is no doubt one of the reasons the roadster market is waning. Styling, better ventilation, air conditioning and removable roof sections have converted hardtops into more pleasurable automobiles. However, not everyone agrees that the ragtop is out — some people enjoy shouting over wind noise and top flap. If you like a soft top, we might add that the Spider's goes up and down as easily as any manual top we've seen, with just one hand, from the driver's seat.

In both cars, sufficient gauges are well laid out and legible, but the switches and controls are indiscriminately scattered hither, thither and yon.

The clutch and brake are good and bad between the Coupe and Spider. In the Coupe, the power brakes are a mite too touchy, and it's hard to avoid jerking on first touch. Whereas the roadster has a rubber clutch, with which it's impossible

to avoid a yunk-yunk-yunk from standstill unless you slip it a lot. It would seem to us that Fiat should get together with the two cars and use the best of each to make one that's really great.

Now, performance. The only significant physical differences between these two cars are: weight — the Coupe having 100 lbs more; gear ratios — the roadster having closer ratios between one, two and three; and air drag — the Coupe naturally losing again. Those skeptics who expressed certain doubts as to the validity of a similar comparison test two months ago, wherein a Corvette out-dragged a similarly equipped Camaro by only 0.1 second, should be pleased to learn that these two siblings had a logically wider spread on the drag strip, the roadster prevailing by 0.6 seconds at a stunning 17.6 in the quarter. In trap speed, however, the difference is only about one percent, with the roadster winning again at 77.2 mph. Acceleration wasn't spectacular (mainly due to the small engine), even in its price range. Although it beats the MG and the 914, it's slower than the Opel GT and the Datsun 240Z, which has one less cam and one less gear (but more displacement) for a similar price.

Braking performance is another yes/no between the two cars. Although both Fiats have the same tires and same discs front and rear, the Spider stops about 20 feet shorter from 60. Since 100 pounds total weight difference couldn't account for the magnitude of braking advantage, it has to be from the lack of feel through the booster in the Coupe. At an average of 0.86 g retardation for the Spider, its system couldn't be all that bad. So, why Fiat went to a softer, super-sensitive system in the Coupe is a subject for speculation. Even with the occasional right front lockup, though, the Coupe was nearly as stable as the Spider, and neither gave any indication of fade. The fade test must have caused some trauma, because ever since then the Spider brakes shrieked and groaned at certain combinations of speed and pedal pressure.

Our standard handling test produced the expected differences in maximum lateral acceleration. At the limit, the Spider reached a tolerable 0.72 g average, while the Coupe was good for a less tolerable 0.68 g. The Coupe's greater weight and higher center of gravity are a double-edged detractor, the most effect coming from a higher roll angle, which means less front cornering power from lost wheel-camber. This also shows up in greater understeer, or steering angle required, in the otherwise identical vehicles. Throttle response at this limit provides negligible effect since the engine is expending most of its power overcoming cornering friction, and full throttle merely increases understeer while throttle-off reduces understeer only slightly. These handling characteristics are considered to be standard, "safe" qualities for dry asphalt. More horsepower would be useless from a handling standpoint without the use of a limited-slip, because of the large amount of inside rear wheelspin.

Again, there's nothing different about the cars' aerodynamic lift and drag. The Coupe was slightly less impressive in both respects, but both cars matched the medians for other sports cars in the general group. With engine, weight, performance and aerodynamics all of a sameness, it's no surprise that fuel mileage reads out at 22-23 mpg average for each.

As you can see, there was nothing really spectacular about the Fiat 124s. They fit nicely into their price group and aren't necessarily any better or worse than any other car for the money. However, there is one point we've been saving for last, and that is general "feel." By feel, we mean compatibility with the driver. Even though a 124 Fiat may not be doing everything you think it does, nonetheless, you *think* it does, and that's what's important to the sale of automobiles and to the man who has to drive one every day.

One thing Fiat 124s offer that no other car in their price range has (Datsun 2000, excepted) is a five-speed gearbox. Now, the old-line thinking of what a sports car should be is: If you can't work out a little when you're driving it, where's the fun?

In recent years, Fiat has made a big push to be larger internationally, and much of this emphasis has been aimed at the American market. Because of earlier service and faulty engineering problems, Fiat was not a particularly good name to much of the American buying public. Today, however, the products have improved in quality, and parts are much more accessible.

Despite their limited technical achievements, the Fiat 124s drew a dislike from only one staff member. The general consensus was that either the Coupe or Spider are good buys within their price range. ⑤

WERNER BÜHRER DRAWINGS

Road & Track Owner Survey
FIAT 124 SPIDER & COUPE

THE FIAT 124 Sports Spider and Coupe have been on sale in the U.S. since 1968 and during this time they have built up an enthusiastic following. Although they are based on the workaday 124 sedan, they are considerably more than just a prettier body on the same running gear. The 124 Sports models have a double-overhead-cam 4-cyl engine that is larger and more powerful than that used in the sedan (1438 cc and 96 bhp vs. 1197 and 65 though the latest 124 S sedan has the 1438-cc block) and a 5-speed gearbox which is standard on the Spider and optional on the Coupe. They have disc brakes at all corners, a nice seating package for two (Spider) or four (Coupe), and extremely attractive bodies and are, all in all, excellent buys in the $3000-3300 price range.

For this survey, after discarding questionnaires from owners whose cars had less than 5000 miles, we had a total of 249 subscribers participating. This is a larger sample than most marques we have surveyed and was also reasonably evenly divided between Coupes (142) and Spiders (107), numbers that should be sufficient to assure valid conclusions. The average number of miles on the 1968 models was 14,950 and for the 1969s, 11,000. The greatest number of miles for any one car was 33,000.

Reasons for Choice

STYLING was the characteristic of the 124 Sports most often mentioned by the owners as one of the reasons for their choice, a total of 68% mentioning this. Next on the list was handling with 45% and it seems clear that these two characteristics—styling and handling—are those that describe the car best.

Other features influencing the choice of these owners were the double-overhead-cam engine (28%), good overall design (25%), good value for the money (20%) and 4-wheel disc brakes (20%). The excellence of the folding top was mentioned by 20% of the Spider owners and an equal percentage of those whose cars were equipped with 5-speed gearboxes gave that as one of the reasons for their choice. Other attributes noted by 10% or more of the owners were comfortable ride, luxurious interior and efficient use of space. Economy of operation was evidently not one of the major reasons for selecting a Fiat 124 Sports as only 7% of the owners gave this as one of the reasons influencing their choice.

How They Are Driven

THE FIAT 124 Sports Spiders and Coupes are the sole transport of almost exactly half of the owners reporting, the balance owning one or more other cars. Curiously, there were three owners in our survey who owned both a Spider and a Coupe, the first time we have encountered this phenomenon. The cars were almost all bought new (91%) and almost all (95%) are used for daily transportation. More than three-quarters of the owners (76%) also use them for long trips as well and almost a third (30%) use them in rallies.

So far as driving habits are concerned, just about half (48%) reported that they drive "hard," while 36% drive "moderately" and the remaining 16% drive "very hard." We have a saying around the office that good cars like to be driven hard and in this regard it is interesting to compare some of the more popular marques that have been surveyed in this series.

Driven "hard" or "very hard"

Fiat 850............74%	Porsche 911 & 912...66%
Alfa Romeo.........73%	Fiat 124 Sports......64%
BMW 1600, 2002....72%	Volkswagen Beetle...63%
Triumph TR.......67%	Volvo 140.........63%
Datsun sports........67%	MGB..............58%

Maintenance & Service

FIAT 124 Sports owners take good care of their cars, over half (52%) reporting that they have maintained their cars by the book and another 43% "mostly" following the manufacturer's recommendations. As we have found to be typical, over 10% do not trust extended-interval oil changes and actually replace their engine oil more frequently than recommended. Only 5% do not follow the manufacturer's maintenance schedule, an unusually low number.

Fiat dealers fared about as well as other importers when rated by owners. As we have found to be true for other makes, both domestic and imported, dealer service seems to be a matter of luck. Some owners have long sad stories to tell about dealer incompetence and indifference while others have nothing but praise for the treatment they have received. One owner even said this was the third Fiat he had purchased from the same dealer because of the superior service he had received in the past. One common complaint regarding dealers was that those who sold Fiats in addition to an American make were almost uniformly unsatisfactory when it came to service.

Put in proper perspective, however, Fiat dealers don't come off appreciably worse than those handling other imported makes. A comparison with five other popular makes looks like this for the owners' ratings of their dealers:

Owners' Rating of Dealer Service

	Porsche	Alfa	Datsun	Fiat	MGB	Triumph
Rated "Good"	56%	54%	50%	45%	39%	32%
"Fair"	20%	18%	27%	29%	34%	27%
"Poor"	16%	22%	23%	26%	27%	33%

So it would appear from this that Fiat service isn't the worst—or the best—to be found among imported cars.

Best & Worst Features

SORTING THROUGH the questionnaires returned to us by Fiat 124 Sports owners revealed an interesting switch of opinion. While "looks," "beautiful body," "appearance," etc., and all the other descriptions that go under the general head of "styling" were mentioned by 68% of the owners as a reason for selecting their Fiat 124 Sports and "handling" noted by 45%, these two characteristics were reversed when they were asked about the "best" features of the car—62% naming handling as one of the car's best features with only 23% listing styling. We don't think this means that they liked the styling any less than they did before but it does point up the importance of appearance in attracting the prospective buyer—and of handling to keep him happy.

Coming right after "styling" as a "best" was comfort (20%), good brakes (19%) and economy of operation (16%). Not surprisingly, 44% of those who owned Spiders listed the operation of the cloth top as a "best."

Also appreciated by the Fiat 124 Sports owners were overall quality (mentioned by 14%), luxurious interior (14%), 5-speed gearbox (13%) and all-around performance (12%).

The "worst" features of the car were about what we would have predicted—almost a third (31%) of the owners mentioning what they felt to be a lack of torque as the car's biggest drawback. Several owners were vehement about this and almost none who had equipped his car with air conditioning failed to mention his dissatisfaction.

Next on the list of "worsts" came noisy brakes and this was noted by 14% of the owners. And among the Coupe owners, 14% listed the rear window mechanism as one of the car's least desirable features. The electrical system was called out as a "worst" by 8% and this was followed by drivetrain noise. The location of the seatback release mechanism was noted by 10% of those owning Coupes and the 3-point seatbelt arrangement was condemned as clumsy and awkward by an equal number. Also worth mentioning is the fact that a total of 7% of the owners complained about the car's behavior in cold weather conditions—either poor traction and unannounced breakaway in snow and ice or poor starting. Considering that less than half the owners live in climates where such weather conditions are found, the real impact of this particular "worst" is probably greater than the bare number represents.

Also noted by more than 5% of the readers as a "worst" feature was the hard-to-remove oily residue deposited on the inside of the windshield by the vinyl upholstery trim material.

Troubles

WE WERE, frankly, surprised at the number of different troubles shared by the owners of Fiat 124 Sports. There was also an indication that the cars were not always properly prepared before delivery and that the solutions to some of the most common troubles weren't getting passed on to all the dealers.

The most common trouble reported was short sparkplug life. Taking 10,000 miles as the minimum distance to be expected from a set of plugs in a modern engine, a total of 28% of our owners had this difficulty. These ranged from the first plug change being required after less than 300 miles to those that required regular changes at 3000-mile intervals. Obviously, there's something wrong here, some not uncommon engine fault that eats up plugs. Several owners reported they had solved their plug consumption problem by using a transistorized ignition system and NGK (B-6E) plugs and others that NGK plugs alone had done the job for them. Based on this, we would recommend NGKs for any Fiat 124 Sports owner who has this problem.

The next most common problem shared by the owners had to do with wheel alignment. A total of 19% reported having had this trouble. The most common complaint seems to be that the car was delivered with the front wheels incorrectly aligned and that as a result there was premature tire wear and, often, the dealers had trouble in correcting the alignment. Associated with this ailment was excessive tire wear and this was reported by almost 10% of the owners.

The electrics of the Fiat 124 Sports also came in for a good many complaints. Trouble with the turn signals was probably the most common of these troubles but there were also reports of heater motors that burned out, bulbs that expired after very brief use and switches that became inoperative. The ignition system—considered as separate from the electrical system controlling lights and auxilliary controls—also has its problems as 8% of the owners reported trouble with alternator or generator and 6% reported such things as voltage regulator, condenser and points problems.

As we complete more and more of these surveys it becomes apparent that instrument troubles are one of the problems common to almost all makes. The 124 Sports was no exception here as 27% of the owners had one or more instrument failures to report. The most common of these—and especially with 1969 models—was with the speedometer. The main problem was with broken cables and the majority happened within the first 9000 miles. On the 1968 models, the biggest instrument problem was with oil pressure gauges, 12% of the owners of 1968 models having had this trouble. And even this number is probably smaller than actually occurred as several owners reported "low oil pressure—dealer baffled" which may indicate that the gauge was at fault but that the dealer had not discovered it. This difficulty seems to have been solved with 1969 models, however, as less than 2% of the 1969s were similarly afflicted.

Oil leaks were also a problem with more than 10% of the cars, the most common complaint being leaks between the

FIAT 124

head and cam covers. These were almost all present early in the car's life and were corrected under warranty.

Valve work was required within 20,000 miles on 12% of the 1968 models but this dropped to less than 2% for the 1969s. Perhaps related to this were complaints having to do with replacement of exhaust manifold gaskets, a problem reported by 8% of the 1968 owners but by only 5% of those owning 1969s.

Other problems reported in sufficient numbers to be worth mentioning included upholstery (mainly stitching that came undone) and clutch troubles (a variety of ailments adding up to 5% of all owners).

A total of 9% of the owners reported having had no troubles at all. The average mileage for these completely trouble-free cars was 11,700 for 1968s and 7500 miles for 1969s. The greatest mileage reported by a trouble-free car was 28,000.

A comparison with other makes looks like this for trouble-free cars:

Owners Reporting No Troubles

Volkswagen Beetle	..35%	Fiat 850	9%
BMW	11%	Fiat 124 Sports	9%
Porsche 911 & 912	...11%	Alfa Romeo	8%
Volvo	10%	Jaguar	7%
Datsun	10%	Corvette	7%

Note: This information not tabulated for MGB and Triumph surveys.

Life Expectancies

PREDICTING THE life expectancy of the various components of the Fiat 124 Sports—or of any car—is a bit chancey as not all owners report mileages as we ask and we often have the feeling that we are likely to hear more about those things that went wrong than those that wore well and gave no trouble.

Based on the reports of our 249 owners, though, we would make these generalizations. Plug life is apt to be short, about

6000 miles on the average for the original plugs, though this can be increased by the use of NGK plugs. Tire wear, because of the difficulties with alignment, is difficult to predict as some owners were having to replace one or more tires after as little as 8000 miles. Of those getting normal tire wear, replacements were being required at between 20,000 and 25,000 miles, though one owner with 19,000 miles reported that his tires were "barely worn." Brake pad life also varies widely, averaging about 18,000 miles though it does not appear uncommon for replacements to be required as early as 12,000 miles or as late as 25,000 miles depending on how the car was driven.

It is perhaps worth mentioning that no engine overhauls were reported by owners whose cars were given "normal" (not racing) use.

Summary

THE ULTIMATE criterion of owner satisfaction is whether the owner would buy another of the same make. In this respect, the Fiat 124 Sports models come off quite well. Although Porsche holds the all-time record for "would buy another" at 95%, the 124 Sports isn't doing badly at 83%. Here's how it looks compared to other sports models:

Would Current Owners Buy Another?

	Porsche	Alfa	Fiat 124 Sports	Datsun Sports	MGB	Triumph
Would	95%	94%	83%	80%	70%	67%
Would not	4%	3%	13%	18%	19%	30%
Undecided	1%	3%	4%	2%	11%	3%

It is also interesting to note that Fiat 124 Sports owners are more favorably inclined toward buying another 124 than are the Fiat 850 owners we surveyed a few months ago. Of the 850 owners, only 70% would buy another 850.

From the results of this survey we would generalize that Fiat 124 Sports owners are very enthusiastic about three particular features of their cars—the handling, the styling and the comfort. Those owning Spiders also are appreciative of the excellent folding top. What they do not like about their cars is also clear—they would like more power (a characteristic that the soon-to-arrive 1.6-liter, 125-bhp 124 Sports will have), brakes that are quieter in operation and a less bothersome electrical and ignition system.

SUMMARY: FIAT 124 SPORTS SPIDER & COUPE OWNER SURVEY

New or Used?
Bought new......91%
Bought used......9%

About Driving Habits
Drivers who said they drove "moderately"...36%
Drivers who said they drove "hard"........48%
Drivers who said they drove "very hard"....16%

How many current Fiat 124 Sports owners would buy another?
Would..........83%
Would not........13%
Undecided.........4%

Mileages
Avg. miles on 1968 models......14,950
Avg. miles on 1969 models......11,000
Avg. no. miles driven per year......16,000

Problem Areas
Mentioned by more than 10% of the owners

Wheel alignment
Short plug life
Instruments:
  Speedometer ('69s)
  Oil pressure gauge ('68s)

Brakes (mainly '68s)
Electrical system
Oil leaks
Turn signals
Valves (mainly '68s)

Five Best Features
Handling
Styling
Comfort
Brakes
Top (Spider)

How Owners Feel about Fiat Service
Rated "good"....45%
Rated "fair".......29%
Rated "poor"......26%

Mentioned by 5-10% of the owners

Excessive tire wear
Upholstery
Exhaust system

Alternator/generator
Ignition (general)
Clutch

Owners reporting no troubles.............9%

Five Worst Features
Lack of torque
Noisy brakes
Electrics
Rear window latch (coupes)
Drivetrain noise

ROAD & TRACK
R&T
ROAD TEST

FIAT 124 SPIDER 1600

*Added flexibility is the only measurable
advantage of the new 1608-cc version*

IN OUR FIRST road test of the Fiat 124 Spider,
done nearly three years ago, we concluded of it
and its companion 124 Coupe, "Our only major
criticism is that their on-the-road performance
is not quite up to their looks, and we would
respectfully suggest that Fiat consider making
the 125 (1608-cc) version of the dohc engine, which develops 100 lb-ft torque, standard equipment for the American market." Last year, when we did a comparison test of
the Spider against the three other sports roadsters listed in
the Comparison Data box and found the Fiat the best car
of the four, we concluded nevertheless that "Every car in
the group has a serious flaw; the Fiat's is its small, low-
torque engine."

Now, at long last, the 1608-cc engine has found its way
into the 124 Sport models, at a $92 cost penalty that is in
every way justified. A few 1438-cc models remain to be sold
but the 1608 is now for all practical purposes standard.
Ever-tightening U.S. emission regulations have forced a de-
tuning of it so that it no longer develops 100 lb-ft torque;
but its present 94 lb-ft is still a useful increase over the
smaller engine's meager 82.5. The power rating is up by 10

to 104 bhp—quite short of the European version which develops about 125, and the acceleration times through the
gears show no power increase at all.

The better torque is noticeable from the first drive around
the block. The larger engine is decidedly more flexible and
torquey, sounding less hard-pressed as it goes about its work;
less shifting and revving are required to maintain a given
pace. And when the driver decides to whirl it through the
gears to its 6500-rpm redline, it takes on a note that is more
aggressive and more appropriate to a sporting car. In a nut-
shell, the larger engine makes the 124 Sport the car it should
have been all along. But we certainly expected the car to be
quicker through the gears, and it most certainly is not.

The only outward identification of the 1608 version is a
small 1600 in chrome on the rear body panel; the U.S. version lacks the two hood bubbles found on the European
1600. Our test car had the optional (at a reasonable $135)
Cromodora alloy wheels, which dress it up nicely, and door-
protecting chrome-rubber strips on each body side that don't.
Otherwise it was the same pleasant, refined sports-touring
car that the 124 Spider has always been.

A fine 5-speed gearbox has been standard on the Spider

all along. On the last test car we were able to beat the synchronizers when shifting fast, but on this one they never failed. We'd like a little more spring loading to pull the lever toward its 3rd-4th gate—this makes it easier to find 3rd from 2nd or 4th from 5th—but otherwise its action is quite satisfactory. The ratios have been changed, and surprisingly 1st, 2nd and 3rd are shorter than before so that the road speeds attainable in them are slightly lower. This mystifies us a bit, but no matter, as the ratios still work out well in everyday driving and 3rd is a useful passing gear to 74 mph. One ratio we don't like, though, is 5th: it's only the barest stepup from 4th and the engine is still doing 4000 rpm at 70 mph. Especially now that the torque curve is so much nicer could the car use a longer-legged 5th, say about 0.85:1, for quieter highway operation and longer engine life. "Quieter," we say, with the reservation that only in the Coupe would one notice this; wind roar over the ragtop drowns out engine noise at anything over 50 mph in 5th anyway.

Speaking of the ragtop, it is excellent and though we've harped on how much better it is than those of most other sports cars it deserves mentioning again. It goes down so easily that the driver can lower it without getting out of his seat. In fairness we must mention that MG, the make we've railed at most on this point, has had the Italian firm Michelotti design a new, easy-folding top for the MGB. Another noteworthy point about the 124's top is its rear quarter windows, which fold with the top: they provide rearside vision that most sports cars don't offer.

Another nice thing about the Spider is its handsome, real wood dash and handsome, legible instrumentation although neither speedometer nor tachometer is accurate. Here Fiat has met a U.S. safety regulation—the one requiring a warning of some kind when one opens the driver's door without·

removing the ignition key—in an absolutely superior way: with an orange light rather than a buzzer. We suspect that most owners wouldn't even bother to disconnect this as they do the buzzers. On the minus side, though, are the top latches over the windshield and these look lethal, sticking out above the padded sun visors.

Our test car had a new kind of Pirelli tire, the Cinturato H CN36. It appears to have a more "aggressive" or sticky tread pattern than other Cinturatos and, though we didn't drive this car in the rain where this would matter, the mild roar it makes when traveling in a straight line reinforces the impression. When testing the Spider for stopping distance from 80 these tires acquitted themselves nicely with a 0.78g deceleration rate—better than the Michelins on our first Spider (which did only 0.62g) but not quite so good as the older Pirelli design on the Coupe we tested at the same time. Handling qualities remain the same as before: moderate body roll, strong understeer and an intimate feel between tires and steering wheel. The steering is a bit heavy at low speeds with these tires but at speed the relationship between driver and road is exemplary—this is what makes a sports car fun to drive on a winding road, and ultra-high cornering power (which the Spider does not have) isn't necessary. The chassis is not too firmly sprung, the well-controlled live rear axle behaves itself as well as any live axle and in all the 124 Sport is a proper sporting convertible.

The brakes perform well, too; fade resistance was better in this car than in our earlier Spiders and within the tires' limits the panic-stop performance is good. But in everyday use these brakes (solid discs at all four wheels) are less than happy. They squeal embarrassingly and the pedal feel is spongy; the latter trait is one we've found sporadically in the various and sundry 124 spiders, coupes, sed ns and wagons

FIAT 124 SPIDER 1600

we've driven. We thought it was cured but, alas, it's back again. The handbrake is weak too.

As sports convertibles go, the 124 Spider is long on comfort. It has an excellent driving position—arms-out but not designed for gorillas; good seats, good ventilation and workable controls. And there's a decent amount of trunk space for that cross-country vacation which should be great fun in a Spider. Routine maintenance intervals are in keeping with modern practice. On the other hand, reliability and durability are not its forte, as our Owner Survey of last year pointed out.

The strength of its fine and balanced combination of acceleration, handling, braking, comfort, finish and style is easily enough to offset the prospect of somewhat more than the usual mechanical work and the disappointment of no power increase, though, and we unhesitatingly recommend the 124 Spider in its new, improved form.

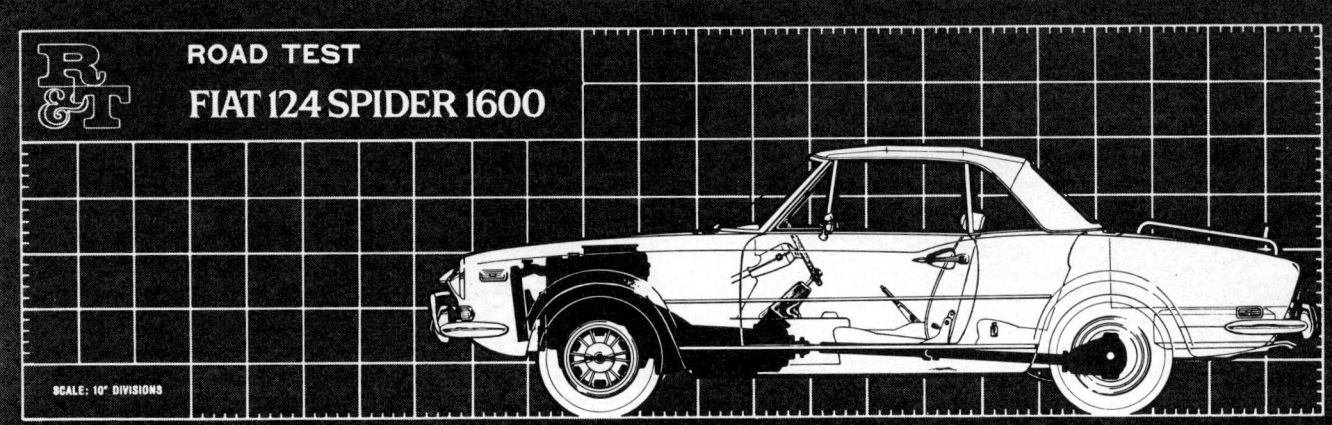

ROAD TEST
FIAT 124 SPIDER 1600

SCALE: 10" DIVISIONS

PRICE

List price, east coast........$3535
List price, west coast........$3572
Price as tested, west coast...$3812
  Price as tested includes AM/FM radio ($85), alloy wheels ($135), side protection strips ($20)

IMPORTER

Fiat-Roosevelt Motors, 532–540 Sylvan Ave, Englewood Cliffs, N.J. 07632

ENGINE

Type..............dohc inline 4
Bore x stroke, mm......80.0 x 80.0
  Equivalent in........3.15 x 3.15
Displacement, cc/cu in. .1608/98.1
Compression ratio...........8.5:1
Bhp @ rpm...........104 @ 6000
  Equivalent mph............106
Torque @ rpm, lb-ft...94 @ 4200
  Equivalent mph.............74
Carburetion..1 Weber 40 IDF (2V)
Type fuel required.......premium
Emission control....engine mods

DRIVE TRAIN

Transmission.... 5-speed manual
Gear ratios: 5th (0.913).....3.74:1
  4th (1.00).............4.10:1
  3rd (1.41).............5.78:1
  2nd (2.18).............8.93:1
  1st (3.80)............15.56:1
Final drive ratio..........4.10:1

CHASSIS & BODY

Layout.....front engine/rear drive
Body/frame............unit steel
Brake type: 8.9-in. disc front and rear vacuum assist; rear limiting valve
  Swept area, sq in.........297
Wheels..........cast alloy 13 x 5
Tires.Pirelli Cinturato H 165 HR-13
Steering type....worm & roller
  Overall ratio...........16.4:1
  Turns, lock-to-lock........2.8
  Turning circle, ft..........36.0
Front suspension: unequal-length A-arms, coil springs, tube shocks, anti-roll bar
Rear suspension: live axle on trailing arms & Panhard rod; coil springs, tube shocks

ACCOMMODATION

Seating capacity, persons....2+1
Seat width..............2 x 19.0
Head room..................40.0
Seat back adjustment, degrees..25

INSTRUMENTATION

Instruments: 140-mph speedometer, 99,999 odometer, 999.9 trip odometer, oil pressure, fuel level, coolant temperature, clock
Warning lights: brake system, directionals, headlight flasher, lights on, high beam, remove key

MAINTENANCE

Service intervals, mi:
  Oil change...............6000
  Filter change............6000
  Chassis lube............12,000
  Minor tuneup............3000
  Major tuneup............6000
  Warranty, mo/mi.......12/12,000

GENERAL

Curb weight, lb............2190
Test weight................2540
Weight distribution (with driver), front/rear, %....55/45
Wheelbase, in..............89.8
Track, front/rear.......52.9/51.8
Overall length............156.3
  Width..................63.5
  Height.................49.2
Ground clearance...........4.9
Overhang, front/rear....29.8/36.7
Usable trunk space, cu ft......6.2
Fuel tank capacity, U.S. gal...11.9

CALCULATED DATA

Lb/bhp (test weight).........23.1
Mph/1000 rpm (5th gear)....17.7
Engine revs/mi (60 mph)....3400
Piston travel, ft/mi.........1785
R & T steering index........1.01
Brake swept area sq in/ton....235

RELIABILITY

From R&T Owner Surveys the average number of trouble areas for all models surveyed is 10.6. As owners of earlier model Fiat 124 Sports reported 14 trouble areas, we expect the reliability of the 124 Sport Spider 1600 to be below average.

ROAD TEST RESULTS

ACCELERATION

Time to distance, sec:
0–100 ft.................... 3.4
0–250 ft.................... 6.7
0–500 ft.................... 10.0
0–750 ft.................... 13.1
0–1000 ft.................. 15.9
0–1320 ft (¼ mi).......... 18.6
Speed at end of ¼ mi, mph.. 72.5
Time to speed, sec:
0–30 mph................... 4.1
0–40 mph................... 6.1
0–50 mph................... 9.0
0–60 mph.................. 12.2
0–70 mph.................. 16.9
0–80 mph.................. 24.5
Passing exposure time, sec:
To pass car going 50 mph... 8.1

FUEL CONSUMPTION

Normal driving, mpg........ 23.2
Cruising range, mi........ 275

SPEEDS IN GEARS

5th gear (6300 rpm)........ 112
4th (6500)................. 102
3rd (6500)................. 75
2nd (6500)................. 48
1st (6500)................. 28

BRAKES

Panic stop from 80 mph:
Max. deceleration rate, % g.. 77
Stopping distance, ft....... 319
Control............ very good

Pedal effort for 50%-g stop, lb.. 20
Fade test: percent increase in pedal
effort to maintain 50%-g deceleration rate in 6 stops from
60 mph..................... nil
Parking: Hold 30% grade?..... no
Overall brake rating........ good

HANDLING

Speed on 100-ft radius, mph.. 32.9
Lateral acceleration, % g.... 0.723

SPEEDOMETER ERROR

30 mph indicated is actually... 28.0
40 mph..................... 37.5
60 mph..................... 56.0
70 mph..................... 65.0
80 mph..................... 75.0
Odometer, 10.0 mi.......... 9.5

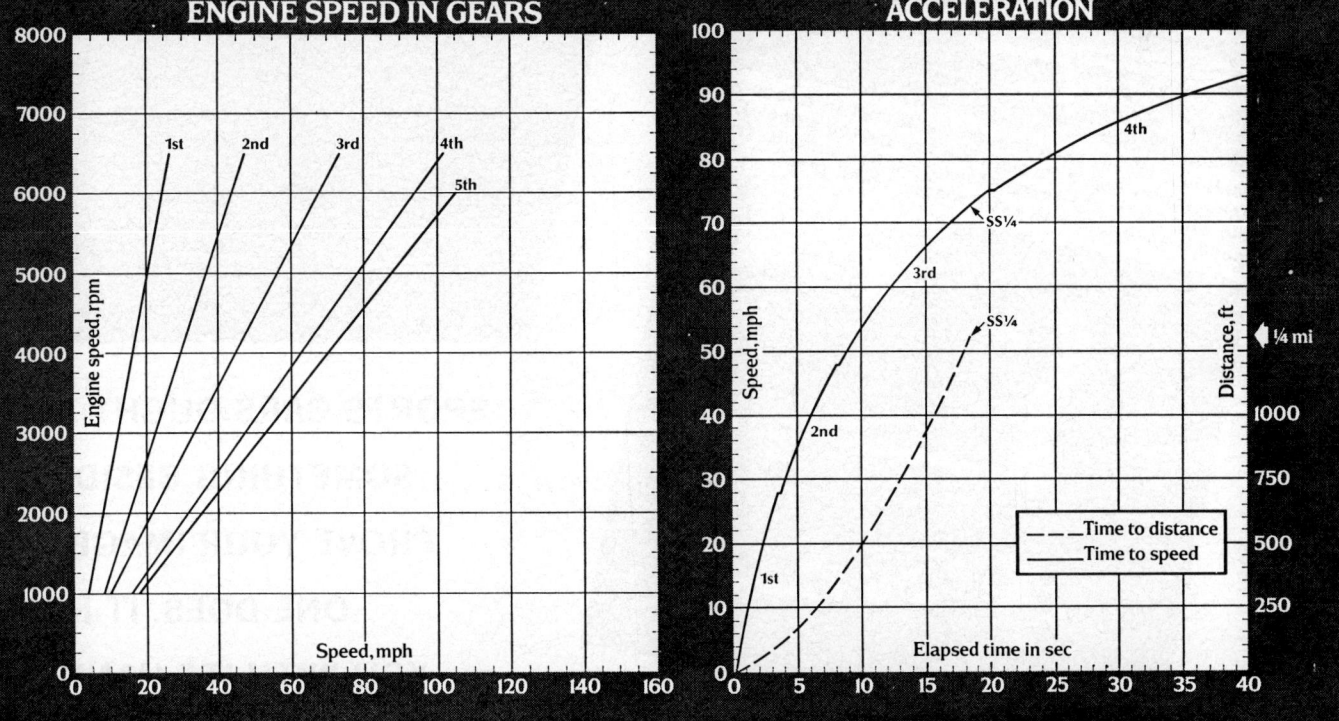

FIAT 124 SPIDER

ROAD TEST

Dashboard layout good though traditional with tach and speedometer visible through the two-spoked wheel. Console with radio and gearshift lever divides cockpit. Trunk space is adequate with extra space behind seat.

SPORTS CARS OUGHT TO DO SOMETHING BESIDES IMPROVE YOUR IMAGE. THIS ONE DOES. IT HOOKS YOU WITH ITS HANDLING.

■ Fiat buffs are going to have a bit of a time telling the new 124 Spider from last year's model, at least, from the external appearance. The side marker lights are oblong and larger this year; the Fiat nameplate has been removed from the engine hood in front and our test car had a stripe running from front to back right through the door. The first real difference that will grab you is the performance of the current engine with its higher horsepower.

The first 124 Spider we drove, more than a year ago, proved to be a fine handling automobile and this version is even better. With the higher horsepower the engine is no noiser than the previous model if you allow for the exhaust resonance that any sports car ought to have. The suspension hasn't changed. The coil springs have been retained with wishbones, anti-roll bar and shocks up front balanced by four trailing arms and a transverse rod locating the live axle rear suspension. The 89.8-inch wheelbase "ragtop" just utilizes the extra horses with a flair that is making this particular Fiat a must with most of the people who know and write about imported sports cars.

Fiat's importer here, incidentally, predicts a sale in excess of 60,000 cars for 1971. The Spider will be a big portion of this figure.

Without doing a rehash of previous reportage on the 124 Spider and for the benefit of readers who missed the original story, we'd like to mention some of the features that made us want to keep the test

FIAT 124 SPIDER

SPECIFICATIONS

Wheelbase (inches)	89.8
Weight (lbs.)	2046
Length (inches)	156.3
Height (inches)	49.2
Width (inches)	63.5
Steering turns lock to lock	2.7
Turning circle (ft.)	34
Engine type	4 cylinder
	In line, dohc
Cooling method	liquid
Displacement	96.48 cu. in.
	1608
Compression ratio	8.5:1
Horsepower (SAE)	104 @ 6000 rpm
Torque (ft. lbs.)	94.0 @ 4200 rpm

car longer than the period for which it had been loaned to us.

The steering is one of the better features of this car. The wheel is far enough away so that you can go with your arms almost straight out in front of you yet the pedal arrangement is such that you can get the clutch all the way down to the floor without having to hitch the seat all the way forward. Your knees are never pulled up so high that your legs get tired. In fact the thigh rests on the seat and this certainly proves valuable on long trips. The back of the seat, too, is nicely designed with ade-

quate support all the way up the back. Visibility is excellent for a soft top coupe like this and although the little rear side windows go down with the top making it just a little harder to lower they tend to reduce the closed-in feeling most imported convertibles have.

The car stops well with its disc brakes front and back. This allows you to move quickly in and around town, of course. The five speed gear box contributes to this mobility even if you don't get up into the fifth gear that often in city driving. The difference in the new engine is really felt in the middle gear ranges, incidentally. An effective gear ratio change was made here and that's where the engine comes into its own. It did take us a little while, however, to shift down from fifth to fourth gear effortlessly. The car is so well set up, though, that it took most of the rises normally calling for a downshift easily without loss of power in fifth. This was especially true when you really got rolling out on the highway.

We never attempted to get anywhere near the top speed of 112 miles per hour the company claims for this car. We did cruise frequently at sixty-five and seventy

CONTINUED ON PAGE 85

124 Sport 1608 cc. Engine

owering the top is an easy one man job
nce you get used to having the little rear
quarter" windows recess with the top. Two
ood sturdy fasteners bind it to the top of
he windshield and the back-light is not too
ifficult to fold without wrecking it per-
anently. The overhead engine with in-
reased horsepower this year just makes a
ood thing better (see our Service test on
age 38 this issue). The 1608cc double OHC
ngine is mated to a five-speed transmission
nd offered as standard equipment. Quite a
ackage!

Supertune
Fiat Firepower

This time the tweak is for the Fiat 124 Sports 1600.
Result, 30 percent more power/By John Christy

For a number of years now, Fiat has been bringing in a delightful device known as the 124 Sports in both four-seat coupe and two-seat roadster form. It is equipped with a twin-cam version of what Fiat refers to as the 125 family of engines, the DOHC setup being unique to the sports models, the 124-S sedan and wagon having pushrod-operated valves. Originally, this Lampredi-designed 4 displaced a miniscule but strong 1438 cc. However, with the emissions handwriting writ large on the world's walls, Fiat lengthened the stroke by 8.5 mm, to bring the displacement up to 1608 cc, and reduced the compression ratio to 8.5 from 8.9 to 1. In Europe the 124 sports could be had with a pair of 40 DCOE Webers and 125 bhp. In the one we get here the carburetion is a single two-barrel progressive Weber 26/39 DCF, meaning that the primary throat is 26 millimeters in diameter and the secondary

is 39 mm wide. In this version the advertised flywheel horsepower is 104 at 6000 rpm. Actually the engine speed at which peak occurs is 6300, as we found out when we got it on the dyno.

Our subject for this round on the Geraghty Automotive & Marine dynamometer is a show-car-cum-demonstrator in the process of being prepared by Geraghty's Glendale neighbor John Rich of John Rich Fiat. Rich is a red hot enthusiast and fields an 850 Spider in SCCA's H Production class that not only terrorizes that class but G Production as well. By way of business, he also handles a full line of Fiat speed equipment. The car had wide Shelby wheels, fat tires and flared fenders but was at the moment dead showroom stock otherwise—in fact it still had the clear plastic over the seats that many imports are shipped with.

The first thing we noticed was that, like Italian high-winders of an earlier,

more carefree era, there was little power under 3000 rpm, but over that figure it took hold and seemingly went on forever, right up to 7000. Use of the overdrive fifth gear was pointless at anything less than 70 mph, but with proper selection of the intermediate ratios the thing was deceptively quick.

On the dynamometer the reason became clear. At 2000 rpm the power at the rear wheels was a weak 12 horses. At 2500 it was 16 and at 3000 it was only 21. From 3500 on up, though, it started pulling power in healthy increments, reaching a peak of 52 hp at 6300, falling back to 47 at 7000. It was also a little dirtier than it should have been with an initial CO reading of four percent and the hydrocarbon level at 530 parts per million at idle. With carburetor adjustment, we could dial in a CO reading of three percent, but at the expense of driveability. At cruise, the CO dropped to 2.5 percent and the HC also

Fiat 124 Sports		
RPM	Stock	Tuned
2000	12	17
2500	16	22
3000	21	27
3500	28	33
4000	33	40
4500	40	46
5000	44	52
5500	46	59
6000	48	62
6300*	52	64
7000	47	58
*Peak power.		

Left: Carburetor changes are totally simple, only the two main jets being changed and, if you have a grappler-type screwdriver the top doesn't even have to be removed or any lines or linkage disassembled.
Below: As the hydrocarbon and carbon monoxide gauges show, the Fiat 124 is cleaner than most similar engines after the dynotune with 400 ppm HC and 2.25% CO.

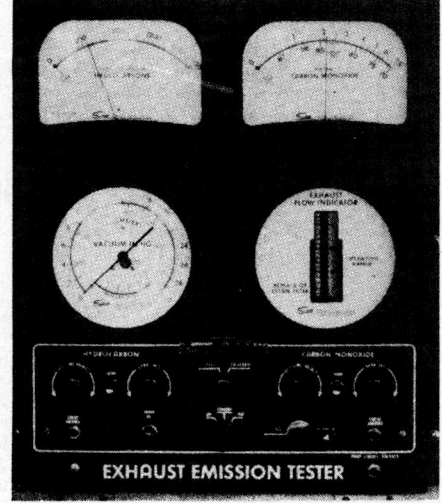

dropped, so you couldn't exactly call it a gross polluter. Part of this may have been due to a broken secondary advance spring in the distributor which allowed it to advance to 20 degrees BTC at 2000 rpm—much too quick, too soon. From there, though it was the usual low and slow curve, still slowly advancing to 35 degrees at 3800. Obviously, the first point of attack was here. The springs were changed to give a curve that started more slowly then moved up to give a peak advance at 2600 rpm.

One would normally be led to think that if a car idled with too fat a mixture that it was generally too rich throughout the range, but that is strictly a function of the idle circuit and has little to do with partially-open or wide-open throttle. The air-fuel meters indicated that while it idled fat, it leaned out a bit much in both high and low cruise, richening only momentarily in the power phases. The primary and secondary jets are No. 125 and No. 155

or .046 and .059 respectively. These were richened slightly and the vacuum diaphragm that operates the secondary butterfly was reset to come in a little earlier. Nothing else in the carburetor was touched. The spark plugs were clean and unblistered so they were left alone.

Back on the dynamometer, it showed a curve that was similar in shape to the stock curve but was considerably stronger all through the range. There was only 17 horsepower at work at 2000 rpm but at 2500 22 got on the job and at 3000 there were 27 of them at work. From 3500 rpm on up the power came on strong, finally reaching a peak of 64 rear wheel horsepower at 6300 rpm and holding 58 at 7000.

We also had a cleaner Fiat. We were able to get an idle that would produce a CO reading of 2.25 percent and 400 ppm of HC. The CO stayed steady, only rising momentarily at deceleration. The HC reading also stayed put, rising only when the point of peak

power was past and the efficiency dropped. We had no measuring equipment to check NOx.

On the road this fattened power curve showed up in increased flexibility and it didn't have to be rowed with the shift lever when we wound through traffic. We *could* flail the gearbox and get some exciting bursts of performance but it wasn't necessary if we wanted to maintain a more leisurely pace. It still liked to be in the 4000 rpm-and-up area but it would allow less without fuss.

As usual, the dyno time will result in an available kit by the time you read this—at least for the 1608 cc version. The address for those interested is Geraghty Dynotuned Products, 4062 Verdugo Road, Los Angeles, Ca. 90065. And for those who are interested in something more, John Rich either has now, or will shortly have, more good things both for legal street use and for all-out racing. Stay tuned in; we just may come back to this subject in the near future. /MT

FIAT ABARTH 124 RALLY

**A larger-engined 124 Spyder with independent rear suspension which could improve Fiat's chances in rallying.
Michael Bowler reports**

Fiat's competition department may not exist in name but the organisation responsible for Fiats in competition has suddenly become an effective force in the rallying world; in 1972 they came 2nd to Lancia in the Rally Championship of Makes and Raphaele Pinto won the Drivers' Championship and the Mitropa (Middle Europe) Cup, both in the 124 Sport Spyder 1600.

But it started as far back as 1965 when Fiat supplied servicing facilities for vintage Fiats taking part in rallies and touring events. This was diverted to helping Fiat private entrants in modern rallies, until this had grown by 1969 to providing a chosen team with works prepared cars and financial help. A works team was formed in 1970 with Alcide Paganelli and Pirelli engineer Hakan Lindberg using the 124 Sport Spyder and the 125S. This continued in 1971, the year of Fiat's complete acquisition of Abarth. This year has seen Pinto, Lindberg and Paganelli competing regularly in international rallies and Maurizio Verini in local events, all with 124 Spyders using the 1600 cc unit.

The man behind the Fiat end of things is Ing. Sgvazini who somehow finds time to direct operations as well as control Fiat's production lines. But the develop-ment of the latest version has been carried out by Abarth engineers in conjunction with the men from Fiat. With the enlarge-ment of the 124 Sports engine to 1800 cc, Fiat decided to produce a special Abarth version to make the car even more competitive in rallying.

Adding power as well as reducing weight is the accepted way of modifying production cars for competition, but for rallying you have to be rather more care-ful with the weight paring as strength is all important. The fact that the 124 Sport 1600 won the Acropolis with team-mates 4th and 7th underlines its basic strength. In addition Fiat have improved the roadholding with the help of a new independent rear suspen-sion.

Power starts at 118 bhp for the standard 1800; Abarth add a couple of downdraught Webers on a special manifold, new cams and a fabricated exhaust manifold to get 128 bhp. It isn't a breath-taking increase but provides the basis for getting about 160-170 bhp in Group 4 form.

The gearbox starts as a four-speed with the five-speed box as an option on the Spyder. Fifth is very close to fourth at 0.88 : 1 and on the 4.3:1 final drive gives 17.2 mph/1000 rpm. Initially Fiat's fifth gear was contained in a separate housing bolted to the back of the four speed box but it is now an integral one; for rallies dog-clutch engagement will replace the synchromesh.

The rear suspension starts as a live axle with radius arms and a Panhard rod. Abarth have made a chassis mounted alloy differential casing which is three point mounted through rubber blocks, one on the rear and one at each end of a carrier bolted transversely across the nose. The drive shafts are fitted with twin universal joints, incorpo-rating plunge. The independent rear suspension now used is a variation on the Macpherson strut theme as used on the Fiat 130. A spring/damper strut is bolted to the top of the upright, while the lower link is an inverted wishbone with its sharp end on a bracket behind the differential casing. Fore and aft control is exercised by a torque arm running from the outer end of the wish-bone to one of the pick-up points for the standard system, both ends being rubber bushed.

And the body started as a unitary steel structure with a hard-top. The structural part is still the same but the boot, bonnet and roof are made of glass-fibre, and the doors and scuttle are skinned in aluminium. A four-point roll cage is bolted in as standard which probably helps with stiffness. Although this sounds quite a lot of lightening, the actual final gain is only 48lb. for a total weight of 18½ cwt.

The method of assembly is rather long winded as Abarth do the non-standard bits. Fiat send engines transmissions to Abarth; he modifies the engines and sends them back to Fiat together with rear suspensions. The body arrives at Fiat from Farina. Fiat bolt it all together, take it to Abarth for individual testing, and it then returns to Fiat for sale at a bit over £2000 in Italy. The standard Spyder 1800 costs about £1400. An application for homologation in Group 4 has been filed and should be agreed from January; the appropriate build of 500 is already under way.

DRIVING IMPRESSIONS

I had driven both the previous 124 Spyders, the 1438 cc and the 1608 cc versions, both with the five speed box. They were nice modern sports cars, comfortable and practical with 0-60 mph taking around 9½ sec. and maxima of 106, and 112 mph respectively. So I felt fairly well at home in the 1800 Abarth with its nice comfortable thigh-gripping seats, a small leather covered steering wheel whose rim hides the water temperature and fuel gauges—I don't share colleagues' enthusiasms for oversmall wheels —and good all round visibility for my size.

The important instruments, rev counter, oil pressure and speedo are straight ahead through the wheel top and the smooth engine fairly thrashes up to the yellow line at 6200 rpm. It is noisy as

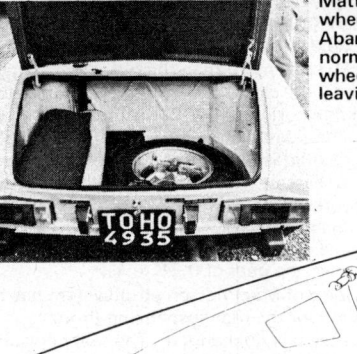

Matt black panels and alloy wheels distinguish the Abarth 1800 Rally from the normal Spider. The spare wheel fills the usual hole leaving a useful boot

there isn't much sound deadening but torquey and it feels unburstable. A quick check on a 0-100 km time on a damp surface gave 9.2 sec. with a lot of wheelspin and a squeaky twitch on the first two gearchanges; 60 mph came up in third. Under better conditions with our normal test loading it should take around 8.9 sec. to 60 mph. The quoted maximum speed is 118 mph which means 6800 rpm; it certainly went up to the start of the red sector at 6500

very easily and held 7000 rpm on the flat, so it should manage 120 mph.

The gearbox ratios aren't brilliant as there is quite a gap between second and third, and fifth is very close to fourth—only a 700 rpm rev drop from 6500. It's a nice change though, with the Alfa pattern gate. The box was quiet but the axle growled on part throttle when maintaining speeds up to about 85 mph, at which point the back end vibrated, but you were through this very quickly.

The springing is set to be pretty firm so that for normal main road motoring it feels fairly similar to the standard softer live axle ride, but at least on the bumpy Bracco Pass in Italy, where we tried the car, the wheels stayed on the ground. It was fairly easy to get the inner rear wheel spinning on the damp surface but the car was nicely balanced with understeer on trailing or steady throttle which could be overcome by

power. The steering kept you informed of front end grip. The tyres fitted were Pirelli 185/70—13 with the blocky CN36 pattern which is a good compromise rally tyre.

There was some wind noise around the side windows but the hardtop seems to fit well and the car is quite practicable as normal road transport, especially in Italy. There is space behind the seats— I used one of the earlier cars as a three seater—and a reasonable boot. The roof comes off with four clips, and if you want to go sprinting the windscreen comes out with four bolts and you can fit an aero screen. The matt black bonnet is held down by rubber clamps—it flaps, so these are essential—and the car certainly looks the part.

Its predecessor which was just a modified production car earned a good solid reputation. With a more carefully conceived version, designed with rallies in mind, Fiat stand a good chance of bettering even this year's record.

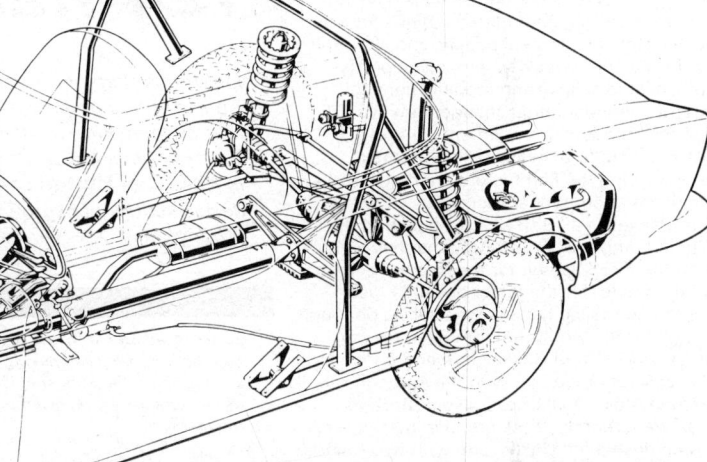

New rear suspension and roll cage are visible in the cutaway; downdraught Webers dictate a pancake filter, below

GENERAL SPECIFICATION

Engine

Cylinders	Four in line
Capacity	1756 cc (438.9 cu. in.)
Bore/stroke	84 x 79.2 mm (3.31 x 3.12 in.)
Cooling	Water with thermostatic fan
Block	Cast iron
Head	Light alloy
Valves	Belt driven dohc
Valve timing	
inlet opens	15 btdc
inlet closes	55 abdc
ex. opens	55 bbdc
ex. closes	15 atdc
Compression	9.8:1
Carburetters	Two Weber 44 IDF
Bearings	five main
Fuel pump	Electric
Max. power	128 bhp (DIN) at 6200 rpm
Max. torque	117 lb ft (DIN) at 5200 rpm

Transmission

Type	5 speed synchromesh
Clutch	7.9 in. dia. sdp diaphragm
Internal ratios and mph/1000 rpm	
Top	0.88/17.2
4th	1.00/15.2
3rd	1.36/11.2
2nd	2.10/7.2
1st	3.66/4.1
Rev	3.53/-
Final drive	Hypoid bevel 4.3:1

Suspension

Front	Independent with double wishbones, coils, anti-roll bar
Rear	Independent with struts with lower link and radius rod with coils and anti-roll bar

Steering

Type	Worm and roller
Assistance	
Toe-in	0.08 in.
Camber	½° negative
Castor	4½°
King pin	13° 40'
Rear toe-in	1½° negative

Brakes

Type	8.9 in. dia. discs all round
Servo	Yes
Circuit	Twin
Rear valve	No

Wheels

Type	Alloy 5½J x 13 in.
Tyres	Pirelli CN36 185/70 VR 13
Pressures	24F, 27R

IN competition terms the Fiat Abarth 124 Rally is a "homologation special". That suggests that somehow it is a cheat — which it isn't. The fact that a major manufacturer is prepared to go to the trouble and expense of building however many cars the regulations for his chosen class of competition demand is an indication of how serious they are about it. A limited production run of uncompromising race or rally cars can provide the factory with something more competitive than the higher volume "standard" model, gives the enthusiast a chance to buy an exciting and unusual road car — and can often contribute to the eventual improvement of the car's less sophisticated relatives. If you doubt that, look at the various sporting Escorts and the Porsche Carrera RS.

In Fiat's case they had come almost to the end of the useful development of the 1600cc 124 Spider which could be accomplished within the Group 4 Special Grand Touring Car rules. They had initially chosen the 124 Spider for their rally effort because its power-to-weight ratio was better than any of the other models in the cheaper end of their range. What the car needed, said the drivers, was independent rear suspension, less weight and more horsepower. The latter was partially satisfied by the arrival of the 1800cc engine as fitted to the 130 saloon, which could be quite extensively modified under Group 4 rules. But since 1971 lightweight body panels have not been allowed as homologated options for a car which normally has steel panels, and although people like Ford get away with some pretty sophisticated suspension modifications for Group 2, a fundamental change from live axle to an independent arrangement isn't on.

After a couple of seasons finding their feet in rallying the Fiat factory team gained significant international success in 1972. In their first year — 1970 — they had won the Italian Championship. At that time they were using the 125S saloon for the rougher events and the Spider for the faster ones. By last year the sports car had shown itself to be tough enough for the worst that European rallying can provide — and Hakan Lindberg, a Pirelli engineer from Sweden, won the Acropolis and Austrian Alpine Rallies to prove it. Both of these were rounds of the premier International Championship for Makes, and with two rounds to go Fiat were still in with a chance of pipping their Lancia cousins for the championship title. In addition, Raffaele Pinto and Gino Macaluso won the complicated 24-round European Drivers' Championship as well as the Mitropa Cup, held over six events in Austria, Germany and Italy.

The works 1600cc Fiat 124 Spider on its way to victory in the 1972 Austrian Alpine Rally — inspiration for the new model

Fiat Abarth 124 Rally

Lightweight spider from Fiat — with Abarth-tuned engine and independent rear suspension — has been built to meet the rally rules but is now on general sale in Italy. **Ray Hutton** *drives it, and describes the background to its production*

Easily recognizable by the black bonnet, hardtop, boot lid, and wing extensions, the 124 Rally has a lighter body than the standard model. The usual bumpers are replaced by rather impractical rubber blocks

The decision to build a minimum of 500 special 124 Spiders to qualify as an additional model under Group 4, came at a convenient time. Fiat had recently completed a total takeover of Abarth, the Torinese tuning firm who had produced modified versions of Fiats for many years as well as running a lucrative business in exhaust systems. Ing. Gianfranco Sgvazzini, technical director of Fiat's automobile division and the man behind their entry into rallying, was also put in charge of Abarth.

The rally team was moved to a workshop adjacent to the Abarth factory where the special parts for the 124 Rally are produced — the cylinder head, transmission and rear suspension. There are no car assembly facilities there, so the parts are transported the 8 km to Fiat's Lingotto plant to meet up with the body-chassis unit from Pininfarina. The cars are built on a special production line and then sent back to Abarth for tuning and final preparation.

Abarth's modifications have been devised in collaboration with Fiat's engineering department. The 1756cc twin-cam engine is now at its maximum bore. In the standard 124 Spider 1800 it gives 118 bhp at 6000 rpm (10 bhp more than the old 1600). Bigger valves, new camshafts with greater overlap, twin downdraught 44 IDF Weber carburettors and a fabricated steel-tube exhaust manifold bring a modest increase to 128 bhp for the 124 Rally, but with plenty of tuning potential — the works team cars have 165-170 bhp. The Rally has the five-speed gearbox, which is optional on the standard car; this gives an overdrive top gear of 0.88 to 1.

A form of MacPherson strut system has been adopted for the rear suspension (front suspension is unchanged). The rear coil spring / damper units are mounted on the top of the wheel uprights with inverted lower wishbones and trailing arms to ensure accurate location. A rear anti-roll bar is fitted. The differential alloy casing is mounted to the chassis at three points by rubber bushes — two on supporting struts where it joins the two-piece propellor shaft and one behind the crown wheel and pinion. The drive shafts each have two constant-velocity type ball joints. As on other cars in the 124 range, rear disc brakes are standard. Cromodora alloy wheels, 5½J and 13in. diameter shod with 185/70 VR Pirelli CN36 tyres are the standard wear.

The bodywork follows the outward appearance of the works rally cars closely. The black glass-fibre hardtop, an option of the standard car, is part of the Rally's equipment and conceals a hefty braced roll-over bar. The hardtop is in fact still removable, but there is no provision for a hood and Fiat clearly intend this to be a closed car. Plastic wheel spats contain the wider wheels and the bumpers have gone — to be replaced by four simple rubber blocks. There are a couple more air intakes at the bumper line for brake cooling. A reduction in kerb weight of a little less than ½cwt (to 18.5cwt) has been achieved by substituting well-fitting glass-fibre panels for the bonnet and boot lid and replacing the steel scuttle and outer skins of the doors with light alloy. This means that the structural strength of the integral body/chassis is unchanged, that the doors close as they should —even if they are outwardly vulnerable. The interior has been simplified, the console and glove box omitted and a simple central switch panel is easily removed to give room for extra rally equipment. It is plain and functional — with more room inside than the average sports car. A clear view of the instrument binnacle is somewhat obscured by the small, thick leather-rimmed wheel. Standard seats are high-backed bucket-type; the car we tried had optional Recaro competition type seats with high gripping sides and corduroy centre panels.

Plain but sensible cockpit has plenty of space and a dashboard designed to incorporate extra equipment. The seats are special ones of the competition variety and very comfortable

Above: Bonnet and boot lid are well made in glass-fibre. Bonnet is double skinned at the edges, retained by rubber straps — and flaps at speed. Spare wheel fits in regular boot space

Right: Cut-away of differential unit, drive-shafts and mountings. The alloy casing is supported on struts at the front and directly on to the casing at the rear

Below: 1800cc twin-cam engine is outwardly similar to ordinary 124 Spider. Twin-Weber carburettors have pancake air cleaner

.We tried the 124 Rally over a 100-mile route in Northern Italy including the Bracco Pass, sometime part of the Mille Miglia route. It is clearly designed to appeal to the young Italians' boy-racer instincts, with its black roof, bonnet and boot contrasting with a light pastel-shade body. It's noisy and rorty to match. The accommodation, however, is thoroughly practical, the competition seats providing a good, slightly reclining driving position. Visibility all round is excellent.

The suspension is firm, to the detriment of ride, which doesn't matter much for a car of this type. It was rather disappointing to find that it was quite badly put off line over bumps which could set up a head-jerking resonance.

It was short on tyre grip too; at least it seemed to be on roads which, admittedly, alternated between dry and damp. On the other hand it felt very nicely balanced and could be powered round smooth mountain corners in a most satisfying way. The steering is precise; the brakes, effective, if a little over-servoed.

The engine is a very willing unit in this tuned form. Though it is noisy — both mechanically and in its fruity exhaust — it feels strong and rushes up to the 6500 rpm red line in every gear with no trouble at all. On the Genoa-Le Spezia *autostrada* it wound round to 7000 rpm in top, corresponding to a maximum speed of just on 120 mph. We would estimate its 0-60 mph acceleration time to be in the region of 9 seconds.

The five speeds in the gearbox are arranged Alfa-pattern with fifth to the right and up, opposite reverse. It is a good gearchange, once one learns not to fight it. Spring loading brings the lever gently into the 3rd/4th slot. The snatch change from third to second is a delight. The stubby gear lever falls conveniently to hand. Fourth and fifth gear ratios are not really far enough apart to make 4th a useful driving gear.

So that is Fiat's "homologation special". The works rally cars with 40 more bhp and other modifications are probably something else again. But if you live in Italy you can buy a 124 Rally that looks like the works cars, and goes and handles better than the normal 124 Spider for around £2250, compared to £1540 for the ordinary open 124. But just as there has never been a right-hand-drive 124 Spider, neither are there any plans to sell the Abarth 124 in England.

Four works Abarth 124s started the Monte Carlo Rally and the team will contend most of the remaining European events in the newly instituted World Rally Championship. The prototype 124 Rally took part in last year's Portuguese TAP Rally. Clearly it was a true prototype, a precursor of a production reality, and not simply a racer taking advantage of the free Group 5 rules. Sgvazzini doesn't believe in those: "It is a question of philosophy. We think that we have to use cars like our normal production models. Otherwise we would put on the road monsters, with no reference at all to the cars we sell".

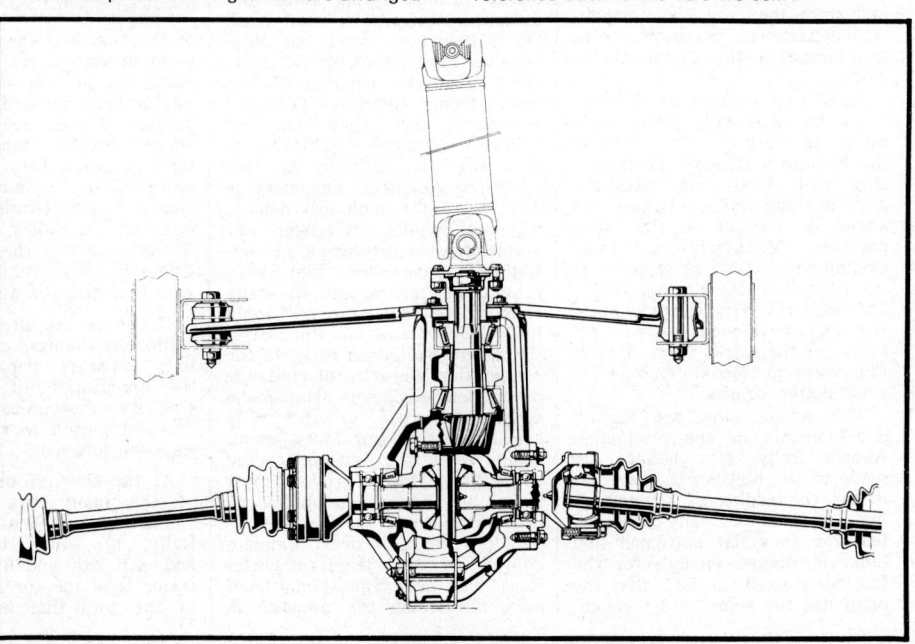

FIAT GOES RALLYING

Too heavy, not enough power . . . the critics were wrong. Fiat and Abarth developed the 124 Spider into a formidable rally weapon

Above : the works team have two of these magnificently equipped support vans, plus four 125 saloons as service cars. Right : a works Abarth 124 Rally Below : a test driver demonstrates the handling and performance of a works rally car

When Fiat went Grand Prix racing, they did so with cars that were technically so advanced that the opposition was continually tempting away their chief engineers to design rival machines. In rallying, however, they have concentrated on the development season by season of a very good but orthodox production car, the 124 Spider, into one capable of taking on the rear-engined Alpine and Porsche and the front-engined front-wheel drive Lancia.

They began rallying the Fiat 124 Sport Spider in 1970, choosing this model because of its rugged contruction. Even so, experience showed that the hull could do with some strengthening at various points, and all these modifications were later incorporated in the Fiat Abarth 124 Rally which went into production at the end of 1972. In addition to the strengthened hull, the Abarth 124 Rally is powered by a 1756cc engine in place of the 1600cc engine with which the normal Spider had been fitted, and with independent rear suspension, specially developed by Abarth for the car. Fiat bought control of Abarth two years ago, and since then the Fiat competition department has been housed in a special section of the Abarth works.

After two seasons of development, the Fiat rally team really made its mark in 1972, winning the European Drivers' Championship with Pinto and Macaluso, and finishing 2nd to Lancia and ahead of Porsche in the International Manufacturers' Rally Championship. All of which was achieved with the normal 1600cc 124 Spiders. With the advent of the rally-developed Abarth 124 Rally for the works team in 1973, Fiat were justified in hoping for even better results.

The works cars are further developments of the production Abarth Rally. No changes are made to the hull which now that it has the additional strengthening and such rally-developed features as a flat bottomed fuel tank, is rugged enough for the job. So rugged, in fact, that the team use the same cars throughout the entire season—unless something drastic should happen to them. For instance, one car needed replacing after the Portuguese TAP Rally last March during which Waldegard went off the road and 180 yards down the side of a mountain where the car rests to this day.

Minor modifications include transferring the battery to a shelf in the boot on the rear bulkhead and mounting the electric fuel pump alongside. The switches, too, are grouped on a single panel in the cockpit. The engines are specially prepared by Abarth and in 1800 form are developing around 171-176 bhp. Fiat now also have an 1850cc engine with bigger valves and Kugelfischer indirect fuel injection from which they are hoping to get 190 bhp. The works cars also have an oil cooler incorporated in the bottom of the radiator block and a separate tank into which oil vapour is fed. The worm and roller steering box, too, is modified to provide a ratio of 12:1 instead of 16.4:1.

No major changes are made to the suspension, but constant development takes place, mainly in trying various spring rates and damper settings. The road holding is now very good, but chief engineer Fernando Russo who has taken over the running of the team from engineer Giovanni Sguazzini says they do not believe they have yet achieved the best that is possible in this direction. Engineer Sguazzini is director of the technical department of Fiat's passenger car group and his increasing responsibilities have left him with insufficient time to run the rally team as well. But that he should have been doing so emphasises the very close liaison between the competition department and the production engineers who make considerable use of the rally cars for testing and development. As a result, the lessons learned in rallying have proved most useful and have been applied to production cars.

Before he took over complete control of the team, engineer Russo had been Sguazzini's chief aide, overseeing the preparation of the cars and then running the team in action. He told me they start the season with 28 cars, 14 for recceing and 14 for competing. These are all works entries, for the department does not prepare cars for private entrants, but in addition to the Group 2 and Group 4 cars for international rallies, Fiat also run Group 1 cars in the Italian Rally Championship which they have won four years in succession.

The cars are prepared by 34 skilled mechanics, and there are four separate departments for the preparation of the engines, electrics, mechanical items and the body, each in the charge of its own foreman.

At the time of our visit most of the team cars were away competing in the San Remo Rally, in which they finished 2nd, 4th, 5th and 6th. The chief tester took me for a run in one of the cars that had been left behind, however, and demonstrated its performance by violent acceleration up and down one of the runways of the airport adjacent to the Abarth factory which Fiat use for testing. He then demonstrated the road holding in spectacular fashion by a series of high speed swerves from side to side of the runway followed by some spin turns. From all of which I emerged impressed by the rugged stability of the car as well as by its vivid performance.

Talking of future plans engineer Russo said they were against prototypes in rallying, and although the use of Groups 2 and 4 cars was okay, they would be very happy if international rallying was in future restricted to Group 1 cars. He did not think Fiat would enter for the 1974 World Cup Rally, but they were considering running some 124 Abarth Rallies in the next East African Safari.

Standing by a works Fiat Abarth 124 Rally in a courtyard in the centre of the Fiat Competitions is the head of the department, Ing. Fernando Russo

Normally, both sides of this long shop are lined with Abarth Rallys being prepared for next event; at the time of our visit most of them were competing in the San Remo Rally

A Fiat Abarth 124 Rally driven by the works crew of Barbasio and Macaluso in action in the 1973 Elba Rally

THUNDERSTRUCK

SPIDER

. . . or how to play Kill The Giants According to Fiat. At least, that's what Sloniger, our hard-punting European correspondent, reckons.

WHEN IT comes to competition cars, it's hard to argue with the champ. The Fiat Abarth 124 Rally — or rather the works prototype of this new limited-production GT — won 10 major rallies outright in 1972, it carried the European Rally Champion Drivers and finished second in the European Rally Championship for Marques.

Obviously, Fiat and its recently-acquired tame tuner named Abarth are doing something right.

And who would have thunk it? This Pininfarina Spider with its sweet little twin-cam engine and beam back axle had become almost a classic by now — the ideal car for a rich man's mistress or just a rich kid starting out at university.

But then Fiat decided to launch it as a rally weapon.

And it was canny enough to let proper rally drivers rebuild the basics into a car which now can more honestly wear the badge "Rally" than any off-the-shelf machines I know.

We aren't talking about kinky stripes or a boulevarde ride behind the matt black bonnet now: the 124 Rally in customer trim is sudden, loud and only sophisticated in a pure engineering sense. But it provides all the requisites the Works team needs and gets it homologated.

Obviously enough you won't buy this 124 Abarth and beat works machines with it as is. And a quick run through the customer competition option list would cost at least $A2000 for a start. But still the basic bolide is capable of going quicker from point-to-point than most club drivers could manage anyway.

For openers, the engineers lifted the 1.8-litre twin-cam four to 128 bhp peaking at 6200 rpm, meaning you don't have a lot of urge low down. It might pull from 2000 where the torque curve flattens somewhat, but the Abarth's heart isn't in it.

Still, our machine would idle through rush-hour traffic in Turin without loading up, choking or running hot. It was a lumpy idle at about 1050 rpm but it never quit. At any other extreme you can drive hard and oil pressure will stay at 55 psi, water temperature hang just below 212 deg F.

The new-found power comes from classic means like a pair of big 44 Weber dual-throat down draft carbs, a cam with more overlap (15-55-55-15) and a steel-tube exhaust manifold. They moved the distributor to the right cam (cdi electronic ignition optional) but left compression at 9.8:1.

More important still — and a tribute to Fiat engineers willing to consider their total package — the 124 Abarth has a new and competitive rear suspension system.

This has a sort of reversed lower wishbone mated to spring/shock legs and long trailing arms for location with half shafts of course. It will still tramp momentarily when you do drag strip starts but only because the five-speed box is geared so powerfully.

Fiat really believed the name it hung on this machine and gave it short gears capable of registering 9.5 seconds for 0.60 mph runs with the tach needle crowding its 6500 red line in first almost before you're underway. Top speed in the strongly "overdrive" 5th cog is a "mere" 115 mph according to the factory. Just on 110 seemed closer, I found.

A pure rally box in other words: blinding acceleration when you remember the relatively small capacity and over a ton of curb weight and a fifth put there only to ease the strain between special sections.

Incidentally, it is also one of the easiest off-by-itself fifth gears to grab fast. The whole gate is taut with the lever spring-loaded to the third/fourth side.

Driven slowly over rough gravel, the car weaves and wallows hust like a pukka rally machine. On long, paved straights you get a small measure of rear-suspension steering. But shove it along fast and the bumps are ignored as this Rally gets on with its specialised job.

You don't want to use the loud pedal carelessly out of slippery bends, of course, because this one with its minute wheelbase and 58 percent of the weight up front will swap ends sooner than burp. But the potential for fast times in the mountains is there for those who can use it. That is something very different to "speed".

Steering is both very quick via the ultra-thick-rim, leather-covered wheel and also fairly heavy, requiring strong shoulders since you must sit with arms out to have the legs even half-way comfortable. Optional full-bucket seats to hold the torso in place are a big help.

The 124 Abarth is not an easy car to drive both hard and with that professional silkiness which posts fast times. Get slightly out of step in a series of bends and it will jink and jive all over the road, acting like a captious steer until you slow right down and start over at building a tango.

You will notice a fair amount of flap in things like the fibreglass bonnet lid held by both an internal latch and two rubber rally catches. The glass top doesn't mate that well with the side windows and you don't want to slam the boot lid or alloy doors for that matter, but the body proper is very rigid. A fully braced roll bar helps. In theory you could remove the top but not easily.

While ignoring niceties like arm rests on the doors or a glove box lid Fiat did put a piece of carpet in the boot.

It skimped not at all in dials — apart from large speedo and tach on either side of an oil pressure gauge (which is the one you need most here) there is a fuel gauge half-hidden by the wheel rim to the left and water temperature ditto on the right. Usual Fiat wands control wipe/wash and light functions.

In short, this thing is a club rally car with a comfort pack and typical Abarth exhaust boom thanks to twin outlets and big-bore pipes. And one impression which surprised me by being absent: there is no trace of tricky clutch. Despite the power going through and the inevitable brutal shifts, clutch action is soft and progressive.

For plain fun driving a car which will top 95 with a gear to go, take the esses with half-turns of a tiny wheel and challenge muscle cars at the lights is hard to beat in any of the three colors: white, sky-blue or "racing" red.

We should be seeing the title Fiat Abarth 124 Rally in the laurel-wreath lists quite often from now on, paired as often as not, I imagine, with the name of some owner-driver amateur.   *

SPECIFICATIONS

Engine: Inline four, twin-OHC, 1756 cc, 84 x 79.2 mm, 9.8 to 1 compression, 128 bhp at 6200 rpm, 117 lb/ft at 5200 rpm. Two dual-choke Weber 44 downdraft carbs.

Power train: Single, dry plate clutch of 7.9 inches, five-speed gearbox. Ratios: 3.66, 2.10, 1.36, 1.0, 0.881. Final drive 4.3 to one.

Chassis: Independent front suspension, coil springs, stabiliser lower transverse arms. Independent rear, swing arms, coil springs, stabiliser. Four-wheel disc brakes, dual circuits. Worm and roller steering, 2.75 turns lock-to-lock, 185/70Vr 13 radials, 5.50 J alloy rims.

Dimensions: Wheelbase 89¾ in., front/rear track 55-3/8 in. and 55 in. L x W x H 154 in. x 64 in. x 48 in., boot 6.35 cubic ft, turning circle 36 ft, weight 2067 lbs, permitted load 360 lb. Tank 9.8 gallons.

Performance: Speedo error 5 percent at 100 mph. Top speed 110 mph at yellow line, 115 mph at red. Gear speeds (indicated) at yellow line (6200 rpm — red 6500) 30, 45, 72, 96 mph. 0-60 in 9.5 seconds.

FIAT 124 SPORT SPIDER

*Now entering its second decade of production, it
has survived to become a classic in its own time*

FIAT FIAT'S 124 SPORT SPIDER made its debut
at the Turin Auto Show in 1966; this
makes it one of those rare models that
survives to enter its second decade of production. In its original
form, the Spider (and its Coupe counterpart) had a 1438-cc
double-overhead-cam inline 4 with 96 horsepower, a top speed
of 106 mph and a basic list price of $3225. In 1976, as the
sole surviving 124 in the U.S. market—the Sport Coupe is no
longer sold in the U.S. and the lesser 124s have been phased
out in favor of the newer, more modern 128s and 131s—the
engine is now almost 1.8 liters, the power output has diminished
to 86, the top speed shrunk to 95 and the price inflated to
over $5000. On one hand you could say that the Spider is a
remnant of a time that has now passed. On the other hand,
however, it is necessary to say that it is still an attractive,
appealing sports car that has much to offer the sporting driver.

We've always liked the looks of the 124 Spider. It was styled
by Pininfarina and has the classic virtue of wearing well. It
didn't look avant garde when it was new and it is a tribute
to the excellence of the job that it doesn't look out of date
even now.

In case you've forgotten, the 124 Sport Spider and Coupe

aren't simply open and closed versions of the same machine.
The Sport Coupe is a genuine 4-seater, an excellent design
since it retains the essential sportiness while accommodating
four passengers in something approaching comfort. The Spider,
on the other hand, is a 2-passenger vehicle, really, and never
mind the little upholstered rear bench. This token seat is not
habitable for people with legs and should be considered handy
space for extra luggage or parcels, not for carrying passengers.

The Spider is smaller than the Coupe, having a wheelbase
of 89.8 in. while the Coupe shares the 95.3-in. wheelbase of
the 124 sedan and wagon. The Spider is only marginally lighter
than the Coupe, however, since the additional structure required
to achieve acceptable rigidity with the open-topped body adds
considerable weight. The latest version of the Spider is about
350 lb heavier than the original, by the way, thanks to the
extra bulk required to meet the U.S. bumper and safety standards.

The Spider has had three—actually four—versions of the
cogged-belt dohc inline 4 engine. At its introduction in 1966
it had 1438 cc from a bore and stroke of 80.0 x 71.5 mm. In
1971 this displacement was increased to 1608 by increasing the
bore to 80.2 mm and the next year, because of a European

tax break for cars displacing less than 1.6 liters, the bore was reduced by a millimeter and the capacity brought down to 1592. The smog-controlled U.S. versions lost power with every change in the emission regulations so the engine was enlarged again in 1974, this time by increasing the stroke to 84.0 mm to give 1756 cc. That's where we are at the present time.

Even these changes in displacement haven't been able to keep up with the power losses resulting from emission controls, however. As a result, the performance of the Spider is even less sparkling than it was in its original U.S. form back in 1968. In a 1968 test of the Spider we recorded a standing quarter-mile time of 18.3 seconds. The 1976 version takes an even 20.0 seconds to cover the same distance.

The engine is smooth for an inline 4 and it is mechanically unobtrusive as long as it's not being thrashed for maximum performance.

The 5-speed manual transmission is very good, the shift lever is where you expect it to be and it operates the way it should. The shift pattern is the traditional H for the first four gears with 5th up and away to the right. In our opinion this is the right place for 5th gear and because the movement toward 5th requires additional effort there's little temptation to overshoot into 5th when it's 3rd you want. Reverse is also outside the H—out to the right and then toward the rear. You must depress the lever by pushing down on the shift knob before reverse can be engaged so there's little likelihood of grinding into reverse when going from 5th to 4th. All in all, it is a very satisfactory 5-speed transmission, which is not a statement we would make about all 5-speed gearboxes.

Fifth gear is an 0.88:1 overdrive, by the way, giving an overall ratio of 3.78:1 and making the Spider comfortably long legged in open highway cruising.

Also contributing its bit to the favorable impression of the Spider is its highly civilized ride and handling. It rides extremely well for a sports car. The springing is relatively soft, the damping is firm on rebound rather than on bounce and the suspension travel is generous. It is particularly good over poor surfaces and this virtue is further enhanced by the rigid and absolutely rattle-free body.

The handling is as outstanding as the ride. It handles in what might be called typical Italian fashion. That is, with moderate body roll, a lot of understeer, an intimate relationship of feel between tires and steering wheel, and very light steering. The tires are rather small (165-13) and while the absolute cornering power isn't sensational, the Spider is highly stable and predictable through any corner.

Even over really bad surfaces the live rear axle, located by trailing arms and a Panhard rod and sprung by coils, shows itself to be very much equal to the job. Even the expected tendency to hop when cornering hard on a rough surface is minimal, thanks to the soft spring rates. We're inclined to think

that a good handling car must have independent rear suspension but cars like the Spider show just how effective the proper combination of spring rates, damping and suspension travel can be.

There are disc brakes at all four corners of the Spider rather than just at the front as is common on most lesser open-topped sports cars. These are vacuum assisted and give light, well modulated braking in all normal driving.

Much as we like most things about the Spider, we are able to find fault with the driver accommodation. For the taller driver the steering wheel is too far away and the pedals too small, too close to each other and too close to the driver. The steering wheel sits low as well as too far away and for a 6-ft or taller driver it's almost mandatory to crank the adjustable

seatback to its bolt upright position in order to reach the wheel comfortably. And when this is done, it brings the top of the driver's head into contact with the roof. Also annoying is the narrow space between the steering wheel rim and the left hand door pull. If you don't have a slim knee, it won't fit in this space, making it awkward to get the left foot back onto the clutch.

The instrumentation and the layout of the accessory controls are both very good. All the dials and gauges are located directly in front of the driver where they belong. All the switches and knobs are easy to reach, our only complaint being that the interior ventilation is almost non-existent. You can stir up a bit of interior air by turning on the blower (it operates independently of the heater) but this is noisy in operation and not

all that effective besides. The windows can be rolled down part way without creating serious buffeting, however, and this may be the best alternative to suffocation during warm weather.

When the weather is pleasant, you should put the top down. In the Spider this is easy to do. In fact, here is one roadster with a folding top that works the way a folding top ought to work. After unfastening two catches on the windshield header, the driver can fold the top all the way back without getting out of his seat. You can do it while waiting for the light to change. It's that easy.

The fixed rear quarter windows—which aid immeasurably in giving the driver better all-around vision than is common to most roadsters with the top up—fold away with the top in a commendably uncomplicated manner. When you want the top up again, erecting it is an equally simple one-handed operation.

Summing up the 124 Sport Spider isn't difficult. It's a highly refined sports car with appealing styling, excellent ride and handling, and rather modest all-out performance. There are limitations in the size of driver it can accommodate in comfort but it is otherwise a civilized place for a sporting driver to enjoy himself. It isn't as new as tomorrow by any means but it has survived the test of the years to become a classic in its own time.

FIAT 124 SPORT SPIDER

PRICE
List price, west coast	$5410
Price as tested	$5625

GENERAL
Curb weight, lb	2440
Test weight	2760
Weight distribution (with driver), front/rear, %	55/45
Wheelbase, in	89.7
Track, front/rear	53.2/52.0
Length	163.1
Width	63.5
Height	49.2
Ground clearance	4.7
Overhang, front/rear	32.8/39.7
Usable trunk space, cu ft	6.2
Fuel capacity, U.S. gal	11.4

ENGINE
Type	dohc inline 4
Bore x stroke, mm	84.0 x 79.2
Equivalent in	3.31 x 3.12
Displacement, cc/cu in	1756/107
Compression ratio	8.0:1
Bhp @ rpm, net	86 @ 6200
Equivalent mph	112
Torque @ rpm, lb-ft	90 @ 2800
Carburetion	1 Weber (2V)
Fuel requirement	91-oct, unleaded

DRIVETRAIN
Transmission	5-sp manual
Gear ratios: 5th (0.88)	3.78:1
4th (1.00)	4.30:1
3rd (1.36)	5.85:1
2nd (2.05)	9.03:1
1st (3.61)	15.78:1
Final drive ratio	4.30:1

CHASSIS & BODY
Layout	front engine/rear drive
Body/frame	unit steel
Brake system: 8.9-in. discs front & rear, vacuum assisted	
Brake swept area, sq in	297
Wheels	13 x 5
Tires	165 HR-13
Steering type	worm & roller
Overall ratio	16.4:1
Turns, lock-to-lock	2.7
Turning circle, ft	34.0

Front suspension: unequal-length A-arms, coil springs, tube shocks, anti-roll bar
Rear suspension: live axle on trailing arms, Panhard rod, coil springs, tube shocks

INSTRUMENTATION
Instruments: 140-mph speedo, 8000-rpm tach, odo, trip odo, oil pressure, coolant temp, fuel level clock

ROAD TEST RESULTS

ACCELERATION
Time to distance, sec:	
Standing ¼-mi, sec	20.0
Speed at end, mph	69.5
Time to speed, sec:	
0–30 mph	4.9
0–50 mph	10.7
0–60 mph	14.8
0–70 mph	20.5
0–80 mph	30.4

SPEED IN GEARS
5th gear (5250 rpm)	95
4th (6000)	95
3rd (6200)	72
2nd (6200)	47
1st (6200)	27

FUEL ECONOMY
Normal driving, mpg	23.0
Cruising range (1-gal. res)	240

HANDLING
Speed on 100-ft radius, mph	32.5
Lateral acceleration, g	0.704

BRAKES
Minimum stopping distances, ft:	
From 60 mph	170
From 80 mph	285
Overall brake rating	good

SPEEDOMETER ERROR
30 mph indicated is actually	28
50 mph	45
60 mph	55
70 mph	65
80 mph	74

Fiat 124 Spider

A winner by default.

• Ten years ago, Fiat introduced the 124 Spider as a car virtually alone in its class; singular virtuosity in comfort, convenience and finish assured it stand-out status in a world full of noisy, drafty and badly screwed-together sports cars. Ironically, it still stands alone today. Ironically, because while not much has changed on the 124 Spider, a lot has changed elsewhere. Like the total collapse of the low- and middle-buck sports car world. And like the total failure of the remnants of that world to upgrade themselves to levels of design sophistication equivalent to those found everywhere in the 124.

Even the newcomers to the affordable sports car have been few; the TR7 leads what is an achingly thin field. And even that solid, wedgy little car has no convertible top. Thus in all too many senses of the word, the Fiat 124 Spider really does stand alone.

It couldn't happen to a more deserving automobile. The double-overhead cam engine that set us all aglow a decade ago is up front still, in its umpteenth update for emissions, boosted to 1756cc and pumping out a yeomanly 86 hp. And if it's somewhat limp in comparison to the days when a similar unit delivered over 100 Italian ponies to the pavement, well, it could be worse, as a glance at any new MGB's power curve will attest. Moreover, the engine remains a pleasing instrument, a well-tuned device with which you can make the miles at least sound beautiful. It responds to the aggressive throttle foot with throaty resonance, moaning out a delightful hollow howl like an old Offenhauser racing engine.

Mated to a close-gated five-speed gearbox, the cammer also makes the new, sanitized 124 competitive—at least in today's terms. Nobody in a Scirocco is likely to totally humiliate the 124 driver, at least not if he has the sense to stir the transmission slick at the right time and keep his boot into the gas. Like many Italian cars, both pre- and post-emissions, the Fiat likes revs. Lots of them.

The suspension—solid axle on coils in back and unequal-length arms with coils in front—made purists looking for mini-Ferraris in 1968 cringe in disappointment (although they grudgingly admired its four-wheel disc brakes), but seems just fine today. The dampers damp and the springs are about right for any kind of driving short of racing. In other words, the ride is firm but not rocky.

Unfortunately, the interior has remained unchanged in some vital areas too—and the results are disappointing. The classic straight-arm driving style so apparently beloved of Italians demands a driving position most people would simply not fit—in order to reach the top of the

Vehicle type: front-engine, rear-wheel-drive, 2-passenger convertible
Price as tested: $6499 (base price: $6349)
Engine type: 4-in-line, water cooled, cast-iron block and head, aluminum double overhead cams, carbureted

Displacement	107 cu in, 1756cc
Power (SAE net)	86 hp @ 6200 rpm
Transmission	5-speed, all-synchro
Wheelbase	89.7 in
Length	163.0 in
Curb weight	2250 lbs

steering wheel, you have to have the seat right up against the forward stop. And that brings your knees into your chin and your ankles past 90 degrees. Not an ideal combination, especially with smallish pedals and the somewhat mushy clutch feel on our test car.

Most of the other features do a great deal towards mitigating the agony of the driving position, though. The top remains the wonderful design we rhapsodized over in the topless-car test (August, 1976). And Fiat won that twelve-car comparison, for those with short memories or new subscriptions. The vestigial rear seats are wonderfully useful things to have, and the general feel of quality and solidity throughout the car gives a constantly reinforced impression of strength and integrity.

For the Fiat's base price of about $6300, you can, of course, buy a lot of other kinds of automotive enjoyment. In that way, the 124 is no longer the screamin' deal it once was (original list: $3482), but it remains unique. And as its gentle curves grow ever lovelier in a wedge-shaped world, that alone may make it a bargain.

—*Steve Thompson*

Used Car Classic:
FIAT 124 SPORT COUPE & SPIDER, 1968–1972

Inexpensive Italian sports cars of the first order

BY THOS L. BRYANT

PHOTOS BY GORDON CHITTENDEN

SPINNING OFF TWO sports cars from a boxy, 4-door sedan may seem like a feat best left to Merlin the Magician, but Fiat did it quite nicely in 1966 and the cars, the 124 Sport Coupe and Spider, have carved niches in the driving enthusiast's arena. The Spider was the first born, making its European debut in late 1966, while the Sport Coupe followed in early 1967. American Fiat devotees were forced to wait a year, however, as it wasn't until early 1968 that the 124 Sport models were ready for the U.S. and able to meet our safety and emissions standards. Ten years later, the 124 Spider is still being sold but the Sport Coupe was removed from Fiat's U.S. line following the 1975 model year. For the purposes of this report, however, we are covering the 1968–1972 models of the Spider and Sport Coupe because later cars are pricey enough to remove them from the scope of Used Car Classics.

Design & Engineering

THE 124 sedan provided the chassis and drivetrain (with a major engine modification) for the 124 sports cars and its handling characteristics were so good that little alteration was needed for the conversion to the Spider and Sport Coupe. The obvious changes were the bodies, with Fiat's in-house designers taking charge of the Sport Coupe and Pininfarina styling the Spider. The roadster model was built on a shortened wheelbase (89.8 in. compared to 95.3 for the Sport Coupe and 124 sedan) and was fitted with a 5-speed gearbox as standard equipment. Initially, the Sport Coupe used the same 4-speed transmission found in the sedan with the 5-speed an option; however, all U.S. Coupes were equipped with the 5-speed from 1969 on.

The 124 sedan's body/frame was of unit steel construction and this same design was used for the Sport Coupe with an entirely new body laid over the platform. Although the Coupe was 3.3 in. longer overall and 8.3 in. wider, its design resulted in a car with less interior space than the sedan, slightly less trunk room and 3.1 in. less height. For the Spider, however, it was decided to shorten the platform and reduce the wheelbase by 5.5 in. in order to build structural stiffness into the floor of the roadster. This was done by adding undersill box-section reinforcements, a box-section crossmember at the rear and making the wheel housing structures more rigid. The result was a shorter car that weighed some 160 lb more than the sedan derivative—but then the Sport Coupe was another 20 lb heavier than the Spider.

The entire suspension system, brakes and driveline of the 124 sedan went unchanged in the Spider and Sport Coupe with the exception of the final drive ratio which became 4.10:1 (4.30:1 in the sedan) and the track width which grew by half an inch with the substitution of 5-in. rims. The spring rates were raised 19 percent at the front and 14 percent at the rear; the coil springs were shortened a bit to make the sports cars lower, and the front anti-roll bar diameter increased from 20 to 21 mm. Finally, the clutch diameter was increased from 7.4 to 7.9 in.

The big change for the Spider and Sport Coupe was the engine, of course. The 124 sedan engine displaced 1197 cc and was of overhead-valve design with pushrods and rocker arms. (There was also a 1438-cc version which came later and was used in the 124 Special sedan.) For the sports cars, Fiat increased the bore from 73.0 to 80.0 mm, increasing the displacement to 1438 cc, and discarded the existing valve gear, opting for a double-overhead camshaft design with a toothed-belt drive (the first production car to use a toothed belt for twin-overhead cams). With the twin-cam design came new pistons, a special carburetor, different manifolds and revisions to the cooling and lubrication systems.

The 124 sports model's new cross-flow cylinder head was made of aluminum alloy (as was the sedan's) with pent roof combustion chambers. Fuel and air were mixed in a single 2-barrel Weber 34 DFH 1 carburetor with a vacuum-operated secondary butterfly and manual choke and throttle controls.

The new cylinder head and the increased displacement meant a marked increase in output, as the 124 sports cars were rated at 96 bhp net at 6500 rpm compared to 65 at 5600 for the 124 sedan, and torque was 83 lb-ft at 4000 rpm versus 70 at 3800. Our initial reaction to the 124 sports models' torque was that it was rather meager at any speed.

The 124 suspension system (common to the sedan, Spider and Sport Coupe) had unequal-length A-arms, coil springs, tube shocks and an anti-roll bar in the front, while at the rear there were a live axle on trailing arms, Panhard rod and coil springs. Our first road test (R&T, July 1968) characterized the 124s' handling as "outstanding," and went on to say, "They handle in a typical Italian fashion, with moderate body roll, a lot of understeer, an intimate relationship of feel between tires and steering wheel and ultra-light steering. The tires are small (165-13) radials and thus the absolute cornering bite isn't great, but these cars are tremendously stable and predictable through any corner and we'll guarantee they will make a better driver out of any novice."

Along with the excellent suspension design, the Fiat 124s could also boast 4-wheel disc brakes, an oddity in cars in their price class, and worm-and-roller steering with road feel as good as any other comparable rack-and-pinion equipped sports car.

Accommodations in both models rated quite high with our road testers, with the Coupe offering sufficient leg and head room in the rear for two adults, while the Spider could carry the two front passengers in comfort and an occasional third person in the small seat behind the individual front seats. Both versions had identical instrumentation but the dash layouts were different, and in the early models the Spider's dash had wood trim while the Sport Coupe made do with simulated wood. In the 1968 road test we praised the easy-to-read instruments and described all controls as being within easy reach. The roof and window design of the Sport Coupe afforded greater outward vision than just about any other closed car we could think of, while the Spider was given excellent marks for the design of its folding top that was (and still is) a model of simplicity that other manufacturers would do well to study.

This road test concluded, "There's no denying that the Fiat 124 Sports are extremely attractive cars, enjoyable to drive, easy to maintain and highly practical. Both are pleasant to look at too, even if the Spider is rather old-fashioned looking. Our only major criticism is that their on-the-road performance is not quite up to their looks, and we would respectfully suggest that Fiat consider making the 125 (1608-cc) version of the dohc engine, which develops 100 lb-ft torque, standard equipment for the American market."

It was three years before Fiat increased the engine displacement and put the 1608-cc twin-cam engine in the 124 Sports and the 1971 models developed 104 bhp at 6000 rpm and 94 lb-ft torque at 4200 rpm. Considering that the 124 Sports' design was then five years old, it's interesting to note our comments about the Sport Coupe in a July 1971 comparison test with the Datsun 240Z, Opel GT, MG BGT and Triumph GT6 Mk 3: "The Fiat deserves more popularity. At nearly $200 less than the Datsun with comparable equipment, it did so well in our comparison test that it scored nearly as many points . . . Its 4-cylinder engine, the smallest of the group, is nevertheless a most satisfying bit of machinery: quiet, very smooth for a 4-cylinder, and willing to rev happily to its 6500-rpm redline. And the 5-speed gearbox is the best gearbox in the group.

"In road behavior the Fiat scores at the head of the group. Its steering is the most precise, its handling the best; it really shines at high speed in contrast to the Datsun, for it isn't blown about by sidewinds and can negotiate high-speed dips and humps without a hint of losing its composure." High praise, indeed, for a 5-year-old car being compared with the new 240Z. At the time of that test, the 124 Sport Coupe had a basic price of $3292, up some $300 from its U.S. introductory price ($2924). The Spider had started at $3226 in 1968 and by 1972 the price was $3692.

Buying a Used 124 Sports

IN COMPILING the information about things the prospective buyer of a used car classic should look for and be wary of, I always seek expert advice from an enthusiast familiar with the particular car(s) being covered. My source for Fiats is a dandy—Jim Weager, President of a northern California race, rally and touring group called Fiat America (PO Box 1001, Campbell, Calif. 95008). He has owned, worked on, and competed in Fiat 124s and knows the cars well.

Starting with the engine, Weager characterizes the 1.5- (1968-1970) and 1.6-liter engines (1971 and 1972 models) as "good,

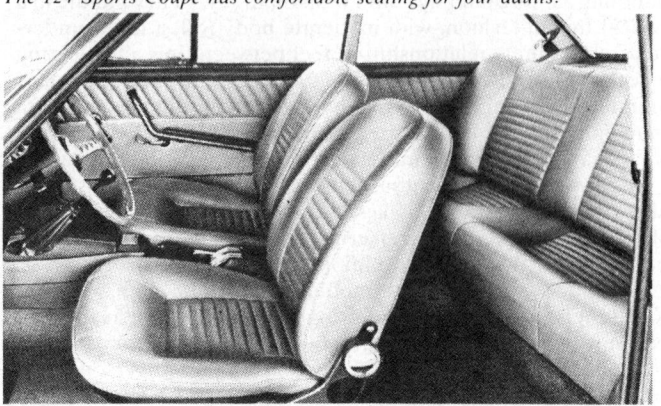

The 124 Sports Coupe has comfortable seating for four adults.

Original double-overhead camshaft engine for the 124 Spider and Sports Coupe displaced 1438 cc; in 1971 displacement was increased to 1608 cc.

strong, durable engines," with few inherent problems although early 1968 models did seem to have occasional valve guide weaknesses that resulted in burned valves. Buyers should look for oil leaks and find few if any with two exceptions: Around the rear cam tower covers some oil may leak out and drip along the flywheel housing and onto the exhaust manifold; the second common leakage problem occurs around the oil sending unit located near the oil filter. The early 124s were equipped with mechanical fuel pumps that seem to wear out after approximately 40,000 miles and this is usually signalled by the engine missing when accelerating at high speeds. Jim also suggested that the fuel inlet line into the carburetor be given a yank—it's a brass tube that is a press fit into zinc and the matchup can wear out to the point where the fuel inlet will pop out.

The 124 Sports gearboxes are worthy of the designation stout although the throwout bearing has a tendency to get noisy after 20,000 miles or so, according to Weager. Also, many drivers don't

Spider version of the 124 used real wood for dash and trim while the Sports Coupe made do with fake wood. Instrumentation is excellent.

Luggage compartments of Spider and Sport Coupe are spacious.

PERFORMANCE DATA
From Contemporary Tests

	1968 Coupe	1968 Spider	1971 Coupe
0-60 mph, sec	11.3	11.9	12.4
Standing ¼ mi, sec	18.6	18.3	18.6
Avg fuel consumption, mpg	24.0	25.0	22.1
Road test date	7-68	7-68	7-71

BRIEF SPECIFICATIONS

	1968 Coupe	1968 Spider	1972 Coupe	1972 Spider
Curb weight, lb	2110	2090	2220	2180
Wheelbase, in.	95.3	89.8	95.3	89.8
Track, f/r	53.0/51.8	53.0/51.8	53.0/51.8	53.0/51.8
Length	162.0	156.3	162.3	156.3
Width	65.8	63.5	65.8	63.5
Height	52.8	49.2	52.8	49.2
Engine type	dohc 4-cyl	dohc 4-cyl	dohc 4-cyl	dohc 4-cyl
Bore x stroke, in.	3.15 x 2.81		3.15 x 3.15	
Displacement, cc	1438		1608	
Horsepower @ rpm	96 @ 6500		104 @ 6000	
Torque @ rpm	83 @ 4000		94 @ 4200	

TYPICAL ASKING PRICES*

1968-1970 Sport Coupe	$800-2000
1968-1970 Spider	$1000-2200
1971-1972 Sport Coupe	$1300-2400
1971-1972 Spider	$1600-3000

*Prices are estimates based on cars that are in reasonably good condition but not restored to like new. Cars in excellent condition will, of course, command higher prices, while poor examples will be cheaper than the range given here.

The raising and lowering of the convertible top on the 124 Spider is a model of simplicity; note rear glass windows that fold down with top.

take the trouble to pause briefly in neutral while shifting and failure to do so can often damage or weaken the synchronizers. A car being considered for purchase that is marked by gear clashing during shifts *may* indicate rather rough treatment by a previous owner. The rear axle bearing seal may leak and coat the rear wheels with oil—if that's the case, chances are good it's the axle seal as the brakes themselves rarely display any leakage tendency, although they do seem to squeak on almost every 124.

The front end should rarely if ever be a problem, Weager says, and if there is something wrong it usually indicates the car may have been hit or involved in a crunch. The steering box can weaken with mileage and age, however, resulting in loose play in the steering wheel. Another potential front end problem on the earliest versions concerns the ball joints which have grease fittings on the top that are often neglected during servicing. This is not a load-bearing joint and the car can go thousands of miles without giving any trouble even though neglected in this area, but Jim had the experience with his early 124 Spider of having the ball joint slip out and punch into the fender well. He learned from the experience that if the ball joints are making noise while the car is being driven, it's a good idea to consider replacing them. Also, many cars have a howl in the rear end coming from the ring and pinion gears; Jim's advice is to live with it as it's not causing any major problem and doesn't warrant replacing the gears. On the positive side, Jim says he's never known of oversize wheels and tires causing any sort of fatigue problems to spindles or suspension pieces, even with cars that have run 7-in. rims and 215/70 series tires. Other positive aspects of the 124 Sports are that there are few general electrical problems; shock absorbers can last many thousands of miles and body rust is not a major problem. There are, however, a few likely rust places to be aware of: The rocker panel on the Spider is made of three metal pieces and as a result there are corners, nooks and crannies where water can be trapped and eventually cause rust. Also, the floor area can get wet from water seeping in from the box-channel support member to the fender inner liner and then into the door sill area. There are drain plugs in the sill area but, as with many older cars, they are often plugged by debris.

The 124 Spider has one of the easiest to use and most efficiently designed tops of any roadster, but water can leak around the latches at the top of the windshield—Weager says he tried all sorts of fixes for this problem and eventually just learned to live with it. The identification plate on the top of the cowl on early 124s was affixed to the car with hollow rivets that allowed water to leak down into the fuse box and cause shorts in the electrical system, but later cars were equipped with solid rivets and the problem was solved. Fender rust is not a general complaint of Spider owners but the Sport Coupe can't boast as good a record and prospective buyers of the closed 124 model should pay closer attention to fender inspection. Also, the coupes have a tendency to rust at the corner of the top where it meets the rear fender line because the rear vent wings collect water; and many coupes have rust problems along the base of the windshield.

All in all, the Sport Coupe and Spider are regarded by people who have owned them as durable, reliable cars with few idiosyncracies of a troublesome nature. All of the 124 owners we talked with were enthusiastic about their cars and the main theme that kept coming through was the fun-to-drive aspect. As each person thought back over the history of his or her car and noted whatever problems had occurred, they still concluded: "I just love driving the car."

Driving Impressions

PHOTO BY DOROTHY CLENDENIN

MARGE STEVENS is one of those people we read about but rarely ever meet: She won a car, a Fiat 124 Spider in a raffle in 1969. The car now has just under 55,000 easy miles on it and Mrs Stevens takes great pleasure in driving the car daily. Several years ago, she loaned it to her daughter for two years while the girl was going to college, but other than that hiatus, it's been hers since new and I have the feeling she wouldn't part with it for anything.

Over the 9-year period she has had the 124, Marge says it has been remarkably trouble free, and she can only recall a problem with burned valves about a year ago, a starter solenoid that gave out, and a new driveshaft that was installed some three years ago. The driveshaft went bad because she was car pooling during the energy crisis with two men and the regular carrying of three adults evidently was simply too much weight.

I reached Mrs Stevens through Bert Jakobs, proprietor of Bert's Foreign Car Service in Santa Ana, California, who has been doing work on the Stevens' car for years and who also takes good care of the 124 Sport Coupe that belongs to our Managing Editor, Dottie Clendenin—her report on Owner Impressions follows this one.

Driving the 1969 Spider for even a limited time gave me a glimpse of why all the 124 owners I talked with are so pleased with their cars. The 1438-cc engine fires up readily and while it's admittedly a bit low on torque, it does offer lively performance. In combination with the excellent 5-speed gearbox, the engine makes spirited driving or easy loping a pleasure.

The chassis is one of the best I've encountered in doing these Used Car Classic reports, especially for a roadster, with ride and handling characteristics to please the most demanding driver while giving the non-enthusiast ample comfort—and no surprises. On bad pavement with ripples and small irregularities, the Fiat 124 Spider is a moving testimonial to Italian (and more specifically, Fiat) know-how in designing suspensions. Although the springing is relatively soft, there is plenty of suspension travel and the damping is firm on the rebound rather than jounce.

There is moderate body roll during cornering, considerable understeer and a sensitive and pleasing amount of feedback through the steering wheel as to just what's going on at the front tires. In really fast driving, the 124 Spider displays excellent transient response through turns and sticks to the road impressively. At the risk of offending other nationalities, I'd have to say that when it comes to building sports cars that handle every driving situation with dash and competence, the Italians are up front, and in its price class, the Fiat 124 is second to none.

—Thos L. Bryant

FIAT 124 SPIDER

CONTINUED FROM PAGE 6
really *too* quiet to be a sports car.

The driver has a sensation of extreme lightness. The clutch is light and precise. The accelerator travel is long but very light. The brakes are power-assisted and the steering is so effortless you'd swear the Fiat was rear-engined. It just feels like the original nine pound car—except that everything is so sturdy and solid. At 2093 pounds the Fiat is the lightest in its class but only 40 pounds less than the Datsun 2000. Apparently Fiat put the weight in just the right place to obtain a quality feel that is missing with the brand X-machines.

One of the greatest hardships associated with the traditional sports car has been the top. Even though vast improvements have been made in the last few years they're not even in the same league with the Fiat. You can put the Spider's roof down without ever leaving the driver's seat. Just unhook the clips at the windshield and push it back. The whole apparatus, including the *glass* rear quarter windows, disappears behind the seats and still leaves room for a large suitcase back there. It couldn't be easier. And erecting it is no more difficult. Visibility is superb because of the large window area. Moreover, the unique glass rear quarter windows assure that weather sealing is the best we've ever seen in a sports car. Fiat even has the answer to the ballooning top problem. They just tie the skin to the bones. Why doesn't everyone?

We see the Fiat 124 Spider as a milestone—the beginning of the end of the hardship sports car. It's the only machine in its class in which we'd enjoy taking a long trip. Not only is it quiet and comfortable but everywhere you look are features normally found in cars costing far more. Vent windows that open, a vanity mirror on the passenger side visor—and to top it all off, an electropneumatic horn. Honest. That's what they call it. You may call it an air horn if you like, but we'll stick with the Italians. Regardless of what it's called, it's the finishing touch for that irresistible Italian personality.

We don't say everything is perfect. The curved outside rearview mirror that makes the truck riding your back bumper look like it was half a block away deserves criticism and we've already discussed the shift linkage and the handling.

Even so, the credits far outnumber the debits on the desirability ledger. If the Fiat 124 Spider isn't a resounding sales success, it will prove, once and for all, that the rest of society is right to dismiss all sports car enthusiasts as incurable masochists. ●

CONTINUED FROM PAGE 11
readily removable timing belt cover plate. Valve adjustment is handled by replacement of shims on the inverted cups or buckets on top of the valve stem and springs.

The engine block is the sturdy, five main bearing cast iron type used in the 65 hp 1197cc 124 sedan. Enlarging the bore by 7 mm. increased the displacement to 1438cc or 87.8 cu. ins. The new design aluminum cylinder head has a double wedge type of combustion chamber that allows the use of large diameter angular displaced valves that offer better combustion at high engine revs and loads.

Fuel is fed by a mechanical pump through a dual barrel vertical Weber carburetor that provides a barrel for each two cylinders, and burned gases are exhausted through a dual branch manifold.

Power output is 96 hp at 6500 rpm, a very creditable figure from an 87.8 cu. in. engine with a 8.9 to 1 compression ratio. A peak torque of 83 lb. ft. is developed at 4000 rpm (64.4 mph in 4th speed). Despite the high output characteristic of the engine or "state of tune" the usable power range extends from 2000 to 6800 rpm where the red line starts on the tachometer. Fiat blandly states that at 88 mph only half the horsepower is being used.

Other interesting aspects of the engine include double oil filtration through a full flow replacement element filter on the lower left side of the engine and a centrifugal type mounted on the camshaft pulley. An electromagnetic cooling fan is used and it operates when required and thus reduces horsepower draw and provides improved fuel economy at higher cruising speeds.

The power is transferred to the road through a 4-speed stick-shift on the coupe and a 5-speed with 5th and overdrive on the convertible. Low rolling resistance radial ply 165 x 13 tires on 5K rims are standard. Roadholding is said to be exceptional.

Our man on the continent Sloniger, in a soon to be published road test of the 124S, says in commenting on Italian driving style: "The real reason 124S' drivers hold their arms out straight is to embrace that engine." ●

FIAT SPIDER 2000

*Thoroughly
modern memories*

PHOTOS BY JOE RUSZ

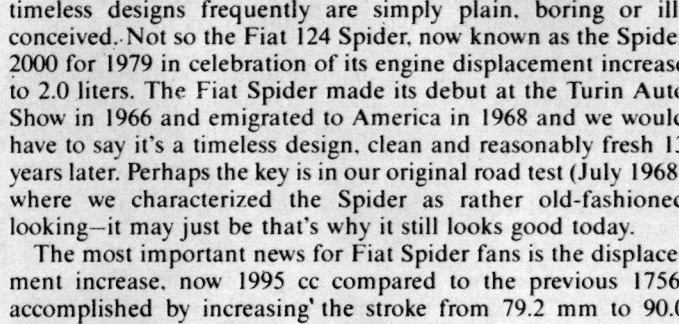

FIAT TIMELESS DESIGNS OFTEN aren't. In fact, what some automobile manufacturers call timeless designs frequently are simply plain, boring or ill-conceived. Not so the Fiat 124 Spider, now known as the Spider 2000 for 1979 in celebration of its engine displacement increase to 2.0 liters. The Fiat Spider made its debut at the Turin Auto Show in 1966 and emigrated to America in 1968 and we would have to say it's a timeless design, clean and reasonably fresh 13 years later. Perhaps the key is in our original road test (July 1968) where we characterized the Spider as rather old-fashioned looking—it may just be that's why it still looks good today.

The most important news for Fiat Spider fans is the displacement increase, now 1995 cc compared to the previous 1756, accomplished by increasing the stroke from 79.2 mm to 90.0 while maintaining the bore at 84.0 mm. The primary benefit is a 17-percent gain in torque which now measures 104 lb-ft at 3000 rpm versus 89 at 2800 last year. Horsepower is also up slightly, with federal versions boasting 86 bhp at 5100 rpm compared to 83 at 5800 with the 1800 (actually 1756-cc) engine. Two-liter California Spiders, however, are rated at 80 bhp at 5000 rpm, and that's the model we used for this road test.

In translating these figures to road test numbers, the Fiat Spider 2000 shows lively acceleration: 0–60 mph in 10.6 seconds, which is nearly a full second quicker than a 1978 Fiat 124 Spider with the 1800 engine we tested for the *R&T Guide to Sports & GT Cars*. Quarter-mile performance is improved too: 18.1 sec at 77.0 mph compared to 18.6 sec at 75.0 mph for the previous model. There's one additional factor in the performance equation, a change in the final drive ratio—it's now 3.90:1 instead of 4.30:1. The 5-speed manual gearbox ratios remain the same, so the upshot is the increased displacement more than compensates for the numerically lower rear-end ratio except on the top end, where the 2000 can barely boast 100-plus-mph speed compared to the 108.0 mph of its smaller-engine predecessor. Frankly, we find that

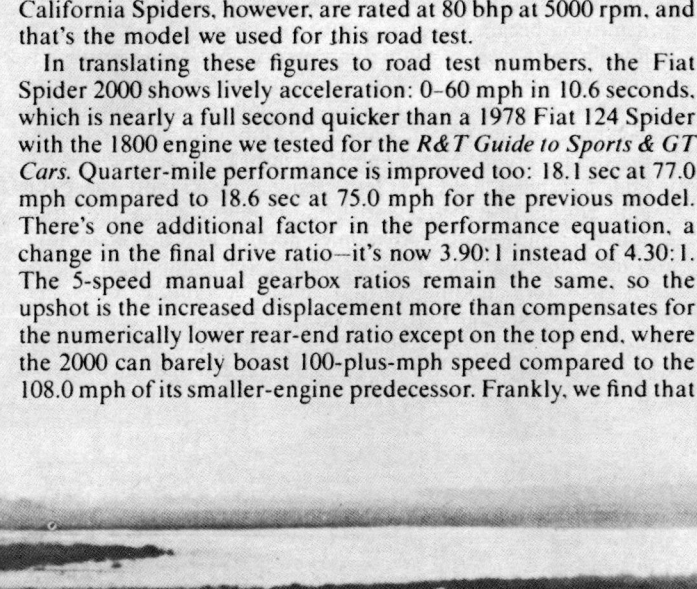

quite an acceptable tradeoff, as there is rarely an opportunity to drive at speeds approaching the century mark in this country anyway.

There's more to discussing engines and their performance than mere acceleration, however, and the Fiat's 2-liter powerplant gets decent marks for cold starting and driveability, only fair grades for high-rpm running because it gets rough, noisy and sounds strained from about 4500 rpm to the 6500 redline, but excellent ratings for flexibility. It will pull from 1500 rpm in 5th gear without whimpering, modest power becomes evident at 2000 rpm, and as the tach needle approaches 3000, the power comes on with a relative rush. Very nice. To control HC emissions when the engine is cold, the throttle is held open between shifts, but this isn't distracting to the point of annoyance and goes away when optimum operating temperature is reached.

Engine power is transmitted to the rear wheels via the 5-speed gearbox, which has short throws, positive definition of gear slots and a feeling of stoutness. Our test car had few miles on it when delivered and shifts were quite stiff initially, but with break-in the transmission became a joy to use for most everyone on our staff, although there were a couple complaints that shifts up to 5th (upper right) and back to 4th were somewhat notchy. For those who want to avoid shifting (what a shame), Fiat is offering a 3-speed automatic transmission on this model for the first time.

Besides the engine and the new transmission, changes for 1979 include a restyled hood with larger bulges giving more space for engine compartment accessories; a spoiler beneath the front bumper for improved aerodynamics, cooling and fuel economy; and inset door handles, outside mirrors and windshield wipers redesigned for smoother airflow and hence more miles per gallon. It's clear that Fiat engineers have been given the word that fuel efficiency is paramount. Also new are the taillights, which more closely follow the body line, and styled steel wheels with aluminum trim rings.

Inside, the reclining seats have increased lateral support, better lumbar support and new-style adjustable headrests. Other changes are relatively minor but appreciated. The steering wheel is now a leather-wrapped 3-spoke design, a wood shift knob replaces the previous plastic one and Fiat has discovered color coordination. Our test car was equipped with optional electric window lifts, which cost $165 and offended the sense of propriety of our more traditionalist sports car staffers.

Fiat made one well intentioned but poorly executed change: a slightly taller rag top that provides a bit more head room, but increases wind noise (77 dBA at a steady 50 mph versus the previous 75) just enough to make it obtrusive. Everyone who drove the car commented on it. Another complaint is a sin of omission rather than commission. With the new steering wheel, we would have hoped for a change in the wheel angle to alleviate the Italian-syndrome driving position of arms stretched and legs splayed wide. Unfortunately, nearly everyone on our staff still found himself having to get accustomed to the car's pedal/seat/steering wheel relationship.

But the proof of any car is in the driving and here this Fiat scores highly. The convertible top is simplicity itself to raise and lower and is the standard by which we measure every other ragtop. Release the two latches at the top of the windshield, push the top back and you're ready to enjoy open-air motoring. With the top up, fixed glass rear quarter windows ensure good vision for lane changing and the plastic rear window is sufficiently large to afford the driver a good view of all he's left behind.

Finding that favorite sinuous road will reveal the Fiat's ability to provide driving fun within its design limits. The live rear axle on trailing arms is a testimony to the Italian talent for building cars with good handling characteristics. As one staff member noted, "This would be the ideal learner's sports car; it's forgiving, has reasonably good handling and adequate cornering power so the neophyte can feel like he's going hard without hurting

AT A GLANCE

	Fiat Spider 2000	Triumph TR7	MGB
List price	$7515	$7695	$6795
Curb weight, lb	2365	2470	2335
Engine	inline 4	inline 4	inline 4
Transmission	5-sp M	5-sp M	4-sp M
0-60 mph, sec	10.6	11.2	13.9
Standing ¼ mi, sec	18.1	18.2	19.8
Speed at end of ¼ mi, mph	77.0	76.0	69.0
Stopping distance from 60 mph, ft	170	171	177
Interior noise at 50 mph, dBA	77	72	75
Lateral acceleration, g	0.737	0.772	0.698
Slalom speed, mph	55.8	60.6	53.0
Fuel economy, mpg	21.0	27.5	18.5

himself or the car." There is moderate understeer all the time, which makes the Spider predictable, but the steering is rather slow and not particularly precise, especially on center where there's a fair amount of play.

The ride characteristics are exemplary for a sports car. The suspension soaks up dips and lane-divider dots nicely and there's only a minimum of bouncing around on rough pavement. Two people can travel all day in the Spider 2000 and enjoy the trip without feeling they'd been cooped up in a small tin ball and dribbled down the road. The occasional rear seats are a point of division among our staff, about equally split between those who thought the space could be better used for luggage and others who felt they could serve quite well for children.

The Fiat Spider 2000's all-disc braking system brings the car to a stop in fine order under normal driving conditions, but we were disappointed with their performance in our simulated panic stops from 60 and 80 mph. The front brakes exhibited severe locking and mild slewing in the stops from both speeds, and this produced the relatively long distances: 170 ft from 60 mph and 298 ft from 80. A sports car with the performance and handling capabilities of the Fiat should offer shorter stops and better control. Blame the vacuum assist. Fiat places too much emphasis on low effort at the expense of pedal modulation and sensitivity.

Overall, the Spider 2000 can be fairly characterized as the best of the vintage breed of roadsters. Increased engine displacement has enabled Fiat to improve performance, and helped by aero-dynamic modifications and the taller final drive ratio the Spider returns 21.0 mpg, which is respectable and certainly competitive with other sports cars in its class. We've made mention of a number of small annoyances but with the top down on a warm and sunny day, alone or with an agreeable companion, the Fiat Spider 2000 will once again bring back memories of why you became a sports car enthusiast in the first place—sheer driving pleasure. ◉

PRICE

List price, all POE	$7515
Price as tested	$8133

Price as tested includes elect. window lifts ($165), AM/FM stereo/cassette ($366), all-weather coolant ($7), dlr prep ($80)

GENERAL

Curb weight, lb/kg	2365	1074
Test weight	2475	1124
Weight dist (with driver), f/r, %	53/47	
Wheelbase, in./mm	89.7	2278
Track, front/rear	53.2/52.0	1351/1321
Length	163.0	4140
Width	63.5	1613
Height	48.2	1224
Trunk space, cu ft/liters	6.0	23
Fuel capacity, U.S. gal./liters	11.4	43

ENGINE

Type	dohc inline 4
Bore x stroke, in./mm	3.31 x 3.54 ....84.0 x 90.0
Displacement, cu in./cc	122 1995
Compression ratio	8.1:1
Bhp @ rpm, SAE net/kW	80/60 @ 5000
Torque @ rpm, lb-ft/Nm	104/141 @ 3000
Carburetion	one Weber (2V)
Fuel requirement	unleaded, 91-oct

DRIVETRAIN

Transmission	5-sp manual
Gear ratios: 5th (0.88)	3.43:1
4th (1.00)	3.90:1
3rd (1.36)	5.30:1
2nd (2.10)	8.19:1
1st (3.66)	14.27:1
Final drive ratio	3.90:1

CHASSIS & BODY

Layout	front engine/rear drive
Body/frame	unit steel
Brake system	8.9-in. (226-mm) discs front and rear, vacuum assisted
Wheels	styled steel, 13 x 5J
Tires	Pirelli Cinturato P3, 165SR-13
Steering type	worm & roller
Turns, lock-to-lock	2.7

Suspension, front/rear: unequal-length A-arms, coil springs, tube shocks, anti-roll bar/live axle on trailing arms, Panhard rod, coil springs, tube shocks

CALCULATED DATA

Lb/bhp (test weight)	30.9
Mph/1000 rpm (5th gear)	19.4
Engine revs/mi (60 mph)	3100
R&T steering index	0.92
Brake swept area, sq in./ton	240

ROAD TEST RESULTS

ACCELERATION

Time to distance, sec:

0-100 ft	3.5
0-500 ft	9.6
0-1320 ft (¼ mi)	18.1
Speed at end of ¼ mi, mph	77.0

Time to speed, sec:

0-30 mph	3.1
0-50 mph	7.3
0-60 mph	10.6
0-70 mph	14.4
0-80 mph	20.4
0-90 mph	28.4

SPEEDS IN GEARS

5th gear (5300 rpm)	102
4th (6150)	102
3rd (6400)	79
2nd (6400)	52
1st (6400)	30

FUEL ECONOMY

Normal driving, mpg	21.0

BRAKES

Minimum stopping distances, ft:

From 60 mph	170
From 80 mph	298
Control in panic stop	fair
Pedal effort for 0.5g stop, lb	25
Fade: percent increase in pedal effort to maintain 0.5g deceleration in 6 stops from 60 mph	40
Overall brake rating	fair

HANDLING

Lateral accel, 100-ft radius, g	0.737
Speed thru 700-ft slalom, mph	55.8

INTERIOR NOISE

Constant 30 mph, dBA	71
50 mph	77
70 mph	83

SPEEDOMETER ERROR

30 mph indicated is actually	29.0
60 mph	58.0

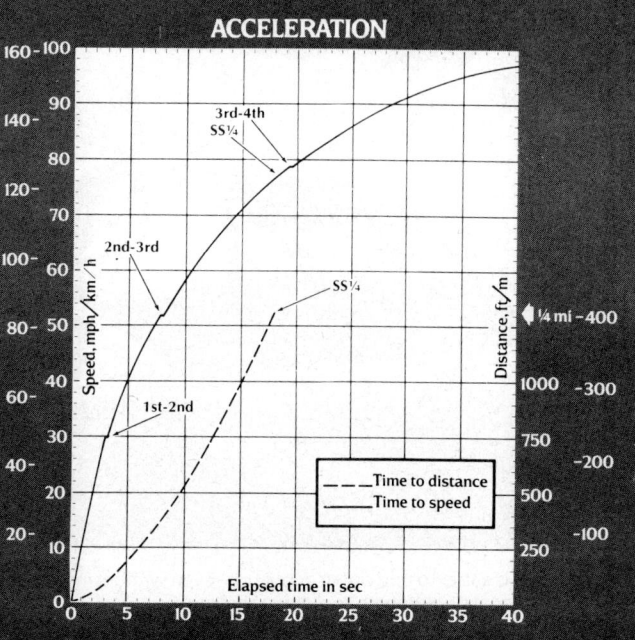

ACCELERATION

FIAT BOASTS that its "new" Spider 2000—originally introduced as the Fiat 124 Sport Spider at the 1966 Turin (Italy) Auto Show—is a "timeless design (that) will never go out of style."

True, it looked great when it was launched in the latter part of the Sixties. And the automotive press waxed enthusiasm over it, some even calling it a "baby Ferrari." A car some said was outstanding if only because of what it offered at its then-$3300 price.

But, is it up to what's come from Fiat the past few years? We don't think so. The X1/9 and Strada, for example, are what you expect from Fiat at this point. Modern, of this generation. What the 2000 is not.

What the 2000 is is a forget-me-not in a corsage of orchids. It's not of this decade—having now been in production for 14 years. That's long enough. It should

The Fiat's top is easier to take down or put up—even without instructions. As with most convertibles of this size, it looks better with top down than up.

A "timeless design"? Or, "timeworn"?

FIAT 2000

We compare it to the Triumph TR-7 —
its major competitor — and find it comes off
second-best. At least in most respects.

be allowed to fade away gracefully. Not die an ignominious death, in sack-and-ashes because it's out of step with the times.

If that seems a harsh judgment, look at its major competition: the Triumph TR-7. A modern style. Macho. Five years old in design, but still remarkably fresh.

Against the Triumph TR-7

How do the two cars compare on the road? Keep in mind that both models were 1979½s. That the Fiat had automatic (one of the first available—an option offered mid-year). That the Fiat now has a more powerful engine, upped to 102 hp on the standard California model and optional 49-state model; this is an increase of 16 over last year's 49-state model and 22 over our test car and this year's standard 49-state model.

—Handling is about the same for both, with a slight edge to the TR-7. Straightline steering is not as self-centering; you have to work at it more to keep it arrow-true. Yet, the worm-and-roller steering of the Fiat is responsive. The independent front suspension (coils and sway bar) and rigid rear axle (coils) of the Fiat are not quite up to the Triumph.

—The ride also comes off second-best, being somewhat choppier. But, like the TR-7, once you get off the straight, flat roads and wend your way over serpentine trails, the driver is not only happier, but so is the passenger. It's also then you realize why the Fiat has fairly stiff shocks.

—The 2000 doesn't have as comfortable a driving position. You also seem to sit *on* the semi-bucket seat, rather than *in* it. (We call it "semi" because it doesn't hug your body.) You sit fairly high and can rest your right leg against the console, which isn't as comfortable as the larger, padded TR-7 console. The wheel is tilted forward at that crazy near-horizontal angle in so many Italian cars.

—The 2000 has the advantage of 2 + 2 seating, but to accommodate rear seat passengers, front legroom is cut to less than minimum. The rear bench seat is really little more than a package shelf.

—Strangely, the performance of the Fiat didn't *feel* quite as good as the TR-7, yet when we compared figures, we found it was *better*. Instead of being at the mercy of the automatic, the GM Strasbourg transmission lets you select manually, if you prefer. In this way, you can keep the engine at its optimum power level for top performance and response. With the added power in the '80 model, this will really help. With our test car cruising at 55 mph, the engine was turning but 3300 rpm, and at 70, only 4100, nearly 2000 under redline.

—In fuel economy, the edge goes to Fiat, a surprise in that it's an automatic model and the Triumph was a 5-speed overdrive. The differences were less than one mpg overall average, in favor of the 2000. Neither car, however, has to apologize for test averages of 25.5 (Fiat) and 24.8

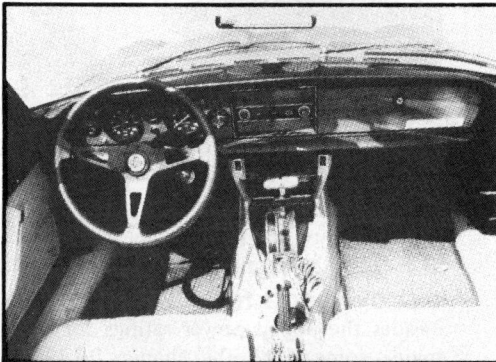

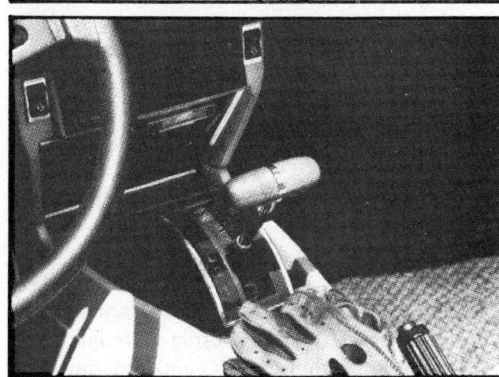

T-handle shift quadrant is located conveniently, has good grip.

Rear seat would be adequate by itself, but requires front seats to be all way forward for any legroom. Top boot fits nicely, snaps on easily.

Accessibility to most components and accessories of the longitudinally-placed engine are good, except for plugs between the camshaft housings and the battery, which is in the trunk.

(Triumph), or their low/high ranges of 23.1 - 27.5 (2000) and 21.0 - 28.3 (TR-7).

Improvements for 1980

Besides the upped power ratings for the engine, some of the other changes for 1980 are these:

• Optional leather upholstery in place of vinyl.

• A new shift gate for automatic.

• Brushed aluminum steering wheel spokes.

• Newly-styled steel wheels with brake cooling vents.

• Optional light alloy wheels.

• A 3-year, unlimited mileage warranty against rust perforation. All Fiats make extensive use of rust-proofing materials, including a standard PVC undercoating on the chassis.

Other Improvements

Some improvements they could make—if

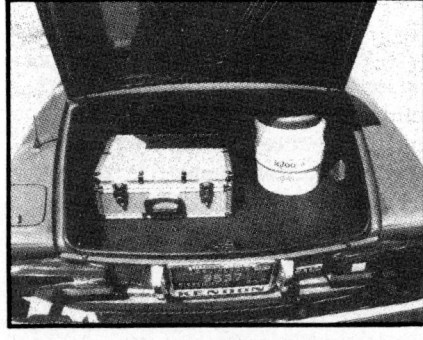

Trunk has fairly good length (31 ins) and width (44 ins), but is only from 6 to 12 ins high. Spare is under carpeted floor; jack in fender well.

they're *really* going to stick with this 14-year-old model much longer—are these:

• Better/more insulation under the floorboard on the passenger's side, where the catalytic converter is located.

• A better seatbelt/harness installation. The belt rides too high, the harness digs into the shoulder and the retract point is located awkwardly halfway down the rear seatback.

• The door handle arrangement is awkward, inside and out. The doors don't stay open on even a slight incline.

Nevertheless . . .

. . . and despite our criticisms, someone out there likes the Fiat 2000. Enough so that it has continued to sell over the past 13 years—and should continue this year as well. And, the automatic seems to make it even more desirable to many. With a production rate set at 20% of the total, sales of automatics last year were running at 28% of 2000s available. What with the additional power this year—and as long as the fuel economy holds—they should continue to do all right.

'79½ FIAT 2000

BODY STYLE	2 + 2 Convertible	**DIMENSIONS & CAPACITIES**	
		Wheelbase, ins	89.7
BASE PRICE	$7931. As tested, $8852 (with automatic transmission, AM/FM/Cassette, power windows).	Track, Front/Rear	53.2/52.0
		Length	163
		Width	63.2
ENGINE	In-line, DOHC 4, up front	Height	48.2 (top up)
Bore/Stroke	3.31/3.54 ins	Curb Weight, lbs	2415
Displacement	1995cc/121.7ci	Fuel Capacity, gals	11.4
Compression Ratio	8.1	Luggage Capacity, cu ft	6.4
Carburetion	Vertical 2V		
Ignition	Electronic breakerless		
Max BHP @ RPM	86 @ 5100 (80, Calif.)	**PERFORMANCE**	
Max Torque @ RPM	104 lbs-ft + 3000 (100, Calif.)	0-60 mph, secs	12.2
Fuel Requirement	Unleaded	30-50 mph	4.8
		40-60 mph	5.9
DRIVETRAIN	RWD	Top Speed (est)	100 mph
Transmission	3-speed automatic (opt)		
Ratios	2.40/1.48/1.0		
Final Ratio	3.583	**FUEL ECONOMY**	
		EPA MPG, City	21
CHASSIS & BODY	Separate frame and body.	MPG Range, Entire Test	23.1-27.5
Suspension	F, independent, with coils, sway bar. R, rigid axle, with coils.	Average MPG, Entire Test	25.5
Wheels/tires	5Jx13/165SRx13 radials	Tank Range (based on above)	291 miles
Steering	Worm-and-roller gear, 34 ft turning diameter.		
Brakes	Power-assisted discs.		

Fiat Turbo Spider 2000

Would you believe Fiat has changed its way of living?

• There is new handwriting on the wall at Fiat Motors of North America, Inc. It says, "Fiat wants to be your sports-car company." This replaces the old handwriting on the wall, which said, "Fiat wants to be your small-sedan company." If you are too far away from the head office to read the writing, you can drop by your local Fiat dealer and have a look at the new Turbo Spider. Company planners hope this freshly breathed-upon two-seater will carry the new message to every hamlet, burg, and ville in America.

The new handwriting is the result of either popular demand or popular lack of interest, depending upon how you look at it. Fiat's sports cars have enjoyed great success in this country—in fact, the Spider 2000 is not sold anywhere else—but the company always thought the two-seater fun car was much too

frivolous a market for an automaker of Fiat's stature and solemnity. So it tried to low-profile the sportsters and push the sedans. It might just as well have been pushing harvard beets the way folks always seemed to find something else, thank you very much.

So in a burst of marketing genius, Fiat is changing the menu. Sports cars go to the top. Much updating of the two-seaters will be done in the next few years. But to make the right people get the message early, Fiat is making a big gesture up front: the Turbo Spider, planned for an April introduction if the final assembly and certification details go as planned.

Not only is this a radical step for Fiat, but it is also being accomplished in a radical way: the turbo conversion has been designed and fabricated by an independent American company (Legend

Industries, Inc.), and it will be installed at the ports of entry. The regular factory warranty applies and spare parts will be available over the regular dealership counter, but the Turbo Spider is one Fiat that's never been seen in Turin.

In fact, the turbocharger itself comes from Japan—an IHI unit marketed in this country by Borg-Warner. IHI is known for its exceedingly compact turbos, and the RHB6 certainly lives up to that reputation. Even with its integral waste gate it weighs only thirteen pounds, and the small-diameter turbines, in addition to not taking up much space, also minimize turbo lag.

In the Fiat, the turbo bolts to a special exhaust manifold and packages down tight against the right side of the block. The air meter for the Bosch L-Jetronic fuel injection stays in its original location. Air now goes through the meter,

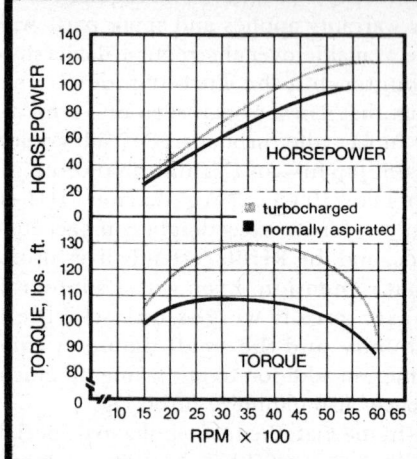

down to the compressor, then up through a cast-aluminum duct over the cam covers to the original throttle body. It's a neat job.

The intent of the conversion was to give the Spider a torquey, big-engine feel rather than a rush of high-end horsepower. The boost starts at relatively low revs—about 1400 rpm if, say, you're climbing a hill in fifth at full throttle—and peaks at 6 psi just over 3000 rpm. In normal cruising the Spider responds quickly to the accelerator—small motions of your foot produce big changes in speed—and the result is quite pleasing. The power seems to tail off at the high end, however, so there is not much incentive to visit the redline. While our sports-car sensibilities draw us to the five-speed version, the turbo seems happiest with the automatic, which is also available, and in our testing the latter turned out to be marginally quicker. The pavement was damp in patches, which may have al-

tered the results, but the closeness of the five-speed's ratios is a disadvantage for a turbo because the boost goes away whenever you shift. It was for this reason that Porsche used a four-speed on the 930 Turbo.

Of course, Fiat of Italy might have used a four-speed too, but that choice is not readily available to someone who installs a turbo at the port. In fact, the Turbo Spider has none of the modifications that are usually present in a factory turbo: no longer axle ratio, no lower compression ratio, no heavy-duty pistons, no enlarged cooling system, and no oil cooler. Detonation is controlled, says Legend Industries, by richening the mixture under boost and backing off the spark timing. The company also claims that durability testing has shown no other modifications to be necessary. This may be true. But the rated output of the turbo engine is 120 hp at 6000 rpm, up 18 percent over the stock engine, and it's clear that the extra 18 percent is being taken out of whatever

Vehicle type: front-engine, rear-wheel-drive, 2-passenger, 2-door convertible
Price as tested: $13,000 (estimated)
Engine type: turbocharged 4-in-line, iron block and aluminum head, Bosch L-Jetronic fuel injection
Displacement............................122 cu in, 1990cc
Power (SAE net).....................120 bhp @ 6000 rpm
Transmission........3-speed automatic or 5-speed manual
Wheelbase ....89.7 in
Length ....163.0 in
Curb weight...................................2400 lbs

ACCELERATION (sec)		
	0–60 mph	¼-mile
automatic	11.9	18.7 @ 73 mph
manual	10.9	18.1 @ 75 mph
automatic turbo	8.6	16.7 @ 80 mph
manual turbo	9.1	17.0 @ 81 mph

durability margin was originally engineered in at the factory. There are those, some in this office, who would say that Fiat's customary margin can't stand any crowding.

We'll have to wait and see on that point. For now at least, Fiat Motors of North America, Inc., just hopes you'll drop by your local dealership and bask in the new emphasis. And if you should happen to see a Spider there that looks just a bit different from the others— bold pinstripes, 14-by-5.5-inch Cromodora wheels with 185/60 Pirelli P6 tires and a nice round boost gauge in the middle of the dash—that's the Turbo. You may also notice that the bottom line of its window sticker has crept over thirteen grand. The new emphasis at Fiat is not confined entirely under the hood. —*Patrick Bedard*

Fiat Spider 2000 Turbo

by Len Frank

PHOTOGRAPHY BY MATT KEEFE

First a short treatise on turbocharging: 1982 marks the 20th anniversary of the production turbo. The 1962 Corvair was the first, the 1982 Fiat Spider Turbo just about the latest (the Spider Turbo was actually introduced about a year ago, but for the sake of symmetry . . .).

The turbo Corvair used the simplest turbocharger layout possible—a TRW (later Rajay) turbo drawing through a restrictive Carter YF sidedraft carburetor. The airflow restriction kept boost pressure down. No fuel enrichment device was necessary, no wastegate to keep boost pressure from going too high, no extra intake restrictor, no water injection, no detonation control, no electronic overrides of any kind.

Results were mixed. Specially prepared, the Corvair was a rocketship, eventually running over 100 in the quarter. But stock, without special (destructive) driving techniques, it was less than wonderful. It had the Dreaded Turbo Lag in abundance. In normal around-town driving and highway cruising, the Corvair never produced use-

ful boost. After a year or so of no/low boost, the exhaust turbine was so carboned that the whole turbo assembly turned into an expensive intake/exhaust restrictor. Since the carburetor was located so far from the intake valves, throttle response was, even in best of times, poor. Which explains why that simple Corvair turbo layout is not ideal and all that enrichment—wastegate—injection paraphernalia is actually useful.

Since the Fiat Spider Turbo has port-type Bosch L-Jetronic fuel injection, the Japanese IHI turbocharger has only air to compress. Due to port fuel injection, throttle response is excellent. The turbo is small, tight, and mounted close to the exhaust manifold, so as soon as the engine makes exhaust gas, the turbo makes pressure. The IHI unit has a built-in wastegate to limit boost to about 6 lb, but full boost comes in at incredibly low speeds—less than 1500 rpm (the primitive Corvair, and many of the rudimentary aftermarket turbo kits,

were difficult to get up on full boost in lower gears, and never before 3000-3500 rpm).

Because the boost remains reasonable, even on a hot day under full load there is no sign of detonation on 91 octane unleaded. And that's when the car does its best—on a hot day, top down, full boost, lots of 2nd-, 3rd-, 4th-gear turns. This Spider will hit rpm redline easily in each of its five gears—only 5th gives the driver time to reflect on courts of law and licensing peculiarities. Acceleration numbers lie as well; in your seat-of-seats you know the car is faster than they say.

Understand, now, that the Fiat Turbo isn't the ultimate anything. The basic Fiat 124 sedan that spawned it is 16 years old. That sedan, in its day, was pretty advanced: coil-sprung live axle with trailing arms and a Panhard rod, more coils front with unequal-length A-arms and a sway bar, 4-wheel discs . . . neat for a family 4-door in 1966. Only the engine was a bit anemic. A couple years later the 124 Sport (coupe) fixed that by using the original 1197cc pushrod developed into a 1438cc hemi with belt-driven overhead

cams. A year after that came the Pininfarina Spider and 5-speed. The whole line was very Alfa-like. Not bad.

The 1438 grew to 1595, 1608, 1800, and finally, 2 liters. Smog-control apparatus, federal bumpers, and ancillary equipment played hell with performance despite displacement increases. With fuel injection (1980), performance got interesting again. Then came the turbo.

Back to that top-down, 2nd-3rd-4th-gear road. The instant boost means that the Spider Turbo can be driven like a non-turbo car. No lag means not having to hammer the throttle entering a turn, hoping that the boost will come in exiting the turn and not just before the apex. It's almost like having a nice little V-8 hooked to a good automatic. Power is smooth and immediate; 3rd, a most useful gear, is good from 1500 rpm through 6000—say 17-75 mph. But the 5-speed gearbox is so nice to use that on a good road you'll find excuses. And more good roads. In traffic, the automatic effect will suffice.

All, however, is not right with the world. The Spider has been around a good long time. What was right is still right: the basic looks that Pininfarina chose to use on a Ferrari as well as the Fiat. But the bumpers, originally beautifully integrated, are now obtrusive and clumsy. Other small details like the side marker lights, the outside mirror, and the turbo identification stripes also lack integration.

Seats are comfortable, with decent leather (a $415 option), but drivers still complain about the seating position because of the steering wheel, which has had the "bus-driver rake" since the beginning. The headlight switch is far left, instrument light rheostat far right. A left-hand long column stalk works the high/low beams. Perversely, high is down, low up. One right-side steering column stalk and one panel switch are used to control the wipers. Heater controls, on the console between the seats, are also ergonomic nonsense. For 1983 minor interior changes are contemplated, including improvement in some of the arrangements criticized here.

Small screws are prone to falling out, plastic hardware could certainly be more durable. At a shade over $3000 (the original price) such foibles were forgivable. Now that the price has gone over 15 thou, not so. Body panel fit is good, paint better than the still-abundant Japanese orange peel. The top was, is, and is likely always to be the slickest one around. When cold, material shrinkage makes erecting the top a bit of a wrestling match. But then, who puts the top down in cold weather? In warm weather it's a 10-sec operation down, 30 up. The vinyl boot is standard.

So are the handsome Ferrari-like Cromadora alloy wheels. Did we mention that Fiat owns both Cromadora and Ferrari? Ditto Weber.

But we left off accelerating out of a turn. If it's in 2nd gear on a bumpy surface, there's likely to be wheelspin. Soon you learn to toss the car into the turn, then bring it out with opposite lock and throttle to counter the inherent understeer. It's not the fastest or most scientific way, but it's about as much fun as you can have in any car today.

The car's tendency to lift the inside rear wheel stems from too much roll stiffness rear, not enough front, and not enough generally. However, to increase overall roll stiffness would be a mistake because the car has been raised to increase bumper and headlight height, thus raising the center of gravity. The marvelous standard-equipment Pirelli P6 rubber allows enough side-bite to get the car leaning at a considerable angle. If roll stiffness were increased, both rear *and* front wheels might come off the ground. Not recommended. The answer is to lower the car—after you buy it.

Steering is heavy, and the sticky P6s don't make parking easier. As speed goes up, steering effort goes down. Because of generally soft suspension and generous rubber bushings, the worm-and-roller steering is not quite razor-sharp, but accurate enough for a good time despite some kick-back.

Four-wheel power-boosted discs may *sound* like the ultimate in brakes but on the Fiat they don't quite make it. They stop the car well enough, but lack consistent feel, probably due to caliper flex and/or line swelling. Front/rear balance is fine and the brakes can be used hard while you're flinging the car into turns without doing anything more than slowing it.

With air conditioning and a turbo, the underhood area is crowded, but anything an owner is likely to want to reach is near the top. Twin cams are driven by a Gilmer-type cog belt that experience says should be changed every 35,000 miles. On the subject of durability, Fiat points out that in European trim, the non-turbo 124 Sport

Fiat Spider 2000 Turbo

has 125 hp; the American Spider Turbo has but 120. Certainly the 124's lower end is strong enough, but the thermal loads imposed by a turbo are higher than those of a normally aspirated engine with the same displacement and horsepower. Some factory turbos use forged pistons, sodium-cooled valves, oil cooling, better valve guides, seats, etc. Fiat (actually Legend Industries) does include an automatic fuel shutoff as a backstop to the wastegate. No reports of upper-end problems have reached us, and as long as boost remains 5-6 lb, Fiat is confident none will.

Ventilation with an open car is seldom a problem. With the top and windows up, fan-boosted air can be brought in through heater or air conditioning (a $695 option). The air conditioning, like the turbo, is a port-of-entry installation, redundant for all but the most sybaritic. The heater and relatively tight top make the car useable in any climate.

The Spider Turbo is an American creature developed for our market by Legend Industries of Long Island, New York. Conversions are done at the ports of Jacksonville, Florida, and Los Angeles. (Strictly speaking, the Fiat Spider Turbo is not even entirely a Fiat. As of last October, Fiat sells mechanical components to Pininfarina rather than Pf selling bodies to Fiat. What this really means for the future remains to be seen.) Of the approximately 12,000 Spiders to be brought here in '82, about 10% will be turbocharged. Prototypes were automatics, but only 5-speeds are projected for future conversion.

Fiat seems to have concluded that it is unable (or unwilling) to compete with the Japanese in the U.S. market and henceforth will import only sports cars (Spider, X1/9, Lancia Zagato). This will allow the company to focus its concentration instead of trying to please the broad spectrum of sedan buyers. And unit for unit, sports cars are more profitable for both importer and dealer.

Which brings us to the last element: the dealers and distribution. Fix It Again, Tony, and Fix It All The Time have ceased being funny to Fiat—or to ex-Fiat owners. Fiat fortunes have cooled and heated almost with the seasons. In the company's best year, about 100,000 Fiats were sold here—this from a company that is currently first in European sales. *All* of the Japanese importers have learned to do a better job, in a much shorter time, of building cars for our market, or at least selling them. Fiat's marketing has been off/on/off. The dealership network, parts distribution, warranty policies, and certain product problems (rust, now presumably cured, and electrics) have put Fiat too far down on the U.S. hit parade. Pity. All Fiats are interesting to drive, and the Spider Turbo is even more. It's genuine fun. **MT**

ROAD TEST DATA

JIM BROWN

Fiat Spider 2000 Turbo

◢ SPECIFICATIONS

GENERAL

Vehicle type	Front-engine, rear-drive, 2-pass. convertible
Base price	$15,300 (incl. $255 freight and $50 port prep.)
Options on test car	Leather upholstery, A/C, Sonata AM/FM/stereo cassette
Price as tested	$16,860

ENGINE

Type	Inline four, cast iron block, alloy head, 5 main bearings
Bore & stroke	3.3 x 3.54 in. (84 x 90 mm)
Displacement	122 cid
Compression ratio	8.1:1
Fuel system	Bosch L-Jetronic fuel injection
Recommended fuel	91 octane unleaded
Emission control	Lambda-sond (oxygen sensor, closed-loop system)
Valve gear	Cog-belt-driven DOHC, inverted bucket followers
Horsepower (SAE net)	120 at 6000 rpm
Torque (lb-ft, SAE net)	130 at 3600 rpm
Power-to-weight ratio	19.8 lb/hp

DRIVETRAIN

Transmission	5-speed manual, all synchro
Final drive ratio	3.43:1

DIMENSIONS

Wheelbase	89.9 in.
Track, F/R	53.2/52.0 in.
Length	163 in.

Width	63.5 in.
Height	48.2 in.
Ground clearance	N.A.
Curb weight	2385 lb
Weight distribution (%), F/R	52/48

CAPACITIES

Fuel	11.4 gals
Crankcase	4.25 qts
Cooling system	8.5 qts
Trunk	6.4 cu ft

SUSPENSION

Front	Unequal-length A-arms, anti-sway bar, coil springs, tube shocks
Rear	Live axle, 4-link trailing arms, coil springs, tube shocks, Panhard rod

STEERING

Type	Worm and roller
Turns lock-to-lock	2.8
Turning circle, curb-to-curb	34.2 ft

BRAKES

Front	8.9-in. discs, single-piston caliper, power assist
Rear	8.9-in. discs, single-piston caliper, power assist

WHEELS AND TIRES

Wheel size	14 x 5.5 in.
Wheel type	Cromadora alloy
Tire make and size	Pirelli P6 185/60HR14
Tire type	Steel-belted radial
Recommended pressure (psi), F/R	28/28

◢ TEST RESULTS

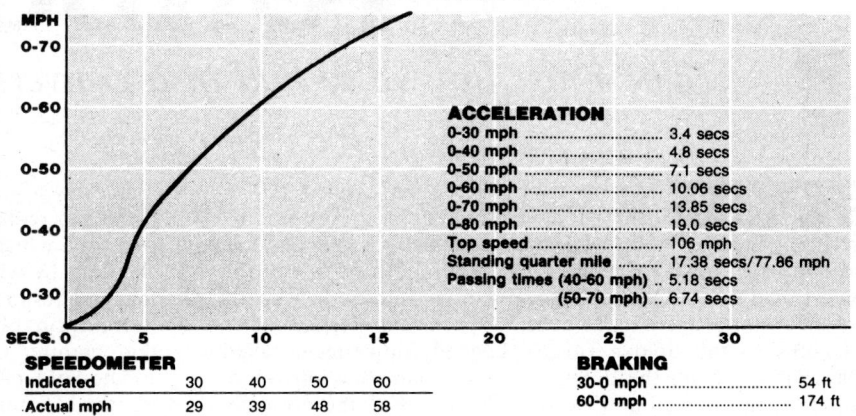

ACCELERATION

0-30 mph	3.4 secs
0-40 mph	4.8 secs
0-50 mph	7.1 secs
0-60 mph	10.06 secs
0-70 mph	13.85 secs
0-80 mph	19.0 secs
Top speed	106 mph
Standing quarter mile	17.38 secs/77.86 mph
Passing times (40-60 mph)	5.18 secs
(50-70 mph)	6.74 secs

SPEEDOMETER

Indicated	30	40	50	60
Actual mph	29	39	48	58

BRAKING

30-0 mph	54 ft
60-0 mph	174 ft

FIAT SPIDER TURBO

The most fun we've had in a convertible in a long time

PHOTOS BY JOE RUSZ

FIAT TAKE A POPULAR, custom-bodied Italian convertible with one of the slickest folding tops in the industry, add a well engineered turbocharger package and you have the Fiat Spider Turbo. You also have one of the sassiest road cars in America, a popular wind-in-the-face sports car whose understated looks belie its spectacular performance.

Thanks to the Spider Turbo's Legend Industries-installed turbocharger setup, the dohc Fiat powerplant develops more torque all the way from 1900 to 5500 rpm than the normally aspirated engine does at its torque peak. The boost comes on

incredibly low at 1400 rpm and continues all the way up to th 6000-rpm redline. In short, this is an impressive turbo installa tion, one which prompted a staff member to exclaim, "It's th standard by which others should be measured. It has excellen low-end response, a fairly strong top end and nary a hint o detonation nor even a suggestion of overly high coolan temperature."

The Spider Turbo was commissioned by Fiat of North Ame ica, the U.S. importer, in the hopes of selling about 1000 copies year. Legend Industries spent about 1½ years developing, testin and finally producing the system, which would be close to bullet-proof, even in the most careless hands. They succeeded (we didn't have a spot of trouble with the car), probably because maximum boost is set at only 6 psi and guarded by a wastegate and a fuel shutoff switch that turns off the fuel injection should the waste-gate fail. Also contributing to the seeming infallibility of the Turbo is the inherent ruggedness of the Fiat twincam power-plant. As a Fiat spokesman explains it: "The normally aspirated European version of this engine develops as much horsepower without using a turbocharger, yet it is very reliable. So we've deduced that the American turbo engine is operating well within these built-in tolerances."

To give you an objective idea of the Spider Turbo's perform-ance, we'll lay out those two standard test figures which all of us seem to commit to memory, acceleration time from 0 to 60 mph and the standing quarter-mile. For the 5-speed Turbo, these numbers are 9.4 and 17.1 seconds respectively. By comparison, the normally aspirated 5-speed car covers the same distances in 9.9 and 17.3 sec. But there's more to the Fiat Spider Turbo than numbers and it's the subjective impression one forms while driving this car in traffic or down a meandering country road. That's when the turbocharger's flexibility and power really shine and bring out the Villeneuve in every driver.

The Fiat's close-ratio 5-speed with its crisp, direct linkage also contributes to the Spider's sporty performance. The ratio spacing is near-perfect; the proper gear for any occasion is only a snick-snick away and you're never left with the feeling that Fiat fitted ratios merely to generate high CAFE numbers. Just the same, we averaged 22.0 mpg with the Spider despite an enthusiastic driving style that doesn't lend itself to high mileage figures. This led us to the conclusion that if fuel economy became a critical issue, Fiat could install a lower numerical final-drive or 5th-gear ratio without compromising the Turbo's flexibility and power.

Besides the turbo, the Fiat has several other salable attributes. It's a convertible, one of the few members of this diminished breed that is enjoying a resurgence of interest. The car's Pinin-farina lines are clean and curvaceous and Fiat of North America deserves credit for keeping them so, even though the temptation to set this model apart from the normal Spider exists. The distributor has been discreet and the only signs of the Turbo's identity are the wider-than-normal Cromodora wheels, Pirelli P6 tires, a tape stripe, some badges and a boost gauge.

It's easy to be dazzled by the Turbo's performance and to overlook the fact that with or without a turbocharger, the Fiat Spider is a decent-handling sports car whose 15-year-old design does not seriously detract from its road manners. Sophisticated it's not, but it certainly is forgiving and entertaining. Even in the standard 2000 Spider the neophyte can feel like he's going hard without hurting himself or the car, and the same is true for the Turbo. The P6s add cornering power and mask understeer, making the car even more enjoyable than its predecessor. Yes, there are body shake and rattles (it is a convertible, after all), but the ride is well controlled, the steering positive and direct and its feedback quite good. "It's so 'tossable,'" said one staffer, sum-ming up the overall impression one gets after driving the Spider Turbo over proper sports-car roads.

"Tossable" is also the right word to describe the Turbo's slalom

AT A GLANCE

	Fiat Spider Turbo	Alfa Romeo Spider Veloce 2000	Fiat Spider 2000
Curb weight	2385	2540	2385
Engine	inline-4	inline-4	inline-4
Transmission	5-sp M	5-sp M	5-sp M
0-60 mph, sec	9.4	13.2	9.9
Standing ¼ mi, sec	17.1	19.5	17.3
Speed at end of ¼ mi, mph	80.0	73.0	79.0
Stopping distance from 60 mph, ft	see text	165	170
Interior noise at 50 mph, dBA	75	75	77
Lateral acceleration, g	0.754	0.682	0.737
Slalom speed, mph	57.6	est 57	55.8
Fuel economy, mpg	22.0	26.0	26.0

performance. Our tester reported that although heavy steering effort made the maneuver a bit difficult, he was still able to manage 57.6 mph (vs 55.8 mph for the previous Fiat Spider) putting the Turbo through its paces. The turbocharged car was quicker around the skidpad too, achieving 0.754 vs 0.737g.

Track constraints during our day of testing prevented us from updating the Spider's panic-stop evaluation. But the normally aspirated Spider tested in 1979 needed 170 and 298 feet to reach a standstill from 60 and 80 mph. Given the Spider Turbo's larger tire footprint, we suspect that the latest Fiat should do better than the non-turbocharged version.

Criticisms? The odd angles of the Fiat Spider's steering wheel, pedals and seat. It's the old Italian driving position again, meaning that unless you are a contortionist, you will have some difficulty performing textbook maneuvers like heel-and-toeing in the Fiat. All of this serves to remind us that the car is a 15-year-old design.

However, one editor put it eloquently when he said, "The turbo changes the car's spirit so that despite a few shortcomings, driving the Fiat Spider Turbo reminds me of what fun it used to be when all enthusiast cars had soft tops." And "proper" engines, we might add.

PRICE

List price, all POE	$12,995
Price as tested	$14,237

Price as tested includes 14-in. alloy wheels w/P6 tires ($550), leather seats ($415), metallic paint ($232), port prep ($45)

GENERAL

Curb weight, lb/kg	2385	1083
Test weight	2590	1176
Weight dist (with driver), f/r, %	52/48	
Wheelbase, in./mm	89.7	2278
Track, front/rear	53.2/52.0	1351/1321
Length	163.0	4140
Width	63.5	1613
Height	48.2	1224
Trunk space, cu ft/liters	6.2	176
Fuel capacity, U.S. gal./liters	11.4	43

ENGINE

Type		dohc inline-4
Bore x stroke, in./mm	3.3 x 3.54	84.0 x 90.0
Displacement, cu in./cc	122	1995
Compression ratio		8.1:1
Bhp @ rpm, SAE net/kW	120/90 @ 6000	
Torque @ rpm, lb-ft/Nm	130/176 @ 3600	
Fuel injection		Bosch L-Jetronic
Fuel requirement		unleaded, 91-oct

DRIVETRAIN

Transmission		5-sp manual
Gear ratios: 5th (0.88)		3.43:1
4th (1.00)		3.90:1
3rd (1.36)		5.30:1
2nd (2.10)		8.19:1
1st (3.66)		14.27:1
Final drive ratio		3.90:1

CHASSIS & BODY

Layout	front engine/rear drive
Body/frame	unit steel
Brake system	8.9-in. (266-mm) discs front and rear, vacuum assisted
Wheels	Cromodora alloy, 14 x 5½J
Tires	Pirelli P6, 185/60HR-14
Steering type	worm & roller
Turns, lock-to-lock	2.8

Suspension, front/rear: unequal-length A-arms, coil springs, tube shocks, anti-roll bar/live axle on trailing arms, Panhard rod, coil springs, tube shocks

CALCULATED DATA

Lb/bhp (test weight)	21.6
Mph/1000 rpm (5th gear)	17.1
Engine revs/mi (60 mph)	3500
R&T steering index	0.92
Brake swept area, sq in./ton	221

ROAD TEST RESULTS

ACCELERATION

Time to distance, sec:
0-100 ft	3.5
0-500 ft	9.5
0-1320 ft (¼ mi)	17.1
Speed at end of ¼ mi, mph	80.0

Time to speed, sec:
0-30 mph	3.5
0-50 mph	7.3
0-60 mph	9.4
0-70 mph	13.1
0-80 mph	17.3
0-100 mph	29.3

SPEEDS IN GEARS

5th gear (6000 rpm)	104
4th (6000)	90
3rd (6000)	69
2nd (6000)	44
1st (6000)	26

FUEL ECONOMY

Normal driving, mpg	22.0

BRAKES

Minimum stopping distances, ft:
From 60 mph	see text
From 80 mph	see text
Control in panic stop	see text
Pedal effort for 0.5g stop, lb	25

Fade: percent increase in pedal effort to maintain 0.5g deceleration in 6 stops from 60 mph | 40

Overall brake rating | good

HANDLING

Lateral accel, 100-ft radius, g	0.754
Speed thru 700-ft slalom, mph	57.6

INTERIOR NOISE

Constant 30 mph, dBA	72
50 mph	75
70 mph	83

SPEEDOMETER ERROR

30 mph indicated is actually	30.0
60 mph	56.5

ACCELERATION

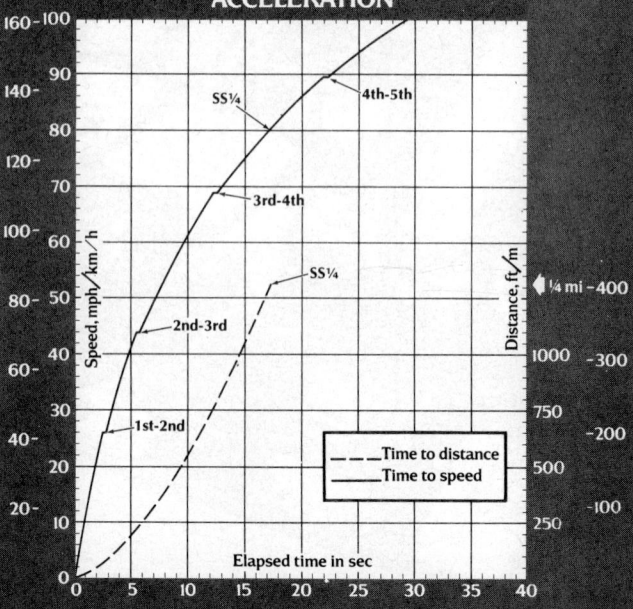

BACK TO BACK
RED DEVILS

Alfa Romeo's Spider and Fiat's 124 soft top are certainly emotive, exciting and entertaining. Chosing between the two is not always as easy as it may seem, as Peter Nunn discovered

oes it come as a surprise to learn that, according to e English dictionary, the word 'spider' can some- mes be taken to mean 'ensnarer'?

In Italy, spider (or spyder) is the general term for open-topped sports car but some might say a spell th one or either of the two delectables above (Fiat 4 Spider on the left, Alfa Romeo 2000 Spider on e right) could well 'ensnare' you for life, especially your test drive happened to take place on a sunny,

twisty road with little traffic about. That may sound daft; it may also sound extremely unlikely, yet be warned – if fresh air frolics are your forte it could well happen . . .

It's not our fault, incidentally, that Alfa's shapely 2000 Spider seems to have an unfair head start in this contest. For, not only does it have The Name (and The Pedigree, come to that) it's also a stunningly good looking car. The 2-litre Fiat 124 Spider, on the

other hand, despite having so many good things in common with the Alfa, is something of an enigma in Britain. It's never been marketed in this country and for that reason can't begin to compete with the Alfa's widespread, fanatical following. The few that have been imported, though, underline only too well the car's basic appeal and overall desirability.

It says a great deal for the quality of Pininfarina's styling and the essential 'rightness' of the two cars that both are still in production close on 17 years after their respective debuts in the winter of 1966. At that time, affordable open-topped sports cars of the Austin Healey 3000, Jaguar E-type, Lotus Elan and MGB variety could still be bought off the showroom floor; today, all four are long gone but remarkably, the Alfa and Fiat Spiders live on, albeit in a rather emasculated form – the bulk of production (as far as the Fiat is concerned at least) being tailored towards the emission-conscious North American market.

More recently, these two 'soft tops' faced competition of sorts from the Triumph TR7 and Jensen Healey. Once again, however, the Italian thoroughbreds, due to clever marketing if nothing else, managed to outlive the British machines although Lancia's Beta 2000 Spyder, introduced in 1976 and still available new, just manages to keep the Latin drophead theme alive in Britain, even if it's not a particularly quick or stylish car. It's fair to say, then, that discounting Anglo-Saxon oddities such as a Morgan or Caterham Seven, both Alfa and Fiat represent perhaps the final flings of what is nostaligically called the 'good old days', when rorty, open-top sports cars for the masses were still a production reality. Sigh . . .

Right from the beginning, the Alfa and Fiat

ith their hoods down and neatly folded away, both Alfa and Fiat are shown to their best advantage

ASSIC AND SPORTSCAR, JUNE 1983

79

57

Hardly the best weather to go Spider motoring! While the Alfa can be tricky in the wet, the Fiat feels more predictable

Spiders have shared a surprising number of similarities. Unless you were conversant with Fiat's huge range of cars and the 124 series in particular, you probably wouldn't realise that ever since 1966 the 124 Spider has 'marked' Alfa's cuttlebone-shaped car pretty closely. True, the Alfa has always been the more glamorous (and expensive) of the two but remember the unsung Fiat also has Pininfarina-styled bodywork, a twin overhead camshaft engine, five-speed gearbox and well-supported live rear axle. Add on the fact Pininfarina built up both bodies in their Turin factory and that both cars are open two-seaters with negligible room behind the front seats and you end up with an almost perfectly matched pair. And the present-day arrangement whereby the Toronese coachbuilders manufacture the two cars under their own name only seems to bring the pair even closer together still.

Developed from Duetto

The story of how Alfa Romeo's 2000 Spider developed from the 1570cc 'Duetto' (itself a development from two Pininfarina Motor Show styling exercises) and its 1779cc successor is a familiar one. Briefly, the Duetto – a car immortalised on celluloid by Dustin Hoffman in *The Graduate* – was Alfa's replacement for the ageing but still beautiful Giulia Spider, launched in 1962 as a successor to the near-identical, smaller-engined Giulietta. Film fans, by the way, might recall at this point that Edward Fox used a Giulietta Spider to good effect in the *Day of the Jackal* until a Peugeot 404 and a tree got in the way!

The Duetto, though, adopted the 109bhp version of Alfa's delightful dohc all aluminium 'four', a five-speed, close-ratio gearbox, wishbone and coil spring front suspension, and a coil-sprung, live axle located by radius arms and A-bracket. Disc brakes were fitted back and front and recirculating ball steering completed the basic mechanical specification.

Based around a shortened floorpan taken from the Sprint GT coupé, first seen back in 1963, the Duetto was certainly a well-proportioned two-seater. Yet in 1967 the Duetto name was dropped when the 1779cc, '1750' Spider Veloce was introduced. Here was a much improved Spider, offering greater refinement and all-round road performance. In particular, engine power and torque were upped considerably and the interior received a major facelift by means of a new facia, console and pair of front seats. Externally little was changed until the 1970 model year cars were shown; in place of the long, graceful tail that characterised the earlier cars, a new, shorter Kamm rear end was incorporated, which made the Spider less vulnerable in confined spaces but, as a penalty, reduced the luggage area.

The mainstream Giulias (boxy saloon, compact

Alfa's 'classic' 1962cc twin cam produces 131bhp

Federalised Fiat 2-litre is smooth but underpowered

GTV coupé and elegant open-top Spider) received a final enlargement to full 2-litre status during the summer of 1971. This was achieved by boring out the 1750's cylinder walls to 84mm each (from 80mm), the result being a throaty, 1962cc 'four' developing a net 131bhp in place of the former's 118bhp. Torque was also increased to 134lb.ft.

The basic formula of open Pininfarina body, Alfa twin cam engine, five-speed 'box and live axle remained from the Duetto and 1750 (and the down-market 1.3 Spider Junior), being carried forward right up until the 2000's official UK demise in 1977. As a driver's car, the Spider 2000 was undoubtedly the best of them all, although some observers still mourned the passing of the Duetto's long tail . . .

At the Turin Show in 1966, Fiat showed for the first time Sports Coupé and Spider versions of their acclaimed 124 saloon. Both cars were based around the 124 floorpan but where the Spider's wheelbase was shortened by some 5ins, that of the Coupé matched the saloon's exactly. Dimensionally, the Spider was also narrower, shorter and lower than the two-door Coupé; the two variants did share the same

1438cc, belt-driven dohc, four-cylinder engine though, (note that the Alfa's cams are chain-operated) developing 96bhp gross. A development of the original 124's pushrod unit, this five-bearing engine featured an iron block, alloy head and a compression ratio of 8.9 to 1.

Transmission was either four or five-speed manual, suspension independent at the front by wishbones and coils with a live axle, coil spring, radius arms and Panhard rod taking care of the rear. Unassisted worm and roller steering and all-round servoed disc brakes were also specified.

The enlarged, long-stroke 1608cc engine, featured first in the quick 125 saloon of 1967, appeared in the 124 Coupé and Spider models during 1969. Power was now up around the 110bhp mark and torque equally healthy at 101lb.ft. For many, these two were the nicest of the attractive 124 series, combining uncluttered good looks, zestful performance and useful gearing with down-to-earth practicality. But the 1756cc 'four', taken from the heavy 132 of the early seventies, provided even better mph and bhp when installed in the Coupé and Spider during 197_, the two cars thus becoming classed as '1800s'. Just to confuse matters, at around this time the '140_' engine was deleted from the line-up and the '160_' re-engineered to produce 108bhp from 1592cc.

Fiat decided the time was ripe to drop the distinctive Coupé in 1975 but the Spider soldiered on regardless, eventually receiving the 80mm x 71.5mm, 1995cc engine in 1978 for its trouble. By now the car was getting pretty long in the tooth but thanks to periodic facelifts and minor revamps, it still managed to survive despite the absurd restrictions of the North American market where, ironically, it remains a popular buy. In Italy, the Spider reportedly available without the energy-sapping US pipework, and also as a fearsome Abarth-tuned hot rod. Wonderful!

Setting up test

During the early stages of setting up this test, we were hoping to put a Duetto alongside a late sixties 1608cc Fiat Spider. Failing that, we considered the possibility of a 1750 Spider Veloce versus an 1800 Fiat confrontation. Of course we could also have gone the other way and pitted a 1300 Spider Junior against an early, 1438cc drophead! In the end though, we settled on a 2-litre Alfa vs 2-litre Fiat test which sounded fine in theory but didn't really work too well in practice.

Michael Jephson's early eighties' Fiat Spider suffers so much from engine Federalisation that its Weber carburettor'd engine produces a puny 86bhp (gross) at 5100rpm whereas the previous 1800 could manage 118bhp at 6000rpm. David Miller's Downton coachworks-refurbished Alfa, on the other hand, turns out a respectable 131bhp of untoxed bhp according to the specification chart. Thus, as we put the two cars through their paces, it soon became obvious which car appealed most to the sporting driver. If only we could have tried one of the US-spec Alfas running with Spica fuel injection as *Car and Driver* did back in 1979, the scales might have been tipped more evenly. On that occasion the $11,325 110bhp Alfa turned in a 0-60mph time of 9.8sec and a maximum of 106mph. Its standing quarter mile time was 17.8sec. The 80bhp Fiat, meanwhile (which then cost $7090) accelerated to 60mph in 11.2sec, achieved a 104mph maximum and did the quarter mile in 18.4sec. On that showing the Fiat certainly gave the Alfa a run for its money, especially in the value for money stakes.

Of course there's more to a car than pure straight-line speed. Michael Jephson picked on his Fiat because he had seen the car in its best light – in sunny 55mph California – and the basic Pininfarina design appealed to him. When scouting around for a new car, just over two years ago, he did consider an Alfa Spider, but at that time low-mileage Spiders in mint condition were both expensive and difficult to find. The Fiat, on the other hand, was to him an unusually desirable car that could be bought virtually brand new for less than the price of a secondhand Alfa.

And that's really the rub in this situation. Because Fiat Spiders are such an unknown quantity

...the bulbous facia cowls mar the Alfa's stylish cockpit?

The neat, well-balanced interior of the Fiat 124 Spider

...tain, it should be possible to pick up a real bargain ...ou shop around. According to our Price Guide, ...average selling price of a Spider 2000 tends to be ...und the £3000 mark (depending, of course, on ...dition) while left-hand-drive Fiats – admittedly ...all of them 2-litres – generally fetch much less. If ...prefer the looks of the Fiat to that of the Alfa, ...ch some reckon is almost *too* pretty for its own ...d, then the attraction of the Turin car becomes ...n greater.

...Conversely, the fact that outlets specialising in ...se Fiat ragtops seem very few and far between in ...UK, and that body spares are reputedly difficult ...btain makes the Fiat less of a practical proposition. ...ht-hand-drive is possible, by all acounts, along ...n detoxification of the engine – but all at a price ...t some might find prohibitive. Spares, expertise ...general know-how to cover all aspects of Alfa ...der ownership are all readily available in the UK, ...vever, and there's also the excellent Alfa Romeo ...ners Club for socialising and advice. Sadly, Fiat ...vers don't seem to go in for the same camaraderie. ...fter a drive in Michael's Fiat, the Miller Alfa ...neo feels positively nervous. On the day of our ...tographic session, the rear dampers and springs ...ded attention but that deficiency didn't mask the ...s underlying characteristics. To drive an Alfa ...der quickly you have to concentrate hard all the ...e (especially in the wet), to keep the built-in ...tchiness of that shortened chassis in check. Yet ...car's responsiveness and overall demeanor is ...oxicating all the same. Performance from the gruff

twin cam is powerful and exciting and the gearchange (apart from the change into second) satisfying despite a rather sloppy gate. Steering, while heavy at rest and low speeds, is exemplary when really moving, allowing instant deflections with no drama. Braking, via twin servos, is equally impressive.

Modicum of space behind seats

From an ergonomic point of view, the Alfa has some excellent features. There's a huge boot, for a start, and even a modicum of space behind the front seats for two legless dwarves. Joking aside, it is *just* possible to squeeze a couple of medium-sized people in, to make a four-up journey possible but not particularly enjoyable. The controversial driving position is perfect if you're 5ft 10in and wear size 8½ shoes (like me!), the pedal arrangement permitting quick heel and toe movements although the splayed leg stance does require some acclimatisation at first. The hood action, though, is superb; the cover, undone by just two clips, folds right down and with practice is said to be a one-man job. There are no clips, poppers or fastners to worry about, either.

While some aspects of the Alfa Spider border on the fussy, the Fiat 124 Spider, in comparison, feels a more conventional kind of car. In essence WYV 608T comes across as a dependable, safe sports tourer that's also beautifully trimmed inside with plush seats and fancy carpeting. In contrast to the Alfa's rather self-indulgent facia, that of the Fiat is kept very simple and is, arguably, all the better for it. Like the Alfa, the Fiat's hood is easy to put up and

down and all-round vision (especially rear three-quarter) is superior to that of the Milanese car. Unfortunately rear seat legroom is simply non-existent so regard the Fiat as a two-seater only and not a 2 + 2.

The strangling anti-pollution equipment means WYV feels underpowered, to put it mildly. There is one bonus, though, it uses two-star fuel! You have to keep the revs really humming to be able to make the Fiat do anything spectacular around corners at which point understeer of sorts occurs but the well-damped ride is both reassuring and smoother than the Alfa's which is a touch jolty in comparison.

In the steering department, the Fiat does not shine so well, the wheel movement having a dead feel to it which mercifully disappears as speed builds up. Both cars have relatively poor locks. As for the Fiat driving position, that requires no special consideration and the gearchange, despite a loose action, generally works well.

So which is better? There's no doubt that if the age gap between the two cars was diminished, the Fiat's emission limitations thrown away and its steering wheel moved to the right, this comparison would have been fairer. As it is, the Alfa has to win this particular round even though the Fiat does equal or better it in some respects. And as a car to own on an everyday basis, the Fiat might actually nudge ahead due to its less exotic temperament and lower running costs – but the knowledge that expert help to keep the car in trim is not always just around the corner could be a worry if you're not a d-i-y man. If you're interested in buying the Fiat, incidentally, the good news is that it's for sale. Ring 01-977 7688 for further details.

Tailpiece: the Fiat's bumpers are perhaps an acquired taste

SPECIFICATION	Alfa Romeo Spider	Fiat Spider
Engine	In-line 'four'	In-line 'four'
Bore × stroke	84mm × 88.5mm	84mm × 90mm
Capacity	1962cc	1995cc
Valves	Twin OHC (chain-drive)	Twin OHC (belt-drive)
Compression	9:1	8:1
Power	131bhp (DIN) at 5500rpm	86bhp (SAE) at 5100rpm
Torque	134lb.ft (DIN) at 3000rpm	110lb.ft (SAE) at 3000rpm
Transmission	Five-speed manual.	Five-speed manual. Auto option
Brakes	Discs front and rear, twin servos	Discs front and rear, single servo
Suspension F.	Ind. by wishbones, coils, anti-roll bar, telescopic dampers	Ind. by coils, wishbones, telescopic dampers
Suspension R.	Live axle, coils, radius arms, A bracket, telescopic dampers	Live axle, coils, radius arms, Panhard rod, telescopic dampers
Steering	Recirculating ball or cam and peg	Worm and roller
DIMENSIONS		
Length	13ft 6in	13ft 0½in
Width	5ft 4in	5ft 3⅔in
Height	4ft 3in	4ft 1¼in
Wheelbase	7ft 4½in	7ft 6in
Unladen weight	20½cwt	20⅔cwt
Tyres	165 HR 14	165 HR 13
PERFORMANCE		
Max speed	118mph	104mph
0-60mph	9.7sec	11.2sec
Standing ¼ mile	17.1sec	18.4sec
Average fuel con.	24mpg	22mpg

Timeless beauty: scalloped side panels blend well with the Alfa Spider's clean overall shape

Dark horse: styled by Pininfarina, the Fiat 124 Spider possesses smooth, unruffled lines

FIAT 2000 SPIDER & SPIDER TURBO

Two versions of a vintage, yet timely roadster

FIAT THERE ARE NO major changes in store for the 1983 Fiat 2000 Spider, nor for the Spider Turbo. And this is fine with us, because both cars are still quite timely.

To say this about a car whose basic production run has gone on for 17 years appears to imply one of two things. Either the car was remarkably right at its 1966 introduction, or we're a bunch of nostalgics sitting around remembering the good old days. Actually, it's a little of both, though matters are somewhat more complicated than this simple dichotomy.

For one thing, the current Spider has gone through quite a few non-trivial revisions. Over the years its engine has grown from 1.4 to 2 liters, and in 1981 Bosch L-Jetronic fuel injection gave the car's now 1995-cc dohc 4-banger exemplary driveability and starting behavior. Shortly thereafter, the Spider Turbo was added. Even the styling has undergone subtle changes over the years, nicely designed impact bumpers being the biggest single alteration.

A second point concerns not the car itself, but rather the changing market place. In the year of its introduction, our listing of available sports and GT cars included a total of 31 (count them: 31!) soft-top cars—and this listing ignored domestic convertibles. The current listing is decidedly smaller; in fact, Fiats make up roughly half of the list, what with these two subject cars and the X1/9 (which isn't really a soft-top car anyway). That the Spider has endured so long says a lot about its attributes.

The first of these, in our view, is the most functional and easily operated convertible top one can imagine. Release two levers, grasp the center handle and toss the top backwards—it's even possible to do while you're seated at the wheel. Those with longish arms could probably reverse the procedure, though most of us would get out to ease the operation along.

Another endearing virtue is the get-up-and-go nature of the Spider's engine, whether it's the 102-bhp normally aspirated version or the Turbo, whose 6-psi boost adds another 18 bhp. Either engine teams with a gearbox and final drive whose ratios are unfashionably short in these days of two-thumps-per-telephone-pole-in-top. Our test Spiders turned 3350 rpm at 60 mph in 5th, for example, which translates into an entertaining close-ratio feel working up to that top cog. Driveability, cold or hot, was excellent with both cars, though the turbocharged version's mid-range kick was a bit more entertaining.

On an objective note, our test equipment sensed the same thing, though not quite to the extent we would have guessed. The normally aspirated car's time to 60 mph was 10.9 seconds; the Turbo's, 10.3. A similar margin continued through the quarter-mile, with the unblown car's 17.9 sec at 76.0 mph comparing with the Turbo's 17.5 at 79.0. Beyond this speed, the Turbo's extra horsepower began to widen the gap. Both cars

Fiat engines: the normally aspirated 2-liter . . .
Musical gauges: boost replaces temperature gauge replaces clock . . .

AT A GLANCE	Fiat 2000 Spider	Alfa Romeo Spider Veloce	Fiat X1/9
Curb weight, lb	2380	2495	2160
Engine	inline-4	inline-4	inline-4
Transmission	5-sp M	5-sp M	5-sp M
0–60 mph, sec	10.9	11.7	12.4
Standing ¼ mi, sec	17.9	18.3	18.6
Speed at end of ¼ mi, mph	76.0	74.0	72.0
Stopping distance from 60 mph, ft	164	152	141
Interior noise at 50 mph, dBA	77	75	73
Lateral acceleration, g	0.754	0.763	0.772
Slalom speed, mph	57.6	57.6	60.7
Fuel economy, mpg	25.0	22.5	27.0

easily reached 90 mph at our test track, but the Turbo got there 3.7 sec quicker, 23.5 versus 27.2. So the Turbo's performance margin is objectively dramatic only at high speeds.

Both cars rolled on identical Pirelli P6s, 185/60HR-14s, previously optional rubber but brought into the standard package during the 1982 model year. Considering the similar test weights (the Turbo was a mere 40 pounds heavier) and identical tires, we confined our brake testing to only one car and the luck of the draw happened to favor the Turbo (our Engineering Editor likes red cars . . .). At any rate, the 4-wheel discs hauled the Spider down from 60 mph in a reasonably short 164 ft; average distance from 80 was 280 ft. In either case (and with either car) the Spider's brake pedal was a sensitive one with which to avoid locking the rear tires, and once locked they seemed to like it that

HOW THEY DIFFER: FIAT 2000 SPIDER & SPIDER TURBO		
	2000 Spider	Spider Turbo
List price	$12,290	$14,995
Time to distance, sec.:		
0–100 ft	3.5	3.4
0–500 ft	9.5	9.4
0–1320 ft (¼ mi)	17.9	17.5
Speed at end of ¼ mi, mph	76.0	79.0
Time to speed, sec:		
0–30 mph	3.5	3.4
0–50 mph	8.1	7.6
0–60 mph	10.9	10.3
0–80 mph	20.2	18.0
0–90 mph	27.2	23.5
Fuel economy, mpg	25.0	22.0

. . and the turbocharged version.

. . but Spider and Spider Turbo cockpits are otherwise identical.

way more than we'd prefer. In fact, purely as a subjective comment, the non-Turbo's brake pedal exhibited a somewhat less linear feel than did the turbocharged car's, though we'd attribute this to nothing more than car-to-car variation.

Quantitative handling data include a slalom speed of 57.6 mph and a skidpad value of 0.754g. The same sort of behavior prevails on the road and in these two settings: fairly strong understeer, due in part to a well located live rear axle that stays out of trouble until the inside rear tire simply runs out of traction.

We've been treating these two cars as very similar, and indeed they are. The conversion from normal Spider to Turbo is actually done in the U.S. Outwardly, the only indication of the Turbo's extra kick are discreet emblems at the front and rear and on its flanks. Drop down into the comfortable, amply sized leather seat (a leather interior is a $415 option), look around for some indication of Turbo or non-Turbo and you'll find it, but not necessarily instantly. Both cars have a proper set of instruments nestled in a handsome wood dashboard, but the Turbo's driver

gets a boost gauge between the tach and speedometer whereas the non-Turbo's coolant-temperature gauge resides there. Turbo drivers do without a clock, because that's where their temperature gauge goes.

The rest of the interior fits the Spider's spirit to a T. Its steering wheel is leather-wrapped, the gearshift's oversize knob is handy and only the Italian knees-up-and-arms-out driving position could possibly interfere with the pleasure of open-air

sports-car motoring. Even tallish sorts will find the seating low enough to keep out of the wind, though your hair will still be tousled a bit by the back drafts—and who would want it any other way?

There's an upholstered seat-like surface behind the real seats, but we tend to think of it as a nice place for your pet or extra luggage. And at the tail lies a relatively shallow trunk that'll accept one decent-size piece of luggage or several of the soft variety.

PRICE

List price, all POE (2000 Spider) $12,290
Price as tested $13,198
  Price as tested includes leather seats ($415), AM/FM stereo ($261), metallic paint ($232)

GENERAL

Curb weight, lb/kg 2380 1080	
Test weight 2615 1187	
Weight dist (with driver), f/r, % 53/47	
Wheelbase, in./mm 89.7 2278	
Track, front/rear . . . . .53.2/52.0 . . .1351/1321	
Length 163.0 4140	
Width 63.5 1613	
Height 48.2 1224	
Trunk space, cu ft/liters 6.0 23	
Fuel capacity, U.S. gal./liters 11.4 43	

ENGINE

Type . . . . .dohc inline-4
Bore x stroke, in./mm . . . . . 3.31 x 3.54 . . .84.0 x 90.0
Displacement, cu in./cc 122 1995
Compression ratio 8.1:1
Bhp @ rpm, SAE net/kW . . . . .102/76 @ 5500
Torque @ rpm, lb-ft/Nm . . . . 110/149 @ 3000
Fuel injection . . . . Bosch L-Jetronic
Fuel requirement . . . . unleaded, 91-oct

DRIVETRAIN

Transmission . . . . .5-sp manual
Gear ratios: 5th (0.88) 3.43:1
  4th (1.00) 3.90:1
  3rd (1.36) 5.30:1
  2nd (2.10) 8.19:1
  1st (3.66) 14.27:1
Final drive ratio 3.90:1

CHASSIS & BODY

Layout . . . . .front engine/rear drive
Body/frame . . . . unit steel
Brake system . . . . . 8.9-in. (226-mm) discs front & rear; vacuum assisted
Wheels . . . . .cast alloy, 14 x 5½JJ
Tires . . . . Pirelli Cinturato P6, 185/60HR-14
Steering type . . . . worm & roller
  Turns, lock-to-lock 2.7
Suspension, front/rear: unequal-length A-arms, coil springs, tube shocks, anti-roll bar/live axle on trailing arms, Panhard rod, coil springs, tube shocks

CALCULATED DATA

Lb/bhp (test weight) 25.6
Mph/1000 rpm (5th gear) .17.9
Engine revs/mi (60 mph) 3350
R&T steering index 0.92
Brake swept area, sq in./ton 238

ROAD TEST RESULTS

ACCELERATION

Time to distance, sec:
  0–100 ft 3.5
  0–500 ft 9.5
  0–1320 ft (¼ mi) 17.9
Speed at end of ¼ mi, mph 76.0
Time to speed, sec:
  0–30 mph .3.5
  0–50 mph .8.1
  0–60 mph 10.9
  0–70 mph 14.5
  0–80 mph 20.2
  0–90 mph 27.2

SPEEDS IN GEARS

5th gear (6000 rpm) 109
4th (6000) 96
3rd (6000) 72
2nd (6000) 47
1st (6000) 27

FUEL ECONOMY

Normal driving, mpg 25.0

BRAKES

Minimum stopping distances, ft:
  From 60 mph 164
  From 80 mph 280
Control in panic stop . . . . . . very good
Pedal effort for 0.5g stop, lb 25
Fade: percent increase in pedal effort to maintain 0.5g deceleration in 6 stops from 60 mph 40
Overall brake rating . . . . good

HANDLING

Lateral accel, 100-ft radius, g . . . 0.754
Speed thru 700-ft slalom, mph 57.6

INTERIOR NOISE

Constant 30 mph, dBA 71
  50 mph 77
  70 mph 83

SPEEDOMETER ERROR

30 mph indicated is actually 29.0
60 mph 55.0

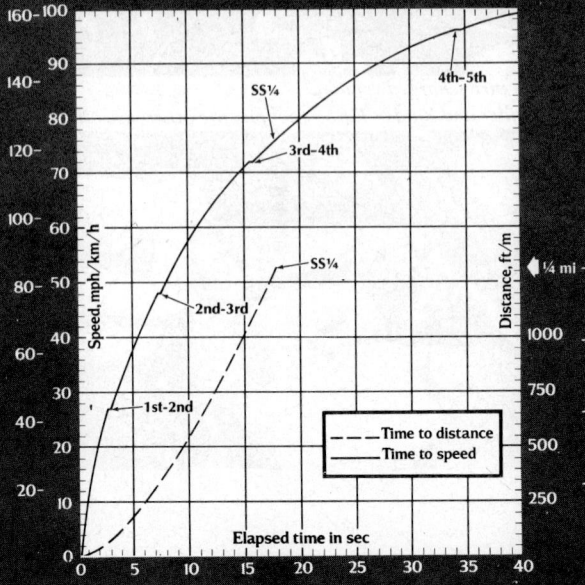

ACCELERATION

1st–2nd
2nd–3rd
3rd–4th
4th–5th
SS¼

Speed, mph/km/h
Distance, ft/m
¼ mi

Time to distance
Time to speed

Elapsed time in sec

This is a car for two people, after all, and we like to think of them as enjoying a tour to somewhere or other.

If their driving is similar to ours, said tourers can expect to use fuel at a rate of around 25.0 mpg (non-Turbo) or 22.0 mpg (Turbo version). On the other hand, we drive somewhat less aggressively in our own touring than we do in test-car evaluations, so maybe we should give these tourers a few extra mpg for their discretion.

The entry fee for all this, as practiced with a 1983 model, isn't firm at the time of this writing. There was, however, a revision of price and equipment level midway in the 1982 model year that resulted in a price of $12,290 for the 2000 Spider and $14,995 for the Spider Turbo. It's easy to put these prices in perspective, simply because there are so few other convertibles or Targas currently available (and we're prepared to argue they're the Spiders' principal competitors). Fiat's own X1/9 is less expensive, Alfa's Spider is more. And either offers tradeoffs of size, performance and exclusivity compared to the Spider duo.

Perhaps more relevant thought should be directed to the trades of Spider Turbo versus non-Turbo. The current price differential of $2705 is about the going rate for a better aftermarket turbo system. And, indeed, the Legend Industries turbo certainly fits this category. It's among the best and it's clearly a system, not simply a turbo connected by some plumbing. Whether its moderately increased performance and flexibility are worth $2705 depends on one's desires and pocketbook, akin to whether a top-line sound system is worth *its* premium. Based on our experience testing both cars, we can add that our Turbo exhibited no downside other than its initial cost. Both cars ran without detonation on unleaded 91-RON fuel. The Turbo's oil consumption was no different than the non-Turbo's during their stint here. Nor were its reactions to ambient temperature, traffic or whatever any different. The car is simply more responsive, a bit quicker and a little less frugal with fuel—primarily because one inevitably takes advantage of these first two characteristics.

Whichever Spider you select, chances are you'll enjoy it.

FIAT 124 SPIDER

CONTINUED FROM PAGE 25
the suspension although it is not as stiff as some of the others in this particular class. Tire pressures, however, can make a difference. The Fiat people here stateside recommend a pound or two more in the front than the book which came with the car does. We found 23 pounds all around (factory recommendation) gave us the best ride over all kinds of terrain. Standard equipment on the Spider is radial ply shoes either Pirellis or Michelins.

We found the door too high to rest one's arm comfortably but there is an arm rest which extends forward and swings up to form a door grab. Putting the elbow on this was relaxing if you wanted to switch from the straight arm bit.

SPECIFICATIONS

Wheelbase (inches)	89.8
Weight (lbs.)	2093
Length (inches)	156.3
Height (inches)	49.2
Width (inches)	63.5
Steering turns lock to lock	2.7
Turning circle (ft.)	34
Engine type	4 cylinder In line, dohc
Cooling method	liquid
Displacement	87.8 cu. in. 1438 cc
Compression ratio	8.9:1
Horsepower (SAE)	96 @ 6500 rpm
Torque (ft. lbs.)	82.5 @ 4000 rpm

Trunk space is never the best in a car with the Fiat's configuration but the 124 has enough that, in conjunction with the space behind the seats, you could tour with two without limiting yourself terribly.

The Fiat 124 Spider is a new car. It isn't that well known here yet. But it has so many things going for it that if Fiat-Roosevelt, Englewood Cliffs, N.J. can get the factory to ship as many as the importer has orders for you'll be seeing lots of them in the next year or so. If we haven't spelled it out up to now we say here that this Fiat is more than just a good buy for the money. It looks like the new "in" under two-litre sports car. They're not kidding around in Turin with this new offering. It will do great things for them in the international marketplace. ●

FIAT 124 SPIDER

CONTINUED FROM PAGE 42
though and always felt that we had enough reserve to pass any time we wanted to. This is a good feeling!

It is always a bore to have to get out of the house in the morning and drive twenty miles or whatever to the office. Doing this in the 124 Spider is guaranteed to remove the boredom from this daily chore. This holds true even in the winter. The heater worked well even with the fan on low and the wipers were most efficient in rain. Fortunately we didn't have the car during a snowy period and therefore were able to get the most out of this hot little performer all the time we lived with it.

One complaint we've heard about Fiats in the past year or so is hard starting on very cold mornings. We got a tip from Fiat which has been issued in the form of a service bulletin but which may not have reached all the owners yet. It seems that incorrect use of the choke and the accelerator may cause flooding. Before touching the choke the accelerator should be pumped to the floor three times. The choke is then pulled out and the ignition turned on. The accelerator should not be touched after the initial pumping until the engine warms up a bit and idles smoothly. We applied this technique in the morning and never experienced a single hard start.

The Spider also never stalled during the time we drove it.

Trunk space is always at a premium in sports cars but the 124 Spider does not come off badly in this area. We had no occasion to use the fancy chromed luggage rack with which our test car was equipped. Careful packing should permit enough stowage for two people unless you proposed to go cross country. Sports car buffs have actually done just that with less luggage space than the Fiat 124 Spider offers.

In summing up, we liked the first 124 Spider and find the new one will do nothing but enhance the Fiat image here in the United States. ●

Pininfarina Azzurra

Now this, dear friends, is a sports car. Call it what you will (Pininfarina Azzurra is the proper name; Fiat Spider 2000 is the only one that means anything to anyone), this classic Italian roadster is one of the precious few automobiles on the market today that can lay unquestioned claim to that title.

We hope you have noticed how, in recent years, the term sports car has had its integrity destroyed. Problem is, there just haven't been many true sports cars built through the last decade, and, in the absence of strong standard-bearers, a lot of pretenders have drifted in to fill the void.

The automotive world has been changing. It's not the same bouncy, rollicking place it was back when names like Triumph and MG were mentioned without nostalgic sighs. As the marketplace has become more sophisticated and consumers less forgiving, most of the front-line sports cars have died out. Left to usurp the label have been weighty and plushly trimmed Nissan ZXs, just because they're sleek and speedy, and uninspiring J-car convertibles because their roofs fold down.

But let's get back to the fundamentals.

by Kevin Smith

PHOTOGRAPHY BY MATT KEEFE

Our copy of Webster's defines "sports car" as "a low, fast, usually 2-seat open automobile." The folks over at the American Heritage Dictionary leaned toward narrower application ("An automobile equipped for racing . . . "), but the illustration they chose shows a lovely little mid-'60s Lotus Elan, top down. For our own definition, we don't want to bury our heads in intransigence, because in the modern context, a car like Mazda's RX-7 should qualify. But ideally we would like to hold to this: "A sports car is a small, simple, fun-to-drive automobile with seating for two and a folding top." Some cars that miss one or two of those requirements might still be admitted to the club, but any that meets them all is surely already in.

Enter the Pininfarina Azzurra.

The what? Well, we said the world was changing. Economic and marketing realities forced Fiat, Europe's largest car maker, off the American scene a year ago. The problems with reliability, rust, and dealer service need not be dredged up here. The point is two lovely sports cars—the Spider

2000 and the X1/9—nearly went the way of the TRs and Healeys. Fortunately, both cars were already being assembled, not by Fiat, but by their respective design houses (the Spider by Pininfarina, the X1/9 by Bertone), and these companies were free to strike their own deals to continue importation of their products to the U.S. market even after Fiat had turned out the lights and gone home.

They ended up making those deals with an organization created for the purpose. Malcolm Bricklin—a man with John De-Lorean's drive but not his legal predicament—formed International Automobile Importers, Inc., and took over importation, distribution, and service of the Fiat 2-seaters. The new arrangement has included a ground-up revamp of the dealer network, lots of detail refinement in the cars themselves, and a general positioning of the products as high-style designer automobiles that are fully worthy of consumers' confidence. (A two-year unlimited-mileage vehicle warranty and an amazing seven-year rust-perforation warranty speak directly to that last item.)

We tested the little mid-engined Bertone X1/9 last month (it stood up well to its modern challenger from Pontiac, the

Mechanically, the Azzurra is about as simple as they come

Fiero), and now we take a look at Pininfarina's traditional roadster, one of the old-guard sports cars that has managed to survive into the mid-1980s. Its original name has not survived along with it, however. The IAI people felt the term Spider had become overused and, besides, a new name would help underscore how different things were going to be under the new regime. Why Azzurra? That was our question. The word means blue in Italian (as in azure), and was the name of the Italian yacht entered in the 1983 America's Cup competition. The nautical theme was considered appropriate since Pininfarina has long been involved in boat design.

That's all well and good, of course, but we have one small problem with the name: On this side of the breezy blue Atlantic, the word doesn't mean a darn thing. Something that conjured more definite images might have been stronger.

After the stylized, sail-shaped "A" of the new trunk badge follows a whole catalog of small updates and improvements aimed at broadening the appeal of the car and smoothing over some of the rough edges that larger, slower-acting Fiat had not handled. The dash vents flow more air, the convertible top seals better and is easier to secure, the trunk has been rearranged to accommodate more luggage and it is upholstered more neatly, the jack doesn't rattle or cause inside-out dings in the sheet metal, and general corrosion resistance is increased. Coming within the year will be wider alloy wheels, larger front brake discs, and a handsome removable hardtop that will fit all Fiat Spiders already out there.

The Azzurra comes in one no-options package, positioned a bit up-market from where it had been as a Fiat Spider. Now listed as standard equipment are leather upholstery, power windows, air conditioning, and an electronically tuned AM/FM/cassette stereo. There's also been a redo of the dash panel and center console, interior and top fabrics are color coordinated, and the apparent finish quality inside has been improved.

What does all this detail upgrading mean? For one thing, IAI is plainly serious about making the car as civilized and modern as anyone could reasonably expect. But it's also obvious the new custodians aren't fooling with anything major on this car. That makes sense financially, since this basic car has already been around for 18 years, and nothing lasts forever (though don't try to tell that to Porsche). But the very fact this thing is still with us after all that time points up the other good reason not to change too much in its formula: It's pretty good and it works fine.

Think again about what we mean when we say sports car, and the Pininfarina Azzurra is an archetypal example. All the key elements are here, starting with its general layout: a neat, clean body design with two and only two seats, plus a canvas top that folds away completely. No pretentious sheet metal, useless +2 rear "seats," or lift-out sunroof here.

Mechanically, the Azzurra is about as simple as they come. The twin-cam four mounts longitudinally in the front, and a 5-speed box transfers drive to the live rear axle. Viewed critically in light of more modern performance cars, this arrangement has plenty of limitations, which start to show up in a reluctance to deliver power smoothly to the ground when pushed hard over bad pavement. But somehow that's okay, because at intensity levels of seven tenths or less, it's so much spirit-soaring fun to be in you just don't mind that it's not an ultra-modern maximum-velocity weapon.

That of course is the real point. Whatever else a car that aspires to the sports car fraternity may or may not offer, if it ain't fun to drive, it doesn't even come close. And the Pininfarina Azzurra truly is a treat to motor about in. We took a leisurely Sunday morning cruise across some of the San Gabriel Mountain roads we use for our Car of the Year test blitz (gee, there's actually some lovely scenery up there), and the combination of responsive controls, willing performance, and that close-to-the-environment feeling that is a convertible's forte made for a delightful day.

◪ SPECIFICATIONS

Pininfarina Azzurra

GENERAL
Vehicle type	Front engine, rear-drive, 2-pass., 2-door convertible
Base price	$16,995

ENGINE
Type & displacement	L-4, liquid cooled, cast iron block, aluminum head, DOHC, 1995 cc (122 cu in.)
Bore & stroke	84.0 x 90.0 mm (3.31 x 3.54 in.)
Induction system	Port injection
Max. power (SAE net)	102 hp @ 5500 rpm
Max. torque (SAE net)	110 lb-ft @ 3000 rpm
Recommended fuel	87 octane unleaded

DRIVETRAIN
Transmission	5-sp. man.
Final drive ratio	3.43:1

CHASSIS
Front suspension	Independent, upper and lower A-arms, coil springs, hydraulic shocks, anti-roll bar
Rear suspension	Live axle, trailing arms, coil springs, hydraulic shocks, anti-roll bar
Brakes, f/r	8.9-in. discs/8.9-in. discs
Steering type	Worm and roller
Turns, lock to lock	2.8
Wheels	14 x 5.5 in., cast aluminum
Tires	185/60HR14 Pirelli P6

DIMENSIONS
Curb weight	1085 kg (2400 lb)
Wheelbase	2283 mm (89.7 in.)
Overall length	4130 mm (163.0 in.)
Overall width	1611 mm (63.5 in.)
Overall height	1263 mm (49.2 in.)
Power to weight ratio	23.5 lb/hp
Fuel capacity	40 L (10.6 gal)

PERFORMANCE DATA
0-60 mph	10.83 sec
Standing quarter mile	18.65 sec/76.6 mph
60-0	153 ft
Skidpad	0.75 g
EPA rating, city/hwy.	25/36 mpg
Test average	26.4 mpg

A whole catalog of small improvements has strengthened the appeal of the car

Performance capability counts in determining the fun factor, but the actual flat-out numbers are less vital than the subjective impression the car's operation makes on the driver. The 2-liter engine Fiat provides pulls flexibly enough to always feel able, even though the Azzurra's 10.83-sec showing in our 0-60-mph sprint hardly qualifies as blistering. More important, the powerplant runs cleanly and responds crisply.

All the controls, in fact, have the kind of immediacy and accuracy that gives a sports car its positive feel. Shift action is direct, steering is generally good (though the upcoming rack-and-pinion gear will likely quicken on-center action), and all the pedals feel silky. Even the stiffness of the ride works to make the Azzurra feel close-cou-

pled and responsive. About the only sensation that occasionally intrudes here is cowl shudder, a flexibility over certain kinds of roughness that makes the car seem less than perfectly tied together.

As you would expect, one assumes the classic Italian driver's posture in this roadster. (Can the foot pedals and the steering wheel really be equidistant from the seat?) Furthermore, the wheel is canted up toward the horizontal in that peculiar Latin fashion, such that it presents only the lower 200° of its arc for actual gripping. Happily, the pose does not bother most drivers for long, and we found ourselves settling comfortably into the cockpit after just a couple of brisk drives.

One thing that requires absolutely no adjustment is the marvelous outward visibility over the low, slope-away Pininfarina

bodywork. Even with the top up, there is no sense of blindness thanks to the slender "C-pillar" panels and the glass rear quarter windows, which come up and down along with the easily operated soft top. (And we do mean easy: If the boot is off, either occupant can raise and secure the top while seated.)

Even the rather plentiful noise has all the right character. Engine rumble, gear whine, road hiss, and wind roar all carry their part in this over-the-road symphony. The sports car experience cannot happen in silence.

And this is, without doubt, a sports car—one that has survived where others of its ilk could not. It's a shame the asking price has climbed to a startling $17,000. That will limit its appeal in the marketplace even though there are no true direct competitors other than the Alfa Romeo Spider Veloce (exactly the same price, comparably equipped). That kind of money buys some pretty serious automotive hardware today.

But if it's the real thing you're after—a true sports car, in the classic, traditional, literal sense—the Pininfarina Azzurra is one of but two or three choices that respect the definition. [MT]

Eh Bellissima

The Italians love their sporting cars and with hands flaying the air naturally enthuse about them. Yet the Fiat 124 Spider — now the Pininfarina Spidereuropa — was an Italian car the Americans took to their hearts like the MGB

Report by Daniel Ward   Photography Peter Burn

THE MGB spawned a sort of sub-breed of owners who required heat-wave conditions before even considering the possibility of putting the hood down. At least drivers of the fastback GT version didn't go in for this pointless self-deception. They were not fresh air fiends and knew it.

In contrast Morgan enthusiasts consider it a matter of honour to keep their hoods packed away unless the rain on the inside of the screen has totally obscured the view. Reflect on how few soft-tops you see in the streets of Paris on blissful summer days and you realise that sunshine and sports cars don't necessarily go together.

And so it is with the Italians. Synonymous with sports cars certainly, but stop and think of the current or recent sports car convertibles, and the list is surprisingly short. After the much-loved Alfa Romeo Spyder and Ferrari Mondial Cabrio, the names come less easily to mind. A car easily forgotten is the Fiat 124 Sport Spider.

From its birth in 1966 on a shortened Fiat 124 floorpan the two-door Fiat has never officially been imported into Britain and, like the 12th man in a cricket team, not had a chance to prove itself here against the opposition of MG and Triumph.

Pity, because the Spider was a copy-book rival to the MGB and the production run of 190,000 between 1966 and 1982 came close to matching the Abingdon total. The North American market was even more important to the Fiat rag-top than the MG. In 1974 Americans looking for the sports car image bought over 14,000 124 Spiders, yet sales in Europe were down to 400 and thereafter it became exclusively a US model. But just like a pop idol built up by the media to be a star, the downfall at the hands of the American "preppies" had an inevitability about it, and so the US market proved to be the Spider's undoing.

With red ink splattered on its balance sheet Fiat took the momentous decision to retreat from North America in 1982; Spider sales were down to about 2000 a year. With the thought that there might still be some mileage left in the ageing soft-top, Fiat suggested Pininfarina take over full production rather than just build the Spider bodies for final assembly by Fiat. This alone explains the dropping of the Fiat name and how the car gained the awful name of Pininfarina 124 Spidereuropa. At about the same time Bertone took over production of the Fiat X1/9, which it had styled for the giant car maker.

With the Spider now on sale in Europe enthusiasts may have hoped that this Italian sports car, to many people's minds enhanced with age and detail improvements, would soldier on for years finding perhaps 1500 customers a year. Sadly, no. Detroit is about to deal it a backward blow, which will mean the last Spider leaves the Pininfarina production line at the end of this year. The company has secured a lucrative deal to design and build the bodies for a new Cadillac convertible, and the Spider can no longer command the factory floor space that stocky Italian workers are busy writing dollar signs on.

This is far from good news for a Nissan dealer in Basingstoke, one Dennis Hands Esq, who since last July has had an agreement with Pininfarina to sell Spiders in Britain, although as "personal imports". They can even be had with the steering wheel on the right side thanks to the freely available supply of bits from Fiat.

Would you buy a "new" 19-year-old Italian sports car for around £9000 which will be obsolete by the end of the year and has zero reputation, compared with, say, an Alfa Romeo? Don't laugh, think about it. For owners of similarly priced Golf GTis, the Spider probably brings thoughts of bailing water out of flooded footwells or trying to go on holiday with the family but just one suitcase. Even for Cabrio drivers who think they would like a sports car, the message must be forget it; fast prams are more your style, so stay with them.

The Spider is all about style and the often indefinable pleasure a small band of drivers gets from being in a car with

Basic design is now 19 years old and Spidereuropa looks like a classic 1960s sports car. Driving position is surprisingly good

just two seats, a cramped cockpit and the roof peeled back, all yielding a sense of driving and travel no mass-production box can match. That is not to say the Fiat is a paragon of engineering design, nor does it set any new standards of roadholding or handling. For those who can't help but like the Spider this is not of real importance.

And there is also rarity in its favour — a strange quality for something that bore the Fiat emblem for much of its life, though this is no criticism; its past, as we have seen, is not steeped in failure. That distinction among Fiats is better reserved for wonderful models like the 130 Coupé with its

breathless elegance, or the odd mixture of Fiat and Ferrari called the Fiat Dino.

As Graham Robson's informative book *Fiat Sports Cars, 1945 to X1/9* recounts, the styling of the Spider neatly continued the theme of the earlier 1500/1600S Cabriolet sports car, although appearing squatter due to its shorter wheelbase and markedly wider track. The Pininfarina lines were certainly simpler and the overall style of the first Sports Spiders less overtly sporty than the MGB, launched some four years previously. Yet the 124 is one of those rare cars which has actually been improved by subtle changes during its life.

When the earlier 1438 cc twin-cam four-cylinder engine made way for a 1608 cc version in 1969 the bonnet was treated to a pair of "power" bulges reminiscent of the glorious bulge in the centre of the Jaguar E-type's bonnet. The steel wheels gave way to distinctive alloy ones, the radiator grille changed style as quickly as women's hem lines, while black door sills helped reduce the perceived height of the body sides. The pencil-thin bumpers of the sixties have been consigned to the defunct pile by Ralph Nader, but even the Federal bumpers hardly detract from the Spider's pleasing form, thanks to a healthy dash of chrome. Pity UK registration plates don't fit the minute slots purpose-made for Roma or Torino numbers.

Proud MGB owners will find it hard to concede that the Fiat started life with a considerably more modern chassis than the B, but the facts are hard to dispute. No-one seemed to mind that the MG's deficent lever arm dampers and crude leaf springs stayed with it throughout its long life. The Spider never suffered such handicaps, as it employed a

coil-sprung live axle efficiently located by torque tube, trailing arms and a Panhard rod; a forward-mounted anti-roll bar checked body roll. At the front it emulated the MG's double wishbone layout. The Fiat stepped up its advantage when the 124 Abarth Rallye was launched in November 1972, complete with independent rear suspension and MacPherson struts with reversed lower wishbones.

Unusually for a sports car the 124 has reciprocating ball steering, rack and pinion only taking its rightful place in 1985 models. From the start the specifications included four-wheel discs, the front ones being upgraded recently to ventilated ones.

Take your place behind the wheel and the impression is one of practical roominess. The generous seat travel makes the Spider infinitely more bearable for taller drivers than the flawed Alfa Spyder and behind the seats there is a broad shelf which for 1985 boasts storage boxes. MGB owners stored their corroding 6V batteries in a similar position. The Italian's boot is deceptively big but hopelessly shallow.

I find myself looking hard at short stocky Italians to see whether they really do have the unlikely proportions of short legs and ape-like arms around which many Italian cars have been designed. When Alfa drew the Spyder the designers worked out the driving position based on a really extreme case. Consequently I find it more easy to grip the steerig wheel, gear lever and door handle of the Alfa with my knees than hands.

By comparison the Fiat is comfortable, largely due to the sensible travel of the seat. I was able to fit into a Fiat 500 for the same reason. The steering wheel is really too far away but certainly manageable, while the

Fiat twin-cam engine (above) gives reasonable acceleration from 2 litres and 122 bhp but lacks refinement. Power bulges on bonnet (below) were introduced in 1969. Hood is very practical

beefy gear-lever falls easily to hand. The instrumentation is no-frills 1960s style, courtesy of Veglia Borletti; the use of familiar-looking Fiat switchgear is inevitable, but the wood facia is an unconvincing effort.

If your definition of a sensible sports car is one where the heater is efficient and the hood both keeps the draughts out and is easily folded down, then the Spider is good sense itself. I can't remember the last sports car I drove where it was necessary to turn the heater *down* in February. To offer the driver an unexpected challenge the heater controls operate in a completely opposite way from the markings.

The engine is more effective than exciting. When the compression ratio was raised to 9:1 power output moved up to 122 bhp, respectable for a 2-litre four-pot; nevertheless, its asset is not outright power but solid mid-range torque. Rev the engine hard to the 5500 rpm red line and acceleration is good rather than enthusiastic; 60 mph is reached from standstill in about nine seconds. Far better to drive the Fiat like a TR7, changing up early and flooring the throttle to

let the lugging power do the work. Get used to driving this way and it becomes a pleasant part of the Fiat's character. Pity though the engine doesn't sound sweeter when revved; Alfa lovers will find it hard to accept that the Fiat twin-cam has the edge on refinement over their "classic all-aluminium" engine. Fuel economy was about 25 mpg — unexceptional.

Strong torque may dull the excitement of an engine's delivery, but it invariably makes a car a swift performer in give-and-take traffic. The Fiat's deceptive speed is undoubtedly complemented by five close and ideally selected ratios. The chrome gear-lever and stitched air-bag type gaiter are pure 1960s nostalgia, and the operation is more rewarding than expected.

The short action lever is both quick and wonderfully direct, the feel refined but strictly mechanical. Matched to this is a heavy clutch that barely needs to be dipped to allow the next cog to be engaged.

Pick your road carefully and the Spider's handling and ride belies its age. On gently undulating lanes with open curves the car impresses with its accurate steering, taut handling and compromising ride. Opt for something more demanding and soon you realise that the steering becomes markedly heavier on lock, subjectively slowing the inputs from the driver. The rack and pinion of the latest cars will be a welcome improvement. The handling becomes less competent, the limits of grip more obvious and the "understeer in/oversteer out of a corner" character more clear. Always controllable, but no mid-engined slot racer.

Make the suspension work for its living and throw in a few pot holes and the body will occasionally shudder as the undue loads excite it. Discernible it may be but it never becomes so marked that the screen shakes in front of your eyes as it did on the "other" Italian convertible we drove recently.

The brake pedal offers reasonable retardation in exchange for a long travel and rather spongy feel. It is not such a bad deal.

It was certainly with regret that we let the Fiat pass from our hands; it had been a surprisingly enjoyable experience. Sadly the last 1500 Spiders are being built this year and then this Fiat will be confined to the obsolete pile. Dennis Hands has 150 right-hand-drive versions available for the sum of £9399 each. Next time you go to Calais to stock up with duty frees bring back a Spider as a personal import; you won't be disappointed.

It is hard to believe but, nearly 20 years after they were announced, two Italian sports cars, one Fiat-based and the other an Alfa Romeo, are still being manufactured, alongside each other at Pininfarina in Turin.

What is even more surprising is that the Spidereuropa, which started life as the Fiat 124 Spider, has never been offered in Britain by Fiat. It's a few years now since Fiat ceased to market the car under its own name, leaving production to Pininfarina, after withdrawing from the North American market in 1982.

Alfa Romeo, meanwhile, continues to market its Spider as part of the family but with production centred at Pininfarina alongside the Spidereuropa. It was sold in Britain up to 1978.

Now both cars are available on the British market. They are imported by dealers, converted from left-hand-drive to right and sold in small numbers, relying on exclusivity for their appeal. Enthusiasts undoubtedly find them appealing, although both companies — Dennis Hands Cars of Basingstoke and Bell and Colvill of West Horsley in Surrey — are talking in small numbers.

PININFARINA SPIDEREUROPA

Until recently, British wanting a Pininfarina-styled Spidereuropa have had to be content with left-hand-drive. Now, however, the import agent for the car, Dennis Hands of Basingstoke, is offering a rig hand-drive conversion of this classic. The conversion uses o genuine Fiat parts, includin new rack, and the whole jo finished off with a neat da board moulding — the result very professional job.

The Spidereuropa dates b only to 1982, but the Fiat Sport Spider, on which the c rent car is based, dates back 1966. Fiat mechanicals are u throughout construction and clude the structural underp engine, transmission driveline components. The ginal car had a 1.4-litre unit, la increased to 1.6 litres in twin format and, in current specifi tion 2 litres with Bosch injection. Power output 122bhp at 5200rpm, couplec 127lbft torque at 3500rpm.

The fairly ordinary-look bodyshell does not immedia strike one as 'Pininfari

ROUTE 66

Two convertible sports cars from 20 years ago are now readily available again. Peter Williams reports on the Alfa Romeo Spider and Andrew Kirk drove the Pininfarina Spidereuropa

although it is unmistakable, nevertheless, for its simple good looks, which have changed very little over the years. Minor modifications have included twin bonnet bulges, which have grown in size, the adoption of Federal bumpers — to meet US safety legislation — and a new square-cut grille. Detail changes have included the fitment of light alloy wheels shod with low profile Pirelli rubber and twin door mirrors mounted, in fact, on the front quarter lights.

The name change from Sport Spider to Spidereuropa resulted from Fiat's deal with Pininfarina, in which the latter took over the complete assembly of the car. It was allowed to rebadge the car as its own product, so the Fiat Sport Spider became the Pininfarina Spidereuropa in March 1982. The 'Europa' was added to show that a European version of the fuel-injected 1995cc engine was on the way.

The car we sampled was one such European version, devoid of external emission control equipment, although internal modifications remain. The specification is similar to that of cars now rolling off the production line in Turin, though more recent mechanical changes include a switch from recirculating ball to rack and pinion steering, larger disc brakes and new-style alloy wheels.

Each car is produced, apparently, to order, other manufacturers such as Talbot and Ferrari providing the majority of work for Pininfarina; with further projects looming, such as a new Cadillac bodyshell, production of the Spidereuropa is likely to finish at the end of 1985 after a 19-year run.

Even in its latest guise, the Spidereuropa is still very much a 60s-style sports car, possessed of all the advantages and disadvantages associated with open-top cars of this era. On the plus side are the classic lines, uncluttered shape and sturdy construction, on the minus side the unrefined — by today's standards — engine and heavy controls. On top of that the basic price tag seems high at £9399, although the basic specification could be hard to match.

The on-paper power output suggests that acceleration and overall performance ought to be close to many current specification sports cars, but this is not the case. Acceleration, in fact, is quite sluggish for a fuel-injected twin-cam unit of this capacity, the car requiring 11.1secs to reach 60mph. Top speed is also a little disappointing at 104mph, perhaps because of the less than aerodynamic body styling and rather high kerb weight (2296lb), although we suspect the reason may be the choice of gearing. Maximum speed is achieved ▶

Main picture: Both cars are now manufactured by Pininfarina in Turin. Left: Spidereuropa 2-litre produces 122bhp at 5200rpm but is a fairly sluggish performer due to high weight, unaerodynamic styling and gearing. Below: Alfa bodyshell has changed little in 20 years

system does not have power assistance and can leave one exhausted after a tight parking manoeuvre. The gear change simply feels old fashioned, the large gear knob and stick possessing a truck-like quality. One gets used to them in time, though they do mar the driving pleasure.

On a more positive note, we were amazed by the overall fuel consumption figure recorded during quite a lengthy test period — 34.6mpg. Clearly the Bosch fuel injection helps towards this. A 9.4 gallon fuel tank is provided and the diet of four-star fuel allows an average of around 300 miles between fills — a ran which many current sports ca cannot match.

Cruising at 70mph proved p ticularly fuel efficient while, this sort of speed, the rat unrefined engine is at a mo subdued hum, though there plenty of road and wind noise contend with, even with the ho raised.

With the majority of weig over the front wheels, 55.1 cent as opposed to 44.9 per cen the rear, the Spidereuropa hibits understeer when push quickly through corners, thou it is more agile than the cumb

◀ in the 19.4mph/1000rpm fifth gear, with the engine slightly over-revving at 5400rpm.

Acceleration in the gears is more acceptable and, here, the torquey 2-litre power unit provides good flexibility for low speed pullaway and fewer gearchanges when negotiating articulated lorries and the like. The 50 to 70mph increments in third, fourth and fifth gears translate to 6.8, 9.0 and 10.9secs respectively.

The heavy clutch, which requires a 40lb pedal effort, and unduly heavy steering and gear-

Top: Alfa Romeo Spider has gained bigger bumpers and bootlid spoiler. Above: Alloy wheels and metallic paint are optional extras on the Spidereuropa. Above right: The Alfa's boat-tail has given way to a squared-off boot. Right: Controls are heavy but economy excellent

change all show up the Spidereuropa's age. They are all excessive by current standards and make town driving more of a handful than one might like. The heavy steering is exaggerated by the wide footprint low profile tyres and the rack and pinion

some initial feel suggests. It is a difficult car to provoke into oversteer, unless really travelling on the limit, and shows good balance and poise in most situations, though it is possible briefly to lift the inside rear wheel without trying too hard and leave it spinning in mid air. The brakes, like the majority of controls are on the heavy side though stopping power is good, thanks to servo assistance and quite hefty sized front disc brakes.

There is more interior space than one at first sight might imagine thanks to the deep footwells. With the front seats half way along their runners, there is also enough room for two small adults in the rear — providing the top is down, of course. Seats have rake adjustment and are stitched up in a waterproof plastic material though they are still likely to leave a driver hot and sticky in warm weather. The quality of finish was high in our test vehicle, the metallic paintwork of a high lustre, the chrome trim contrasting well. Only source of complaint was a faulty boot lock which required more effort than normal to open. The weather equipment is easy to raise and takes only a couple of minutes.

Overall, the Spidereuropa is well packaged and, compared to the Alfa, a fair bit cheaper. It may lack the performance of its close rival but certainly offers as much enjoyment in terms of wind-in-the-hair motoring.

For more information contact Dennis Hands Ltd, West Ham Roundabout, Basingstoke, Hampshire, phone 0256 25783.

ALFA ROMEO SPIDER 2.0

She's a bit more butch nowadays; gone are the pretty nose with perspex light covers and the long 'boat' tail, but Alfa's classic Spider — spell it with an 'i' not a 'y' — is alive and well, once again on sale in Britain.

Everything else is still there. Turn the ignition key after a couple of dabs on the pedal and the 2-litre twin cam engine fires up immediately — that familiar Alfa growl distinguishing it from any pretenders. As you snick the gearlever into first and move off, you know you're in a no-nonsense sports car built only for your pleasure.

The lever comes easily to hand in the Alfa fashion of the period.

Remember you're driving a design that's now 19 years old and which harks back even further to some Pininfarina styling studies of the late 50s. If you judge it by the fluidity of the primary controls — steering, gearlever, pedals — then the Alfa Spider doesn't show its age.

It's the way that the Spider brings together those functions that marks it out from any other sports car I can remember driving. After just a brief taste, 20 to 30 minutes behind the wheel, the Alfa will capture your imagination forever.

Drop the snug, tight-fitting roof down on a bright Spring morning and you will be further inspired to stay behind the wheel of the Spider. The driving position may not be to some people's tastes, your knees are well bent upwards in the traditional Italian ape fashion, but it is comfortable for a six-footer, the flat seats perhaps the only drawback.

The large speedometer and tachometer, left and right respectively, have hardly changed since the car's inception, while the centre console, which houses the neat, cranked, gearlever bears an assorted bunch of minor gauges and controls, including an incongruous modern digital clock.

On the move, you can feel the responsiveness of the torquey twin cam engine through the pendant Giulietta-type accelerator pedal. It develops 127bhp at 5500rpm and 134lb/ft of torque at 4200rpm. That's from an all-alloy unit of 84mm bore and 88.5mm stroke which gives a displacement of 1926cc.

It puts the power down through a five-speed gearbox and live rear axle. Gearing can appear a little strange at first. There's a long throw between first and second, while fifth is an overdrive giving 21.85mph/1000rpm. The final drive is 4.4:1 while in each gear the Spider does 26.7mph (3.30:1), 42mph (1.99:1), 65.2mph (1.35:1), 87.9mph (1:1), and 118mph (0.79:1). Economy is not a strong point — we managed 30mpg.

The Spider easily reaches 60mph in under 10 seconds and runs out of steam at around 120mph. At all times it feels relatively stable but will occasionally hop out of line if the tail is caught out by a road bump in mid bend. It's a well-located axle though, staying well-glued to the ground and generally feeling more like an independent set-up. Coil springs, shock absorbers and

an anti-roll bar complement the trailing arms and central triangulated link locating the axle.

At the front there are unequal length wishbones, coil springs, shock absorbers and an anti-roll bar. Braking is by discs all round and there is a brake regulator to the rear axle to prevent premature lock-up. Other technical highlights include twin Weber or Solex carburettors and an electronic ignition system. On 'our' car there was also a non-standard electric fan arrangement fitted by the importers, Bell and Colvill.

The all-monocoque body of the Spider sits on a 88in wheelbase, but overhang front and rear gives an overall length of 13ft 9in. At 64.1in wide, the Spider has plenty of room for two passengers with room behind the seats on a carpeted shelf for further luggage if it will not fit in the capacious (for a sports car) boot.

After 19 years in production it is still an extremely forgiving and responsive car on the road. Yes, it has a live axle, but the modern Michelin MXV70R tyres mounted on 14in rims — as big as they ever were — help the Spider stay a little better glued to the road than it did in the past.

Only around town does the low-geared recirculating ball system show the disadvantages of its poor lock-to-lock and heavy feel. The brakes are an absolute delight, progressive in the best sense of the word, pulling up the car easily, especially in the wet.

Ride comfort can be a little disconcerting at low speeds. Here the modern tyres have given the Spider a coarser feel than before. It doesn't seem as supple though, at higher speeds, it tends to level out and absorb road undulations better.

Wind noise predominates, of course, when the hood is down and does much to hide the mechanical din at higher speeds. With the roof up, the throaty Alfa twin-cam note is always there, wind noise starts to come in at 50mph and, by the time you're at the legal limit, there's quite a thrash — not unacceptable from a sports car, though. From about 4500rpm upwards, the 2-litre engine is quite extended and some better sound insulation would not be a bad thing.

What the Spider's engine doesn't lack though, is low-down punch. The driver can poodle around town in it quite easily — it pulls so cleanly from 10mph in third — continuing strongly right up the rev range.

Our black example arrived with less than 900 miles on the clock, so was still a bit tight; either this or the gearing prevented it from revving quite as freely as we remember with previous Alfa twin cams. That said, the Spider really has few faults. It proves how good the original design concept was, with the first 1300cc car back in 1966. Since then it has developed, gaining 1600cc, 1750cc and 2000cc engines over the years and then the current square 'short-tail' rear-end in 1970.

Alfa Romeo did export the Spider to Britain until 1978 when it was withdrawn because of Type Approval problems and the company's projected marketing strategy. Since then, the front and rear bumpers have been remodelled and are always coloured black, the rear with an integrated spoiler, while the front gained an apron spoiler.

Overall, Pininfarina's build quality for the Spider is excellent, with a high standard of paint and interior trim finish. One disappointment was the quality of the hood cover clips, while the hood can be a bit of a heave-ho to erect. Another is the finish of the boot carpeting, and there are perhaps one or two too many screw heads about. It's not free of scuttle shake, either. Bell and Colvill has made an excellent job of conversion, though, except perhaps for the loss of the glovebox, reducing oddment space to virtually zero, while the new facia covering looked tacky and did not match as well as it might with the maroon interior.

Bell and Colvill still services Alfas and has readily at hand the parts to convert. A new steering rack is used, Giulietta pedal box and a clever tie-rod connecting the left-hand servo (in its original position) to the new right-hand-drive set-up.

It is well-equipped for £10,995 but metallic paint, alloy wheels, leather faced seats, targa hardtop and a radio unit are all optional extras so you could easily find yourself spending from £11,500 to more than £13,000.

The Spider is a living classic, though, a car that deserves to survive as long as legislation allows it to. With its elegant styling, however, it probably best suits the role of a woman's car.

For further information contact Bell and Colvill at Epsom Road, West Horsley, nr Leatherhead, Surrey, phone East Horsley 4671.

So rarely seen on the road nowadays, a Fiat 124 Sport Spider 1600 leads an even scarcer Sport Coupé 1400

FORGOTTEN FLAIR

Although nearly forgotten today, the Fiat 124 Sport Coupés and Spiders were remarkably advanced in the sixties. Richard Sutton re-discovers these dynamic Italians

How short our memories are. How prejudiced we have become. We who claim to know so much of classic or collectable cars seem to have forgotten one of the greatest and once most popular of them all. Precious little has been written or spoken of them for years, yet they were great competitors of the MGB, were built in similar numbers over a similar period, and at a similar price. Furthermore, on many counts they were far superior cars.

Yet today there are few enthusiasts for them, and even fewer examples left on the road. Only road test reports in contemporary motoring magazines remind us of these remarkable little cars. They were, and still are, highly capable, immensely stylish, cheap and highly desirable, and they will still out-perform many of their modern equivalents.

I speak, of course, of the Fiat 124 Sports. These convertibles and coupés were truly astonishing motor cars. Triumph TR and MGB owners, even Alfa Romeo and Lancia enthusiasts, need read no further if so persuaded by their loyalties. But those interested in acquiring one of the world's finest performance cars, which *Car* magazine once implied would out-handle a Lotus Elan, should continue and rejoice in the realisation that the best need not be the most expensive.

For those unconvinced by such heady praise, a reminder of Fiat's remarkable market status back in the sixties might help. At that time, Fiat was in a far healthier international market position than it had been before or since. In 1967 Paul Frère remarked in *Motor* 'You cannot fail to be impressed when you consider the range of models announced by Fiat in the course of the last three years, everyone of which has considerable technical merit and has met with immediate success.'

Such 'considerable technical merit' saw Fiat topping the import charts in Belgium, Germany and France during the late sixties, to say nothing of successful export drives to Great Britain. Of all those new Fiats, the 124 – in saloon, Coupé and Spider guises – was probably the most important, and undoubtedly the most surprising.

The 124 story effectively begins in 1963, when Fiat were having to consider replacing their then 10 year old 1100/103 saloon. It was a costly period for

Fiat, who were having to budget for massive re-investment in factory modernisation, tooling and design. As the new car would have to be inexpensive and effective, it was to be based on the 1100/103 floorpan but with all-new bodywork and a new, more versatile engine. This new engine was to be the heart of Fiat's production for the foreseeable future. Its design was crucial, and it was left to Italy's best man for the job, Aurelio Lampredi, to execute.

Lampredi's reputation went before him; he had already been responsible for several fabulous Ferrari engines (notably the V12) prior to 1955, and had then designed several six-cylinder engines for Fiat. His brief this time was to design a light in-line four cylinder of 1.0, 1.4 and 1.6-litres with an iron block, and the capability of carrying different valve arrangements. The project was dubbed '124'.

Triumph TR, MGB, Alfa Romeo and Lancia enthusiasts need read no further if so persuaded by their loyalties

At this stage only the saloon was under final development, but the Sports – Spider and Coupé – were soon to follow. All the models carried the same drive-train specification, but engines and gearbox options varied. The specification included coil spring and double wishbone suspension with telescopic dampers and an anti-roll bar to the front, and at the rear a lightweight hypoid bevel axle located by parallel trailing arms, coil springs and telescopic dampers. A clever torque tube arrangement was mated to the front of the differential casing, and both a Panhard rod and anti-roll bar were employed. Such early rear suspension set-ups were significant, as will be disclosed later. The sensitive steering was by worm and peg, and brakes, remarkably, were by discs all round!

For the saloon, revealed in April 1966, the 1198cc version of Lampredi's engine was employed together with a four-speed gearbox. This was an overhead valve pushrod operated unit producing 60bhp. Sure, its Fiat in-house styling was very conservative – a three-box affair with rounded corners – but the little saloon's dynamic qualities were well ahead of the opposition.

Such qualities were put to better effect with the development of the 124 Sport Spider, due to be launched a few months later. As had been the case with the Fiat 850, Fiat delegated the styling of the convertible car to an outside stylist, in this case Pininfarina, while the Coupé derivative was shaped, like the saloon, in-house.

Pininfarina were supplied with shortened 124 saloon floorpans (by 5½ins) complete with drive-trains. The shorter wheelbase, together with certain floorpan reinforcements undertaken by Pininfarina, ensured that the convertible would be suitably rigid, but prevented the Spider from evolving into a full four-seater – 2+2 seating was settled for. Most significantly, with the Spider came the first variant of the Lampredi engine, an enlarged 1438cc version topped with twin overhead camshafts. The camshafts were driven by a single toothed belt powered directly from the crankshaft, a system pioneered by Glas and seldom seen on quantity production cars. Valves were inclined at 65 degrees and cross-flow breathing was incorporated. This meant that inlet and exhaust manifolds now appeared on opposite sides of the engine rather than both on the right, as was the case with the 124 saloon unit. Carburation was by a single downdraught twin choke Weber. This engine was a rugged, reliable and revvable unit producing 90bhp at 6000rpm, and was available with a five-speed greabox.

It was accepted that the 124 Spider would look good and, although somewhat eclipsed at its debut at the November 1966 Turin Show by the Fiat Dino Spider launch, the Sport Spider was very well received.

The bad news was that the Fiat Spider was not destined for the British market, and that it was only to be available with left-hand drive. With the American market squarely in its sights, the Fiat would make dramatic inroads into the MGB's share of the US market. If only it had been available in England …

There can be no doubt that the launch of the Sport Coupé caused more of a stir than that of the Spider. The Coupé was first shown at the 1967 Geneva

The Mark 11 acquired twin headlights and new wings

The press loved the early Fiat 124 Spiders and it was always regretted that the model never made it to Britain

The Coupés looked just as good from behind

Motor Show, this time alongside the new Bertone-styled Dino Coupé. The car caused a minor sensation. It was, after all, styled in-house at Fiat, but it was *so* beautiful. A generous 2+2 seater airy coupé with sharp, unfussy styling, it looked as practical as it was pretty, and was cheap too. The motoring press, in the cheerful knowledge that the stylish little Fiat was due for England's shores, soon with five-speed gearbox, clamoured for press cars.

And so began a remarkable period for Fiat in Great Britain as magazine after magazine raved about the car's sensational roadholding, handling, styling and practicality. It seemed that Fiat, almost by accident, had come up with the world's best family coupé, and by a wide margin.

It should be mentioned here that the Spider might well have received a similar response in Britain, but its non-availability rendered any English reviews pointless and no major tests were carried out. The Spider was built initially in small quantities, and only when US exports began in 1968 did test reports from America start to extol the cars' virtues in the English language. And in America, despite anti-smog paraphernalia which repressed the cars' performance, both the Coupé and the Spider were regarded as outstanding and without competition. The Spider was described by *Road & Track* in July 1968 as being the 'only car of its type being built today that is mechanically modern'. That statement was to hold true for several years to come.

The 124 Coupe caused a minor sensation. It was, after all, styled in-house at Fiat, but it was so beautiful ...

Perhaps some indulgence is permitted here as contemporary road tests make such extraordinary reading. The esteemed L.J.K. Setright was one of the first to try the 124 Coupé, and he immediately adopted it as one of his favourite cars. Such hallowed praise had been lavished only on the original Lotus Elite and various Bristols.

On successive group car test days at Goodwood, run by Total for the benefit of the motoring press, LJK walked away hailing the 124 Coupé as the best car he had driven all day. On two such occasions Maseratis had been hounded and overtaken and it would appear that even larger engined Alfas were defeated by the little Fiat. The 124 Coupé was an outstanding track car. In August 1969 LJK remarked of the Coupé: 'It is absolute bliss and it will take something better than that Alfa GTV behind to catch me.' Earlier in 1967, LJK said of a Spider that had made its way to Britain, 'This was a car that sent everyone wild with delight, several discriminating people clamouring to know when they could buy one.' Of the roadholding of both Spider and Coupé he said, 'It was fantastic. It was inexplicable.'

And by no means was it just the over-the-top temperament of LJK which sparked such enthusiasm, for others consistently said similar of the Fiat Sports. *Autocar* reported, 'Seldom have the *Autocar* test staff been so unanimously in praise of a car ... yet judged absolutely and objectively it is outstanding ...' *Car & Car Conversions* said, 'The worst feature about the 124 Coupé is that everyone who drives it wants one ... it's a real beauty and goes as well as it looks.'

Of course, there were complaints. The steering was considered too heavy at parking speeds, the brakes were rather 'over-servoed', and the pedals were too close together. The car was rather noisy inside, and the driving position, for all but the shortest drivers, really did take a bit of getting used to. Four adults could be seated in relative comfort, but their luggage would have to be minimal. The simulated wood interior trim received little enthusiasm, and the traditional Italian plastic trim did not respond well to hot summer temperatures. But the little Fiat was well equipped, with comprehensive instrumentation, a good heater and even variable windscreen wiper speeds.

The Spider had all of the Coupé's domestic conveniences, but because it was really only a two-seater its 6.2 cubic feet of luggage space was rather more practical. The Spider also came with the world's best convertible hood, complete with glass side windows which retracted automatically as the hood was lowered. It was leak-proof and easy for single-handed operation.

For all the quibbles, Fiat were on to a winner, not least in America, where the Spider and Coupé were offered at near identical money to the MGB. From the year that sales began in the US, 124 production rose dramatically. Between 1968 and 1970 Spider production alone doubled. By the beginning of 1970, annual production of Spiders and Coupés at Fiat's Lingotto factory had risen to 50,000 units – that is about 15,000 more than MGB production.

The first significant changes to the 124 occurred in September 1968. The rear suspension layout was revised, and this modification upset the Sports' impeccable handling characteristics. The modifications involved disposing of the torque tube and substituting a system with two extra short radius arms fitted above the axle tube toward the centre of the differential. The torque tube was dropped because it was found that unless the suspension radius rods were exactly aligned the torque tube would transmit substantial loads on the axle casing on poor roads. As breakages were apparently common, the system had to go. The new arrangement, together with extra rubber bushing, worked well, but the car now rolled rather more and there was a marked tendency toward understeer.

If the rear suspension modifications were a necessary evil, the introduction of the Mark II at the Turin Show in November 1969 was positively malevolent. 'With what woe did I discover its deficiencies. I was appalled,' wailed Setright.

The Mark II should have been everything the Mark I was and much more. The principal difference with this car was the adoption of the 125 saloon 1608cc variant of the twin-cam engine with twin Webers. Performance increased: as power was now up to 115bhp at 6400rpm, the car could reach 60mph in 11.6secs and top 105mph, a healthy increase over the 1.4's 12.8secs and 99.5mph. The Americans would surely be happy, having complained so much at the de-smogged 1.4 car's lack of urge.

But life didn't work out like that. The new car was notably thirstier than the 1.4 and could achieve barely 23mpg. Worst of all, the American specification car turned out to be no quicker than the 1.4 version. The Mark II was much 'softer' too – the handling had lost its edge. The brakes were even more over-servoed and tended to fade. The car rolled more than its predecessor and the gearbox (a five-speed as standard on the 1.6) acquired closer ratios and developed a snatchiness due to the increased torque. It was also a heavier car, and more expensive.

The styling, too, was upset. Twin headlights appeared, and the front wings were modified. Sud-

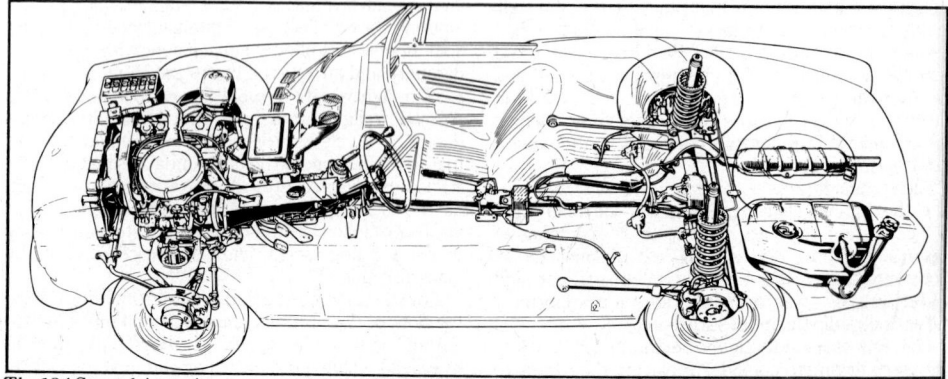

The 124 Sport drivetrain was very advanced in the sixties, as this cutaway of a torque-tubed Spider shows

denly the Coupé became rather plain. Of course, lots of creature comforts inside – better heater, an electric clock and windscreen washers – had appeared, but to what avail? Some housewives were happy, fashion following fancy-frees with cravings for fast roundabouts were not.

The revised Spider was more attractive. Two vestigial power bulges appeared on the bonnet and a new grille adorned the snout. A 1.4-litre version with four-speed gearbox was still available.

Nevertheless, the 1.6 continued to impress. Robert Glenton of the *Sunday Express* sampled the revised machine and sighed 'Believe it or not, this car spoke to me', and *Motor* summed up, 'Although it now has tougher opposition, notably from Ford Capri and Opel Manta, it has, in our opinion, yet to be surpassed by any upstart youngster.'

In the summer of 1972, Fiat introduced the 132 saloon offered with a highly modified Lampredi twin-cam of 1.6 or 1.8-litres. This engine had different block and head castings from its forebear, and in 1973 both engines were offered in the Sports. These revised cars are now known as the Mark IIIs. Power was rated at 108bhp for the 1592cc version and 118bhp for the 1756cc. The 1438cc engine was dropped altogether. Two gearboxes were offered: a four-speed (basically the old five-speed with fifth lopped off) and the new five-speed as fitted to the 132. Performance was up again: the 1.8 Coupé could now top 111mph and reach 60mph in 9.2secs. Those after even more performance could always opt for the Abarth Spider now being offered in limited and expensive quantities – but that's another story, ably recounted in *C&S* in January 1985.

Even if the 1.8 was not as powerful as had been hoped, the Mark III was regarded as much improved over the Mark II. A single Weber carburettor helped restrain fuel consumption to the mid-20s, even if performance was affected. The rear anti-roll bar which had been removed on the Mark II reappeared, and the brakes were revised. These relatively small changes restored much of the Coupé's old character. Nearly all had been forgiven.

But the revised Mark III styling was another matter. The Coupé acquired vast rear lights, extra grilles and very nasty styling trim around the nose. Fortunately, the Spider was largely left alone, although power bulges and bumpers became inevitably larger for the American market.

From 1974, all Spiders were destined for the USA as the open car continued to sell well there, but the Coupé was not as successful and production ended in late 1975. The last cars were sold in Britain in 1976.

From 1975 the 124 Spider continued to be developed and revised for the American market. By this time Fiat had bought Lancia and were hard at work developing the Beta range, the X1/20 (Monte Carlo) and the X1/9. But as long as there was demand for the Spider, Fiat continued to supply. And the American motoring press during the seventies ensured that a demand would be maintained. In August 1976 *Car and Driver* pitched the 124 against 11 other convertibles, concluding that the Fiat 'is the finest all-round sports car money can buy'.

In July 1978 a longer stroke 1995cc version of the 132 engine was fitted to the Spider and a three-

The Mark III Coupé's styling became very cluttered . . .

. . . but its interior was by far the most sumptuous

speed Strasbourg automatic gearbox became available. The car was now called the Spider 2000. It produced only 86bhp, but at least it managed 104lbs ft of torque.

For May 1980, Bosch L-Jetronic fuel injection increased power output to a healthier 103bhp, but sales had now irreversibly slipped. A Turbo Spider was offered through Fiat agents courtesy of Legend Industries of Detroit, but in spite of good performance from the 120bhp car, just over 1000 were sold.

As sales continued to fall, Fiat handed over 124 production to Pininfarina, who then marketed the car under their own name. Supercharged Volumex and Abarth versions were offered, but fewer than 5000 Pininfarina cars were built between the time of the hand-over in March 1982 and the model's final demise in 1985.

Buying any second-hand 124 is an unenviable task as Fiats, perhaps more than any other Italian car, have an appalling reputation for rust. When buying a 124 it is not so much a case of finding a good one as finding one that isn't too far gone! Any second-hand 124 will demand bodywork attention.

Furthermore, Fiats rust everywhere. This is because of inherently poor quality steel used in the car's manufacture rather than too many built-in water traps. Doors fall off, floorpans drop out and holes appear everywhere.

Start your examination with the sills. The inner and middle sills take most of the structural strain, while the outers are largely decorative and their condition is not as critical. Check that the bottom rear corner of the door isn't jutting out – if it is, sill problems are likely. The front floorpans around the outriggers disappear. These are fairly easy to repair, as excellent quality (and very cheap) Lada outrigger assemblies are available off the shelf.

The front suspension turrets rust away. These can be plated, but the job is difficult. Spanish-listed SEAT parts would appear to be available as complete replacement units.

All 124 wheel arches rot and let the water in, and are generally difficult to repair. Check the rear

under-valences too. The bonded-in front and rear 'screens let in plenty of water and rot the scuttles – replacements are not currently available.

Because the Spider's demise is only recent, it would appear that panel availability is very good and rumour has it that panels will continue to be supplied for another three years at least. Spiders also seem to avoid the rust problem rather better than the Coupés, for which most panels are unavailable.

Mechanically, the 124s are for the most part reliable and cheap and easy to repair. Virtually all parts are readily available and easy to fit. Engines should last at least 100,000 miles before serious bore or valve guide wear demands attention. The bottom end is particularly strong, but the cylinder head is apt to warp. A common reason for this is overheating due to blocked radiators which are cheap and easy to renovate. Head overhauls normally transform the twin-cam's performance.

It is crucial that camshaft belts are changed whenever a car is purchased and replaced thereafter every 30,000 miles. A breakage can result in very expensive valve/piston collisions.

Carburettor wear is common in older cars and replacements are cheap. A larger alternative is often advised. All exhaust systems are available but vary a great deal in quality.

A worn gearbox is indicated by excessive slop and a tendency to jump out of gear. Reconditioned units are available.

Brakes and suspension componentry are reliable, and all parts are available. Discs are cheap, Tar-Ox replacements with Mintex pads making a dramatic difference to performance and reliability. Calipers can be troublesome but replacements are cheap. King-pin ball joints wear – replacements are available but ensure only Fiat or Lada parts are used.

When buying a 124, it is not so much a case of buying a good one as finding one that isn't too far gone

It is absolutely vital when considering purchase of a 124 first to join the Fiat Twin Cam Register. This excellent club can help and advise on all aspects of 124 purchase and restoration. They are constantly tracking down parts sources, experimenting with performance modifications (for which there is huge scope) and tracing cars. The club even runs a computerised market place in which vast numbers of Twin Cam Fiats are listed for sale. The FTCR is a young organisation but is deservedly growing fast. Over 200 124s are now on their books and they can be contacted via their membership secretary, Dave Gibbons (whose gold Spider you see in colour here). Dave can be found at 166 Pickhurst Rise, West Wickham, Kent.

Very little outlay is required to buy a Fiat 124 Sport today. There appears to be no difference in values between Mark I, II and III Coupés (termed AC, BC and CCs respectively). A wreck can be picked up for next to nothing, and MoT'd runners for a couple of hundred pounds. Even the best on offer will fetch barely £1000. Having said that, a BC Coupé with delivery mileage was sold last year for £6000. There is clear investment potential!

Spiders always sell for a lot more money than the Coupés and anything up to £10,000 can be paid for Abarth versions of Pininfarina Spidereuropas. But excellent Mark I, II and III cars (termed AS, BS and CS respectively) can all be bought for around £2500 each. A fully restored example may make nearer £4000 and MoT'd runners can be bought for around £1000. Right-hand drive converted cars (undertaken by Radbourne of Chiswick in the mid-sixties and Hands of Basingstoke in 1984-5) are worth significantly more than their standard left-hand drive equivalents, and as yet torque tube suspension cars have no price premium.

There can be little doubt that the dynamic and practical Fiat 124s are among the most under-rated classic cars available today.

. . . he end of the line – a rhd converted Pininfarina Spidereuropa in action 20 years after its ancestor's launch

Hot Performer

Spyderman

Allan went a long way to find his grey beauty

ALLAN TONGE is a Fiat freak and has owned many of the Italian machines over the years. But one car had always been missing from his stable, a convertible — or rather a Spyder, to use the European name.

In the 1960s when Allan was a teenager just getting into the car scene he lusted after a car like the beautiful, gunmetal grey one you see here, but two things stood in his way — lack of money and the fact that the Spyder was never sold in Australia.

A successful career solved the lack of cash but the absence of a car to buy left him with only one alternative — to go to California to buy one. The American home of topless motoring is a fabulous source of rust-free convertibles so Allan bought his Spyder and imported it to Sydney.

There was one other major hassle to be overcome before the dream could finally be fulfilled — the steering wheel was on the wrong side. Allan did the con-

This 2.0 litre twin cam Fiat Spyder was converted to right hand drive by a dedicated owner.

version himself. It's not the sort of work we would recommend you to try to do yourself, but Allan has had a fair bit of engineering experience.

Fortunately the car was designed with left to right-hand drive conversion in mind, but it still took 10 months of hard work in his garage at home before the job was done. A complete steering assembly from a Fiat 124 Coupe was bought from a wrecker's yard and installed in the Spyder. The existing steering wheel and pedals were removed and attached to previously plugged holes on the right-hand side, which were built into the car in Italy.

The brake master cylinder had to be moved across, as did the clutch and accelerator controls. There was plenty of spare underbonnet space on the right-hand side of the car, so fitting things in was reasonably easy.

Then came the dashboard. It wasn't as difficult a job as expected because the dash was symmetrical — the glove box lid and the instrument panel are interchangeable. So the instruments went in where the Yanks had their glove box and the glove box lid went where the instruments used to be — simple eh? Of course the wiring and cables had to be moved over and the panels had to be re-trimmed in timber, but that was no hassle to this Fiat lover.

Mechanically the car is superior to the 124 Coupes which used to be sold in Australia in that it has a 2.0 litre engine. There are bulges on the bonnet, to give clearance to the taller, twin-cam, powerplant.

We took the car on the road on a beautiful summer's evening in Sydney and had a wonderful time. The top was down, of course, and the sound of an Italian engine is something which has to be heard to be fully appreciated. The car is as solid as a rock and has far less body flex than many Japanese open-topped cars we have driven recently. The gearchange was as firm and notchy as in any other Fiat of the 1960s. The wind blew through our hair and people in their air conditioned Holdens and Falcons looked thoroughly

jealous as we went past.

The Fiat Spyder wasn't cheap. It cost about $7000 in Australian money. Then 95 per cent import duty and shipping costs had to be paid and, though the left to right-hand drive conversion cost only about $1000, don't forget the hundreds of hours of hard work which went into the job. Parts had to be bought to restore the car, and spares set aside — just in case. Allan reckons the car owes him about $25,000 and thinks he could get considerably more than that if he sold it. But it is not for sale.

Could you look this wonderful little Italian sports car in the headlamps and then sell it? I certainly couldn't.

Ewan Kennedy